The Colonias Reader

THE
COLONIAS
READER

**Economy, Housing, and Public Health
in U.S.–Mexico Border Colonias**

Edited by

Angela J. Donelson and Adrian X. Esparza

The University of Arizona Press   Tucson

The University of Arizona Press
© 2010 The Arizona Board of Regents
All rights reserved

www.uapress.arizona.edu

Library of Congress Cataloging-in-Publication Data

The colonias reader : economy, housing, and public health in U.S.–Mexico Border
colonias / edited by Angela J. Donelson and Adrian X. Esparza.
      p.   cm.
    Includes bibliographical references and index.
    ISBN 978-0-8165-2852-3 (pbk. : alk. paper)
      1. Mexican-American Border Region—Economic conditions.   2. Mexican-
American Border Region—Social conditions.   3. Public health—Mexican-American
Border Region.   I. Donelson, Angela J., 1971–   II. Esparza, Adrian X., 1957–
    HC137.M46C65   2008
    330.972′1—dc22   2009040699

Publication of this book is made possible in part by the proceeds of a permanent
endowment created with the assistance of a Challenge Grant from the National
Endowment for the Humanities, a federal agency.

Manufactured in the United States of America on acid-free, archival-quality paper
and processed chlorine free.

15 14 13 12 11 10   6 5 4 3 2 1

As editors, we dedicate this book to Flora, Tristan, Phillip, Gabriel, and Jude.

As contributors, we all wish to recognize and support the tireless work of those who seek to improve the border colonias. Proceeds of sales from this book will support a regional borderlands effort, the Rural People, Rural Policy Southwest Network. Launched by the W. K. Kellogg Foundation in 2006, the network of 14 organizations—in fields as diverse as environmental and public health, community and economic development, and housing—has been working to address shared policy issues to strengthen their respective rural border communities in the states of Arizona and New Mexico. For more information about the network and its activities, see http://www.wkkf.org.

Contents

Introduction

There is mounting global concern for the issues of poverty, housing and shelter, and public and environmental health. Many of these issues are hinged to long-standing inequities that divide the wealthy from the poor, the mobility of populations that cross international borders with increasing frequency, and the degradation of natural environments that comes with rapid population growth. Such problems have been the focus of international organizations like the United Nations (2008) and the World Health Organization (2008), which reach out to countries where deplorable living conditions have been documented for decades.

But we do not have to look far to see many of the conditions found in these countries: they are common in the southwestern borderlands of the United States. In parts of southern Texas, New Mexico, Arizona, and California—near the U.S.–Mexico border—poverty is widespread, housing is often unfit for habitation, and public health concerns such as HIV/AIDS, tuberculosis, and diabetes approach crisis levels. Natural environments fall victim to poorly planned residential developments, substandard infrastructure, and air and water pollution. It is perhaps too bold to place the border region on a par with sub-Saharan Africa, but many communities are nearly as destitute.

Even so, few recognize the U.S.–Mexico border region as one of the country's largest pockets of impoverishment. Residents in some of the country's largest cities—El Paso, Tucson, Phoenix, and San Diego—are unaware of the deprivation that lies nearby, so it is not surprising that people in other parts of the country know little about life in the borderlands. The popular press confounds the problem by depicting the border region as a haven for drug smugglers and undocumented immigrants who threaten the nation's security and livelihood. With the rash of sensationalism that fills the airwaves it is easy to lose sight of the deeper problems that color the border region.

Objectives and Themes

The Colonias Reader looks to the U.S.–Mexico border with the aim of describing many of the region's problems and the efforts to overcome them. Although poverty and deprivation are common in the borderlands, the book targets colonias because they house much of the region's poor and have been singled out for assistance by federal and state agencies as well as nongovernmental organizations (NGOs). Colonias are a diverse mix of communities, some dating back well over a hundred years, others sprouting up during the post-WWII era, while still others are only a few years old. Regardless of their history or geographic setting, colonias embody the struggle for equality in a country that too often ignores the poor.

The book offers a compilation of research and experience garnered from years of working in the colonias of Texas, New Mexico, Arizona, and California. The book's contributors focus on three themes: economic growth and development, housing and community development, and public and environmental health. Certainly, other challenges confront colonias, such as political disenfranchisement, racism, and the assimilation of immigrants. But these and other issues are embedded in the book's three themes and surface in many of the chapters to come.

The Colonias Reader does more than report problems and document programs that respond to them. Some of the chapters provide conceptual frameworks that pin impoverishment to institutional and class-based conflicts that perpetuate unequal power in the borderlands. Other chapters challenge the very basis of colonia designations as advanced by government agencies and urge alternative definitions that build on deeper class and cultural foundations. These chapters bring to light the causes of inequality and point to longer-term, sustainable solutions. Most chapters move beyond portraying border dwellers as hapless victims of discrimination and overt racism. Rather, they bring forward residents' deep resolve, creativity, and steadfast devotion to improving conditions through grassroots organizing and community leadership. The book's chapters demonstrate that these efforts vary across the border: some communities are ripe with activism, while others struggle to advance their goals. Despite these differences, nearly all people living in colonias have modest aspirations: a livable wage, safe and decent housing, and basic health care. *The Colonias Reader* showcases many situations in which colonia residents have organized to fulfill these ambitions.

The book builds on two additional themes that warrant mention. First, *The Colonias Reader* brings together scholars and practitioners, each reporting her or his research and lessons from the field. In this way, *The Colonias Reader* crosses the divide between academic research and applied experience. While the majority of contributors hold faculty positions, several chapters are penned by community organizers and activists who work in colonias. Their voices are seldom featured in academic publications, even though community activists have managed praiseworthy success. In many respects, their stories are the most valuable of all. Second, the book is decidedly multidisciplinary. Contributors pursue research in disciplines as varied as anthropology, history, urban and regional planning, economics, geography, environmental science, sociology, and public health. The book consolidates these diverse perspectives to provide readers with comprehensive coverage in a single volume.

Background

Hundreds of settlements known as colonias line the U.S.–Mexico border from Texas to California. They form a network of over 2,500 villages, towns, and cities that house a combined population of well over one million persons.[1] As figure I.1 illustrates, the distribution of colonias varies significantly from state to state. Most colonias (an estimated 2,200) are located in Texas. The combined population of Texas colonias is estimated at 400,000 persons, with significant population growth expected in the years ahead. Over 860 colonias are located in Hidalgo County alone, near the southern tip of the state (Federal Reserve Bank of Dallas 2007). Many of the state's colonias arose as unregulated subdivisions throughout suburban and exurban landscapes in the 1960s, 1970s, and 1980s. They often lacked adequate infrastructure, which led to numerous public health concerns. There are fewer colonias in New Mexico and Arizona, approximately 227, with an estimated population of nearly half a million (Esparza and Donelson 2008). As figure I.1 shows, they

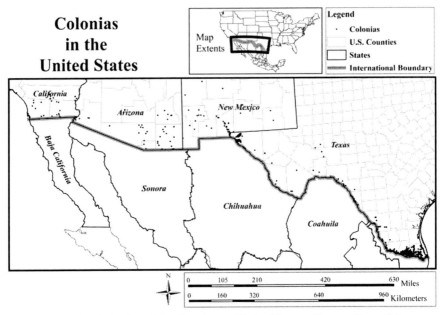

FIGURE I.1 Colonias of the Southwest United States. Source: Laura Norman, USGS

are clustered in southern New Mexico along Interstate 25, which runs from Ciudad Juárez, Mexico, northward through Las Cruces. Many of New Mexico's and Arizona's colonias are sparsely populated (fewer than 2,000 persons) and are located in rural and remote areas of both states. This reflects their historical roots as agricultural outposts or communities that met the labor needs of large mining operations, which are invariably located in remote areas (Esparza and Donelson 2008). The situation in California is far different. There are 32 colonias in California's southern counties. However, many are excluded from federal and state assistance for a variety of reasons. Most are located in agriculturally rich regions of the state where farmworkers endure enormous hardship. It is noteworthy that a handful of colonias are located on tribal lands and thus fall under different jurisdictional governance. Nonetheless, these colonias share many of the problems that apply to colonias, and tribal populations across the country should not be ignored.

The term *colonia* comes from the Spanish for "neighborhood" or "community": a place occupied by people who share a common heritage and have similar social and economic standing (Mandelbaum 2000). The term is fitting, because colonias share many characteristics.[2] Foremost, their populations are overwhelmingly Hispanic: over 60 percent across the border region, and in Texas and California the numbers are much higher. Many colonias lack decent housing, physical infrastructure such as water and sewers, and basic amenities such as electricity and paved roads. Poverty and unemployment/underemployment are also widespread, health care is often difficult to come by, and educational attainment typically lags well behind state and national levels.

The region's poor are not confined to colonias, but their official designation opens the door to federal and state aid. Communities must meet federal and state guidelines to receive a colonias designation. Colonias can be either incorporated or unincorporated communities located in one of the four southwest border states. Nearly all colonias in Texas are unincorporated and fall within the domain of county government; only a few are incorporated towns and cities. The situation in New Mexico is much the same, with the lion's share of colonias classified as unincorporated places. In Arizona and California, however, larger shares of colonias are incorporated towns and cities. Two federal agencies—the Department of Housing and Urban Development (HUD) and the Department of Agriculture, Rural Development (USDA-RD)—require that communities be located within 150 miles of the U.S.–Mexico border. The U.S. Environmental Protection Agency (EPA) requires that communities be located within 62 miles (100 kilometers) of the border. Communities also must demonstrate hardship, either poor-quality housing or the lack of sewer or water delivery systems (U.S. Department of Housing and Urban Development 2006; U.S. Environmental Protection Agency 2008; U.S. Geological Survey 2006). Communities must apply for, and receive, official designation to be eligible for support.

Levels of federal, state, and local support for colonias vary substantially across all border states. Texas has the largest number of agencies and organizations working in behalf of colonias. This is expected given the comparatively large number of colonias and the severity of their problems. In addition to federal programs, several state-level agencies respond to colonia needs in Texas. In contrast, there are few state agencies in New Mexico, Arizona, or California that deal exclusively with colonias. Instead, assistance is available through federal agencies such as the EPA, HUD, USDA-RD, and the U.S. Department of Health and Human Services. For this reason, NGOs and local community activism play a central role in community development. But, as the chapters ahead demonstrate, colonias struggle with a range of pressing problems, despite the efforts of federal and state agencies and NGOs.

It is noteworthy that the formal definition of *colonias* has come under fire because it can lead to the inequitable distribution of resources. First, even though a community may be severely disadvantaged, it will not receive assistance unless it meets locational criteria. Alternatively, communities near the border (within 150 miles) may receive aid even though conditions may not be as severe. At times, therefore, location outweighs need. Second, communities are excluded from some federally sponsored programs if their county population (metropolitan statistical area— MSA) exceeds one million. Such requirements ignore the geography of the Southwest, where counties often cover thousands of square miles, and populations are concentrated in a single large city (e.g., San Diego). Finally, the official colonia designation ignores the deeper cultural and demographic profiles of communities where, historically, the "colonia" referred to a predominantly Hispanic settlement (Rochin and Castillo 1995). Given this alternative, culturally based definition, many border communities would qualify as colonias (Mukhija and Monkkonen 2006; Esparza and Donelson 2008).

Organization and Chapter Descriptions

The Colonias Reader consists of fifteen chapters divided equally into three sections, and a concluding (sixteenth) chapter that reflects on the book's content and proposes directions for future research. The first section, Colonia Economies and Economic Development, deals with the critical issues of economic diversity, farmworkers, employment (and unemployment/underemployment), and the cross-border economy. Chapter 1, written by Oscar Martínez, opens this section by summarizing principal socioeconomic conditions in the border region and providing a historical overview of the border economy. Issues and themes include the maquiladora economy, transborder labor and trade, tourism, and the military presence in the border region. Martínez builds context and background for the remaining chapters in this section by bringing forward factors and forces that have shaped the border economy over time. In chapter 2, Cecilia Giusti explores economic development in Texas colonias. She begins by proposing a broader framework for understanding economic growth versus economic development. Giusti argues that economic development is often narrowly defined so that issues of safety and security, participation and engagement, and community identity and pride are overlooked. She then reports primary research that examines the role of microbusiness in promoting local economic development. She looks closely at how gender affects business operations, and concludes with policy recommendations that enhance the role of microbusinesses in colonias economic development. Chapter 3 turns to economic development in New Mexico's colonias. In this chapter Robert Czerniak and David Hohstadt begin by demonstrating the need for local economic development in the state's colonias, where unemployment rates are high and residents are often forced to commute long distances to job sites. Many of the state's colonias are small, remote, and unincorporated, which means that there is little comprehensive assessment of their needs and economic development potential. Czerniak and Hohstadt respond by using survey research to develop a typology of colonias based on local conditions such as size, location, and infrastructure quality. They also rely on primary research to identify the types of businesses currently found in the state's colonias. In chapter 4, Vera Pavlakovich-Kochi and Adrian Esparza address economic development in Arizona's colonias. They document levels of poverty, income, and unemployment in southern Arizona, then provide an in-depth analysis of the cross-border economy. Using analytical methods, they show how ties to Sonora, Mexico, affect levels of employment, as binational agreements, border security, and seasonal variations alter employment demands. They conclude by using primary data to flesh out factors that constrain local businesses and hamper economic development efforts in the region's colonias. In chapter 5, Vinit Mukhija provides a careful evaluation of farmworkers in California. He begins by pointing to the state's rich agricultural economy, then shows how farmworkers and the poor are excluded from this prosperity. He explains how farmworkers and other low-income populations make up much of the colonias' population; at the same time, he argues convincingly that these officially designated districts fail to capture much of the region's poverty. Instead, he urges a revised definition of colonias that considers ethnic, cultural, and class characteristics rather than location and proximity to the U.S.–Mexico border.

The second section of the book, Housing and Community Development, deals with housing and shelter in the region's colonias. In chapter 6, David and Lydia Arizmendi and Angela Donelson review housing problems and needs in the region's colonias. Drawing on lengthy experience with low-income housing, they point to the need for more citizen-centered approaches, rather than the regulatory-based ones that have typically been directed at critical problems such as predatory lending, land ownership and land titles, unplanned and unregulated subdivisions, inadequate infrastructure, and a variety of housing conditions in the border region. Chapter 7 looks to housing in Texas, the largest pool of colonias housing in the border region. John Henneberger, Kristin Carlisle, and Karen Paup share years of experience as advocates for the underprivileged as they discuss the history of colonias housing in Texas. They trace the development of state-level policies and programs and explain how and why problems with colonias housing grew to such proportions. Henneberger, Carlisle, and Paup also showcase colonias that have confronted housing problems head-on, and share the personal stories of colonia residents. In chapter 8, Angela Donelson and Esperanza Holguin feature recent efforts to build sustainable low-income housing in New Mexico and Arizona colonias. These developments use environmentally friendly building materials such as adobe, straw bales, and rammed earth, combined with "sweat equity" to provide cost-efficient housing for the poor. Donelson and Holguin summarize obstacles that limit the use of alternative approaches, and describe two nonprofit organizations in New Mexico that use more sustainable building materials. In chapter 9, David Henkel Jr. visits the important role that faith-based organizations play in promoting community development. He describes the emergence of faith-based organizations as advocates for the poor and explains how and why they continue to prosper. He also presents examples of faith-based organizations working in New Mexico's colonias. In chapter 10, John Mealey paints a poignant picture of farmworker housing in California's Riverside County. Mealey conveys his decades of firsthand knowledge of the appalling conditions in which farmworkers live. He then turns to efforts by NGOs that are building affordable housing for farmworkers in

Riverside County. He summarizes work of the organizations that shoulder the task of housing the poor and explains how they managed to leverage residential developments with limited resources.

Public and environmental health issues rank high among the challenges that confront colonias and the entire U.S.–Mexico border region. The third section, Colonias Health and the Environment, considers these issues in the borderlands. All of the chapters in this section highlight the close connections between social equity, human-built and natural environments, and public health. They bring forward the critical themes of social and environmental justice and demonstrate how they are linked to human health and well-being. Chapter 11, written by Marlynn May, begins by identifying important health problems in the borderlands, then presents a conceptual model that links health to broader social and political arenas. May discusses obstacles to public health delivery and summarizes principal organizations that target border health. In chapter 12, Sergio Peña and Lee Rosenthal discuss public health and environmental issues in Texas colonias. They define pressing public health concerns in the Texas–Mexico region, and then present a conceptual model that links health to social, political, and economic institutions and class divisions. Peña and Rosenthal argue convincingly that Texas policies have favored physical improvements in colonias while ignoring the human dimensions of health. They also describe how NGOs provide health care to the region's poor through *promotores(as)*, or community health workers. In chapter 13, Samantha Sabo, Maia Ingram, and Ashley Wennerstrom take us to the border of Arizona and Sonora, Mexico, where numerous public health issues are found. They link public health to social and environmental inequities that largely explain health disparities among minority populations. Sabo, Ingram, and Wennerstrom describe two programs that respond to diabetes and obesity, problems that are widespread in the Arizona–Sonora border region, especially among the Mexican American population. As with Texas, promotores(as) figure prominently in these health-care programs. In chapter 14, Laura Norman examines urbanization and environmental degradation in the Arizona–Sonora borderlands. She charts the rapid pace of urban development in the region and shows how lax development regulations have contributed to environmental problems that compromise public health. Norman describes several large-scale federal programs that aim to mitigate environmental degradation and improve environmentally friendly planning in the region. Chapter 15, written by Kimberly Collins, looks at one of the most polluted cross-border environments in North America. She traces these problems to the Imperial Valley's (Imperial County, California) long history of agriculture that favored landed elites at the expense of farmworkers who live on subsistence wages and work long hours in the fields and processing plants. Collins finds that despite substandard housing and degraded environments, Imperial Valley residents are satisfied with their living conditions. She explores this paradox by investigating the meaning of quality of life as it applies to individuals versus more broadly defined communities. Collins describes how residents' high levels of satisfaction have derailed efforts to upgrade housing and the natural environment.

In the concluding chapter, William Smith examines the book's contributions through the lens of praxis—translating ideas into action. His aim is to articulate ways in which academics and practitioners can join hands to mobilize resources in behalf of colonias. He coins the term "Colonia Studies" as a new multidisciplinary field that takes stock of innovative theory as it informs applied practice. Smith's reflections provide fruitful directions for future research and suggest ways for positioning colonias on longer-term sustainable foundations.

The Colonias Reader is the first book that provides a comprehensive assessment of colonias in the U.S.–Mexico border region. It is motivated by the belief, which is shared by all contributors, that people everywhere are entitled to life's basic needs: a livable wage, decent housing, a safe and sanitary environment, and adequate health care. We hope that the book informs readers of the conditions in colonias, the efforts aimed at improving quality of life, and the severity of unresolved problems.

Notes

1. Identifying the exact number of colonias and the persons who live in them is difficult for three reasons. First, there is no census geography for colonias that is equivalent to the county or census tract. This means that singling out colonia populations is difficult and impossible in many situations. Second, colonias are oftentimes home to undocumented immigrants, and many fall beneath the census radar. Third, definitions of what constitutes a "colonia" vary between various federal and state agencies. These varying definitions explain why chapters in the book may report different numbers of colonias and colonia populations.

2. It is important to note that there are differences among colonias even though they share common characteristics. For example, few Hispanics are found in some colonias of New Mexico, Arizona, and California, where populations are overwhelmingly "white" or Anglo. See Esparza and Donelson (2008), and Mukhija and Monkkonen (2006, 2007) for detailed discussions of these differences in Texas, New Mexico, Arizona, and California.

PART I

Colonia Economies and Economic Development

The U.S.–Mexico Border Economy

Oscar J. Martínez

THE U.S.–MEXICO BORDER region comprises one of the largest pockets of deprivation in the United States. Deprivation arises from numerous problems, with economic hardship ranking high on the list. The five chapters in this section of the book focus on colonia economies and economic development in the four border states. Chapters explore issues critical to each state, while this first chapter introduces the borderlands economy more broadly.

The chapter pursues two objectives. First, it summarizes socioeconomic conditions found in the U.S.–Mexico border region. The analysis demonstrates that border counties differ from the United States in terms of the Hispanic/Latino presence, income, poverty, and unemployment. Second, the chapter traces the evolution of the border economy and then examines in detail the following specific sectors: maquiladoras (predominantly foreign-owned assembly plants), NAFTA (North American Free Trade Agreement), tourism, commuters, and immigrants. The intent is to illustrate the dynamic relationship that binds the two sides of the border, especially the cheap-labor system that is ultimately responsible for the colonia phenomenon discussed in this book.

Socioeconomic Conditions in the U.S.-Mexico Border Region

The U.S.–Mexico border region struggles with many problems that arise from lagging economic growth and development. These problems have been documented for specific states (Peach 1997; Ward 1999; Pagán 2004; Esparza and Donelson 2008), but few sources report them for the entire border region. Table 1.1 lists socioeconomic indicators for 24 counties located in Arizona, California, New Mexico, and Texas that abut the Mexican border and house the lion's share of colonias.

TABLE 1.1 Socioeconomic Indicators for U.S.–Mexico Border Counties.

State/County	Total Population (2007)	Percent Hispanic Population (2006)	Median Household Income (2004)	Percent Population in Poverty (2004)	Percent Annual Unemployment Rate (2007)
Arizona					
Cochise	127,866	31.6	$36,585	17.1	4.1
Pima	967,089	32.5	38,687	15.6	3.7
Santa Cruz	42,845	80.6	32,901	19.1	7.3
Yuma	190,557	55.9	34,230	18.4	13.8
Total/Ave.	1,328,357	50.2	35,601	17.6	7.2
California					
Imperial	161,867	75.7	33,674	18.5	15.9
San Diego	2,974,859	30.1	51,939	10.9	5.0
Total/Ave.	3,136,726	52.9	42,807	14.7	10.5
New Mexico					
Doña Ana	198,791	65.0	30,740	23.0	3.9
Hidalgo	4,945	57.0	23,702	21.2	2.9
Luna	26,996	59.7	22,888	24.3	9.2
Total/Ave.	230,732	60.6	25,777	22.8	5.3
Texas					
Brewster	9,239	43.3	30,467	16.9	3.5
Cameron	387,210	86.1	26,719	29.4	6.0
Culberson	2,484	70.5	24,672	22.0	2.7
El Paso	734,669	81.4	32,046	24.6	5.9
Hidalgo	710,514	89.5	26,375	30.5	6.6
Hudspeth	3,294	75.3	22,177	26.6	4.9
Jeff Davis	2,264	37.0	33,755	11.0	3.5
Kinney	3,320	50.9	31,335	18.8	4.8
Maverick	51,656	94.9	24,786	27.9	11.3
Presidio	7,575	83.8	24,915	26.4	9.1
Starr	61,833	97.5	19,775	34.8	10.6
Terrell	934	50.9	27,870	15.1	5.4
Val Verde	48,029	78.6	31,202	22.1	5.4
Webb	233,152	94.8	29,433	26.8	4.8
Zapata	13,605	88.4	26,157	27.2	5.4
Total/Ave.	2,269,778	74.9	27,446	24.0	6.0
All Counties	6,965,593	67.1	29,876	22.0	6.5
USA	301,621,157	14.8	44,334	12.7	4.6

Source: Compiled from U.S. Census Bureau 2008; Arizona Workforce Informer 2008; California Employment Development Department 2007; New Mexico Department of Workforce Solutions 2008; Texas Workforce Center 2008.

Table 1.1 indicates that as of 2007 nearly seven million persons lived in the 24 counties, but a handful of counties claim the majority of the population. These include Pima County, Arizona; San Diego County, California; and El Paso and Hidalgo counties in Texas. These four counties account for 77 percent of the total population and, with the exception of Pima County, are home to principal cross-border cities. The majority of the border population is Hispanic (67 percent), but the numbers are much higher in some counties. Hispanics account for over 70 percent of the total population in 12 of the 15 Texas counties and exceed 75 percent in Santa Cruz County, Arizona, and Imperial County, California. These compare with a Hispanic population of only 15 percent for the country as a whole. The geographical concentration of Hispanics owes much to the troubled history of the border region (Martínez 2006).

The level of economic hardship is reflected in income, poverty, and unemployment data. First, median household income in border counties lags well behind the country as a whole. On average, residents in these counties earned $14,458 less than across the country as of 2007. With a large and wealthy population, San Diego County boasts the highest median household income ($51,939) and even surpasses the nation. Thus, San Diego County stands apart from other border counties. For example, counties in New Mexico and Texas have the lowest household incomes and often trail behind the nation and other border counties. Second, table 1.1 shows that San Diego County records the lowest percentage of population living in poverty (11 percent), about one-third the percentage recorded in Starr County, Texas (35 percent). As a whole, Texas border counties are among the most poverty-stricken in the nation, but poverty colors much of the borderlands: county rates are nearly double those for the country (22 percent versus 13 percent). Finally, unemployment levels are far more variable in the border region, with many counties rising well above the national trend. Unemployment rates in Yuma County, Arizona, and Imperial County, California, are three times higher than in the rest of the country, and Maverick and Starr counties, in Texas, are nearly double the national average.

The data reported in table 1.1 reveal much about economic conditions in the border region. The large and rapidly growing population is dominated by Hispanics, especially in Texas, where the Hispanic population nears 100 percent in some counties. Incomes fall well below other regions of the country, while poverty and unemployment rates tower well above nationwide averages. The chapters in this section look more closely at the reasons for impoverishment in the border region and detail how economic development tries to stimulate growth and prosperity. The remainder of this chapter looks to the economic underpinnings of the borderlands economy.

Evolution of the Border Economy

In the 1880s, with the penetration of the railroads into the resource-rich zones of the U.S. Southwest and of Mexican states such as Sonora and Chihuahua, the borderlands overcame historic geographical isolation that had placed limits on economic growth. In Mexico, the governments of Porfirio Díaz (1876–80 and 1884–1911) succeeded in bringing about greater political stability and advances throughout the country, especially in the northern states. Foreign investment poured into critical sectors such as the railroads, mining, ranching, and agriculture. On the U.S. side, expanded population and modernization stimulated industries linked with Mexico, boosting transnational interaction. It is within the context of the economic rise of the greater borderlands that towns and cities in the boundary region emerged as important trade, transportation, and labor distribution centers (Martínez 1978; Tinker-Salas 1997). Many of the colonias discussed in the chapters to come owe their origins to these burgeoning industries and the cross-border movement of Mexican workers who were vital to regional economic growth and development.

To meet the demands of the growing border population, the Mexican government stimulated commercial activity by creating a free trade zone that functioned from 1885 to 1905. Previously, states like Tamaulipas and Chihuahua had experimented with free trade in their respective border districts, but when the federal Zona Libre took effect in 1885, it marked the first time that the central government had approved such activity along the entire northern border. Free trade would surface as an important issue in the border economy in subsequent generations (Herrera-Pérez 2004).

After the Mexican Revolution of 1910–20, Mexico began a process of political, economic, and social reconstruction, slowly eliminating conditions that had previously precipitated internal civil wars. Meanwhile, sustained economic growth became strongly institutionalized in the U.S. borderlands, engendering a closer relationship with northern Mexico, which, since the latter part of the nineteenth century, had in effect functioned as an extension of the U.S. economy. The more stable environment ushered in during the 1920s shaped the borderlands in ways that differed considerably from earlier periods when underdevelopment and turmoil were the order of the day. Expansion, including a rise in tourism spurred by liquor prohibition in the United States, created new opportunities and drew capital and new residents to the region (Martínez 1978).

In the 1930s, the Great Depression devastated the border region as businesses failed, border transactions fell, unemployment rose, and welfare rolls swelled. In the latter part of the decade, recovery began to be felt, and, once the United States entered World War II in 1941, the trend upward became clear. Both sides of the border received an unprecedented impulse for new growth as a result of the rise of defense-related industries in the U.S. Southwest. The U.S. government expanded existing military installations, created new ones, financed research facilities to develop modern weaponry, and awarded contracts to companies that produced armaments. New industries that served military needs stimulated other economic activity, which in turn attracted increasing numbers of people to formerly slow-growing centers in desert areas. Large U.S. government expenditures also went for improvements in infrastructure such as interstate highways and water projects, substantially raising the capacity of the region to sustain urbanization. Growth was further stimulated by the Korean and Vietnam wars and the increasing shift of economic activity from the industrial Snow Belt to the southern and western Sun Belt (Nash 1977, 1990).

U.S. border cities benefited substantially from these trends, expanding and diversifying their economies beyond the traditional agricultural, ranching, mining, trade, and basic service-oriented activities. For example, by the 1960s El Paso had boosted its agricultural and tourist sectors and had developed substantial labor-intensive industries that employed large numbers of low-wage workers, many of them from Mexico. The need for Mexican domestics rose dramatically as European American women became wage earners in ever-increasing numbers, and, as a result, needed help with housekeeping and child care. As U.S. border cities became more integrated into the national economy, giant corporations established local operations. Soon, modern commercial centers and shopping malls sprang up to serve the mushrooming middle-class suburbs.

The post–World War II boom affected the Mexican border cities just as forcefully, with the result that new waves of job-seeking migrants from the interior of Mexico began to make their way to the northern frontier. The economic growth along the border also reflected trends throughout Mexico, because the postwar years constituted a period of great national economic expansion. *La frontera* (the border zone), with its dynamic, U.S.-driven economy, surpassed most other regions of Mexico in the expansion of trade, industry, and tourism. Commerce also grew rapidly as U.S. shoppers, particularly Mexican Americans, crossed the border in growing numbers to buy a wide variety of Mexican products.

By the second half of the twentieth century the border region assumed a new character, having evolved from an isolated and underdeveloped area into one of the most rapidly growing zones of North America. New opportunities opened when the expanding global economy discovered cheap labor and other border attractions, triggering an unprecedented boom. The highly interdependent transnational economies found in vibrant twin-city complexes like El Paso–Ciudad Juárez and San Diego–Tijuana, and the ties that these communities developed with countries far beyond the boundaries of the United States and Mexico, catapulted them to new heights in world manufacturing and trade (Ganster and Lorey 2008).

Maquiladoras

The emergence of maquiladoras in the 1960s provides striking evidence of the rapidly growing integration of the border region into the global economy. Multinational corporations from the United States, Asia, and Europe found the abundant cheap-labor pools in centers like Ciudad Juárez and Tijuana, and the proximity of these cities to the lucrative U.S. market, as ideal factors in addressing the problems of rising production costs and international competition. Before long, a who's who of leading global companies engaged in a wide variety of assembly operations, and, in time, some high-tech industries made their appearance as well. Routinely, these companies established infrastructure on the U.S. side of the border to support the work in Mexico, including administrative, transportation, and warehousing centers. In that way both Mexican and U.S. border cities functioned as a single economic entity firmly linked to the world economy (Fernández-Kelly 1983; Sklair 1993; Stoddard 1987; Wilson 1992).

Maquiladoras began operations in 1965 at a time of high unemployment along the Mexican border caused largely by the end of the U.S. guest worker initiative known as the Bracero Program. Mexican officials had visited foreign-financed, offshore assembly plants in the Far East and concluded that Mexico could establish similar low-wage factories on its northern border, a region traditionally lacking in industry as a result of physical isolation and noninclusion in the long-standing national development strategy of import-substitution industrialization.

The Mexican government hoped that assembly plants would utilize significant local inputs and also stimulate the creation of domestic industries. From the beginning, however, the maquiladoras have incorporated only minimal domestic inputs, and the vision of thriving border domestic industries never materialized. Thus, maquiladoras have operated as foreign enclaves in the national economic system, with little or no integration into other Mexican industries.

Mexico enticed both foreign and domestic investors to establish maquiladora operations by allowing the duty-free importation of foreign equipment, parts, raw materials, and supplies as long as the final assembled products were exported abroad. Later, NAFTA made it possible to sell maquiladora products in the national Mexican economy. Foreign companies achieved tremendous cost savings, because Mexican manufacturing wages were about 10 percent of U.S. manufacturing wages.

Between 1970 and 2001, the number of maquiladoras rapidly grew from 120 to over 3,700, while the number of employees rose from 20,327 to almost 1.3 million. Historically, most of the plants have been located in Ciudad Juárez and Tijuana, while Matamoros, Reynosa, and Mexicali emerged as second-tier centers of maquiladoras, with Nuevo Laredo, Piedras Negras, Ciudad Acuña, and Nogales as third-tier centers. Select cities in Mexico's interior have also embraced maquiladoras (Martínez 1978; *Twin Plant News* September 2002).

The acute vulnerability of the maquiladora industry to international wage competition and periodic global recessions has been demonstrated repeatedly, but never so dramatically as during the crisis of 2001–2. As a result of sluggishness in U.S., European, and Asian markets, and the devastating impact of the terrorist attacks of 2001, droves of maquiladoras shut down or moved to China, Thailand, and Vietnam, lured there by lower production costs. By 2003, the number of maquiladoras dropped to 2,800, and the number of employees plummeted to one million (*Twin Plant News* February 2004). Since the crisis of 2001–2, the industry has experienced some recovery. In 2006, although the number of factories remained at the same level as in 2002, the number of employees had risen to 1.2 million (*Twin Plant News* February 2007).

In the 1960s and 1970s, critics of maquiladoras pointed out that the original purpose of the program, to alleviate pronounced male unemployment at the border, had not been accomplished. Indeed, at the time, women who had only recently joined the workforce and who could be paid lower wages dominated the maquiladora employee ranks. In recent years, however, the representation of men has increased significantly.

Detractors of the program have noted that rapid industrialization brought attendant social ills, such as inadequate housing, an alarming shortage of social services, increased crime, and family disintegration. Environmentalists have accused the maquiladora program of aggravating pollution problems on the border. Many have also argued that maquiladoras have encouraged more migrants from Mexico's interior to head toward the border, thus contributing to a persisting overpopulation problem. For example, with an unofficial current population of about 2 million each, Ciudad Juárez and Tijuana are among the most overcrowded cities in Mexico. Undoubtedly, the expansion of a low-wage maquiladora economy has contributed to the growth of poor, informal colonia settlements on both the U.S. and Mexican sides of the border. Substandard settlements in Mexico have grown in response to overcrowding and crises of border infrastructure. At the same time, colonias in the United States have expanded as growing numbers of border-area Mexicans have migrated north in search of work.

The North American Free Trade Agreement

The 1960s witnessed a renewed effort on the part of the Mexican government and domestic producers to stop, or at least slow, the overwhelming

consumption of U.S. and other foreign consumer goods by the boom-
ing Mexican border population. Through the Programa Nacional Fron-
terizo (PRONAF), the government sought to expand consumption of
national products on the northern frontier. Although PRONAF achieved
some success, Mexican *fronterizos* (borderlanders) continued buying foreign goods, with people shopping directly in the United States in ever-
increasing numbers. The foreign-oriented consumption patterns on the
border, along with extant acute job reliance on foreign companies and
tourists, underscored the reality of external economic dependence in the
Mexican border region. Acceptance of that reality led Mexico City to
allow more foreign products to enter border communities without paying the usual duties. The practice of exempting fronterizos from tariffs
has its origins in the Zonas Libres of the nineteenth century and various
other free-trade experiments during the first half of the twentieth century (Herrera-Pérez 2004; Martínez 1978).

By the 1970s, the extraordinary pressures wrought by national and
global economic crises prompted the Mexican government to embrace
free trade as a major part of its economic development strategy. Nego-
tiations by Mexico, Canada, and the United States finally produced, in
1993, the watershed NAFTA pact, which eliminated tariffs, some under
a short-term schedule and others over the long term. NAFTA also
removed other obstacles to cross-border trade and business, such as barriers to foreign investment. Responding to concerns by labor unions and
environmentalists, NAFTA established two commissions and a development bank to deal with worker displacement and pollution problems.
However, much to the disappointment of advocates of workers' rights,
the agreement did not allow the free flow of labor across North America
(Hufbauer and Schott 2005).

While NAFTA advocates have proudly emphasized that since the
agreement took effect in 1994 a boom in international trade has stimulated growth and created many new jobs in the three countries, critics
have focused on various perceived negative consequences. U.S. labor
unions and their supporters have charged that NAFTA has encouraged
more plant closures in the United States and the shift of assembly operations to Mexico. El Paso, which once had a substantial textile manufacturing sector, witnessed the movement of most of its garment factories to Mexico, displacing tens of thousands of predominantly Mexican

American female workers as a result. Critics have also pointed out that NAFTA failed to diminish border poverty (Peach 2007). Environmentalists from the three countries have contended that the safeguards created by NAFTA have not dealt with serious ecological problems that plagued overcrowded border cities.

In Mexico, many people have bitterly complained that the increased influx of foreign capital and consumer products has harmed key national industries such as agriculture and has displaced large numbers of domestic workers. Those concerned with dependence have charged that NAFTA allowed the United States to strengthen its long-standing hegemony over Mexican border consumers. That problem has long been recognized by the federal government, which has sought unsuccessfully to integrate the northern frontier economically with the rest of the republic.

Tourism

The economic dependence of Mexico's fronterizos on the United States is also evident in the reliance of border communities on tourist industries. Tourism per se is a beneficial addition to any economy, but certain activities that emerged in Mexican border cities have seriously marred the image of the border zone. Historically, cities like Juárez and Tijuana have been seen by many on both sides of the boundary as wide-open recreation centers for foreign visitors, appealing particularly to U.S. military personnel eager for thrills from sex, liquor, drugs, and other vices. This aspect of border life has been popularized in books and the media, much to the detriment of local residents. Given the powerful image of Mexican border communities as "sin cities," it is important to place the development of border nightlife in proper perspective and underscore ties with U.S. investors and clientele. In the broadest sense, this facet of the border economy started because of frontier economic necessity and thrived because of continued consumer demand and a favorable operating climate.

During the Prohibition years, from 1920 to 1933, border communities acquired infamy as centers of vice and moral abandon. Millions of Americans visited Mexican border cities when the Volstead Act of 1920 made it illegal to produce, transport, or consume liquor in the United States. Mexican fronterizos, while benefiting from the bonanza engendered by

Prohibition in the United States, found themselves on the defensive, having to explain why they tolerated so much drinking, gambling, and prostitution in their communities. With the onset of the Great Depression in 1929, and an attendant decline in tourism, controversies over border vice waned. The border economy worsened in 1933 with the end of Prohibition in the United States and the subsequent closure of many bars, casinos, nightclubs, and other centers of entertainment located south of the boundary.

World War II brought another major upswing in tourism in Mexican border towns. As military installations in the U.S. borderlands enlarged their populations during the war years, millions of military personnel visited Mexican border cities, stimulating local entertainment and other service-related activities. Tourism continued to rise as more Americans traveled in the U.S. Southwest and made short trips across the border, and more visitors spent time at the border in preparation for trips into Mexico's interior. The new earnings allowed fronterizos to make civic improvements and stimulated nontourist activities that aided in economic diversification. Yet the heavy reliance on entertainment, especially its seedy component, reinforced the image of border cities as "Centers of Vice," "Sodoms," "Gomorrah Cities," and other such epithets (Martínez 1978).

By the 1970s, liquor, drugs, and prostitution in Mexico no longer provided the magnetism they once did. The emergence in the United States of topless and bottomless bars, X-rated movies, sexual permissiveness, and the availability of drugs diminished the thunder of Mexican border nightlife. Even so, in the early years of the twenty-first century, foreigners continued to frequent diversion centers on the Mexican side, and, in the process, many needy Mexicans dependent on tourism, particularly women who worked as prostitutes, endured humiliations and indignities in their struggle to survive.

Commuters

An even more important and longer-standing source of income for Mexican border cities has been jobs north of the boundary. During the late nineteenth century, when northern Mexico and the U.S. Southwest experienced rapid economic growth, significant numbers of Mexicans began working for *norteamericano* companies on both sides of the border. The towns adjacent to the boundary became strategic recruiting points of Mexican labor, and soon a system developed by which large numbers of fronterizos, both documented and undocumented, used the area as a jumping-off point, or springboard, for crossing into the United States to work. Over time that labor system became institutionalized and continues to the present day. Transborder workers include commuters who cross the boundary daily and migrants who penetrate deeper into the interior of the United States, working seasonally and making periodic return trips to their border home bases (Martínez 1977).

It is difficult to know the actual size of the Mexican-worker commuting traffic because of data problems, but it includes persons who hold U.S. residency cards ("green cards"), persons who illegally use local crossing permits (issued to shoppers, students, businesspeople, tourists, and others) to work, and persons who cross the border without documentation. It is likely that the three categories of Mexican workers taken together comprise a workforce of several hundred thousand commuters. Another category of south-to-north commuters consists of U.S. citizens who live on the Mexican side and cross the border daily to work in U.S. border cities. Data are likewise not available on these workers, but undoubtedly they number in the tens of thousands. Finally, thousands of U.S. citizens commute from U.S. border cities to Mexico daily to work in maquiladoras as managers, administrators, supervisors, engineers, and technicians, while others work in non-maquiladora sectors of the Mexican border economy such as tourism, commerce, manufacturing, and real estate.

Immigrants in U.S. Border Cities

Since the late nineteenth century, Mexicans have been migrating northward from the interior of Mexico to and beyond the borderlands in search of economic opportunity. With continuous movement over several generations, it was inevitable that many people would establish themselves permanently in the U.S. border region. Some of these immigrants settled in the area fully "documented," while others arrived without documentation. As a rule, the poor immigrants who made the U.S. border region their home have little formal education and few occupational skills. Donelson and Esparza (2007), for example, find that undocumented workers who move to colonias in New Mexico and Arizona often lower the overall quality of life because of low educational attainment and limited employment skills. Most of these workers have found employment in agriculture and urban service industries that typically pay minimum wage. That profile is common among other poor immigrants who have ventured to different areas of the United States (Zúñiga and Hernández-León 2005).

Since the passage in 1965 of a U.S. immigration law that closed the door for most nonskilled laborers to obtain legal residency in the United States, greater numbers of foreign workers crossed the border without authorization as demand for their labor remained high. A heated debate ensued, prompting lawmakers in Washington, D.C., to introduce a number of bills in the 1970s and early 1980s meant to stop unregistered migration. Each proposal, however, was defeated. Then, in 1986, the U.S. Congress passed the Immigration Reform and Control Act, which increased border enforcement, enacted sanctions against employers of undocumented persons, and granted amnesty to undocumented individuals who had lived in the United States continuously since January 1, 1982. This landmark legislation promised to resolve the undocumented immigration problem once and for all, but it only diminished the flow temporarily. *Indocumentados* continued to enter the United States because of strong demand for their services, and employers found loopholes in the new law.

Along the border, many indocumentados took advantage of the amnesty provision to legalize their status. Social agencies and community organizations assisted in the effort to identify people who qualified for amnesty, and also helped with the required paperwork. Across the United States, 2.7 million immigrants received amnesty, most of them Mexicans. Without a doubt, border people constituted a sizable percentage of that number.

Soon the effects of the 1986 law dissipated, and by the early 1990s the undocumented migrants' levels of apprehension resembled those of the pre-1986 period. Frustrated, the U.S. government turned to other strategies. The INS (Immigration and Naturalization Service) strengthened the infamous "Tortilla Curtain" fences and reinforced extant walls on the border. New barriers also went up, including formidable corrugated steel walls along the San Diego–Tijuana sector and the Arizona–Sonora border. More television cameras and electronic sensors monitored strategic points in border cities, while powerful stadium lights illuminated the all-important San Diego–Tijuana crossing. The INS also dramatically increased the size of the Border Patrol and assigned more helicopters, land vehicles, and other equipment to border duty. The militarization of the border was in full swing (Dunn 1996).

The greater presence and assertiveness of border law enforcement agents became evident in El Paso–Ciudad Juárez in 1993 with the implementation of "Operation Blockade." U.S. immigration officials sought to stop immigrants from crossing the Rio Grande with an overwhelming show of force, positioning personnel and vehicles along the riverbank at close proximity to each other around the clock. When critics opposed this military-style campaign, authorities changed the campaign's name to "Operation Hold the Line" in an effort to soften the image in the public's eye. Few migrants could penetrate the line. In the first five months of the operation, Border Patrol apprehensions in El Paso declined by 73 percent in comparison to the same period a year earlier. According to media accounts, most El Pasoans, including Mexican Americans, strongly supported the blockade, but residents of neighboring Ciudad Juárez made their outrage known in street demonstrations, international bridge shutdowns, and boycotts of U.S. stores.

The success of the blockade in El Paso prompted the INS to implement similar campaigns elsewhere. "Operation Gatekeeper" and "Operation Safeguard" followed along the California–Baja California and Arizona–Sonora borders respectively (Nevins 2002). Collectively, the blockades, along with the new formidable walls, proved highly successful in deterring crossings in urban centers, forcing huge numbers of determined, would-be immigrants to head to unpopulated, remote, and increasingly dangerous areas to cross the border. Tragically, deaths became common in desert zones, mountainous terrain, and treacherous stretches of the Rio Grande. Between 1993 and 2003 nearly 3,000 border crossers lost their lives as a result of drownings, accidents, exposure, and homicide.

Controversy over undocumented immigration has escalated in the twenty-first century as concerns over border security in the United States became a major political issue following the terrorist attacks of September 11, 2001. The acute polarization in U.S. society doomed several bills in Congress meant to address the problem, delaying any long-term solutions until after the national elections of 2008. In the meantime, tougher enforcement at the border meant that many former commuters moved permanently to U.S. border cities. Legal commuters sought to avoid chronic delays at ports of entry, while undocumented workers wished to forestall possible apprehension by the ubiquitous Border Patrol.

Summary

Over the last 125 years, the border economy has changed dramatically, evolving from a production system based on basic agricultural and extractive activities to one that now boasts highly diversified commercial, industrial, and service sectors that form part of the modern global economy. Yet much of the activity in border cities continues to be based on assembly operations and other forms of low-cost labor. For that reason the border region remains a magnet for poor, uneducated workers from the interior of Mexico.

From the standpoint of the United States, the availability of large numbers of Mexican workers has been an important factor in the growth and development experienced by Texas, New Mexico, Arizona, and California. That reserve army of labor has been built up over the decades by a combination of push-pull tendencies that have characterized the economies of Mexico and the United States. A natural consequence of that condition is the emergence and growth of poor colonias throughout the borderlands on both sides of the dividing line. Today colonias located in border areas from the Texas Lower Rio Grande Valley to the San Diego, California, area serve as pools of cheap labor in the service of numerous U.S. industries, including agriculture, construction, manufacturing, and sundry service enterprises. The chapters in this book document many of the problems surrounding the border economy.

Microbusiness in Texas Colonias

Cecilia Giusti

THE NUMBER OF COLONIAS in Texas is difficult to pin down, with estimates ranging from 1,400 to nearly 2,400 (Cisneros 2001; Texas Secretary of State 2008). Much of the discrepancy rests in the definition of colonias, which varies between federal and state agencies. In any case, all agree that Texas colonias struggle with a host of health, housing, and economic problems. These are summarized in other chapters of the book; here I focus on the role that economic development plays in improving quality of life in colonias. In this regard, unemployment takes center stage, because it is so prevalent and contributes to many of the problems witnessed in Texas colonias. As discussed in chapter 1, unemployment rates often double or triple those found in Texas and the country.

The persistence of unemployment underscores the need for economic development but raises the critical question: how can we best promote economic growth and development in colonias? Improving educational attainment and job skills will certainly help, but two factors complicate the situation in colonias. First, jobs are inaccessible to many colonia residents because they typically live outside of major towns and cities. This physical isolation means that long-distance commuting is the only way to get to jobs, an option unavailable to many colonias because transportation costs are unmanageable. Second, and perhaps more important, employment opportunities are unavailable in many colonias. Esparza and Donelson (2008) find the same problem in New Mexico's colonias, where residents commute to distant job sites because local jobs are unavailable. For these reasons, development programs that emphasize education and job training yield some positive benefit, but the pivotal issues of job access and local availability are unaddressed.

These constraints suggest that *local* economic development holds the greatest potential for increasing employment in colonias. But in the past, efforts to develop local economies have proven difficult, which means that new and innovative approaches are needed. Local entrepreneurship in the form of microbusinesses or microenterprises is emerging as a promising alternative in the United States and across the globe. Even so, little is known about it in the border region's colonias.

This chapter examines microbusinesses in Texas colonias by pursuing three objectives. First, I present some fundamental concepts and definitions of economic growth and development. This discussion builds a foundation for understanding constraints to economic development and how best to overcome them. Second, the chapter turns to microbusinesses, which many argue hold the greatest promise for bringing sustained economic development. I define microbusinesses, summarize current programs that support them, look firsthand at how and why they emerge, the characteristics of owners, success and failure rates, and other attributes. The analysis draws on primary research that involved 200 microbusinesses active in Texas colonias. Finally, I propose some specific policies and programs that encourage microbusinesses and, more broadly, economic development in borderlands colonias.

Economic Growth and Development

Distinguishing economic growth from economic development is critical to understanding problems that confront colonias. In the first case, economic growth is occurring in the Texas–Mexico border region, as evidenced by indicators such as income, employment, exports, and the overall growth of many border cities (Anderson and Gerber 2007; U.S. Census Bureau 2002). In the second case, even though the region as a whole is improving, some areas lag well behind, creating pockets of poverty that have not benefited from broad-based prosperity. These pockets include the region's colonias: communities that have been the subject of special legislation due to extreme circumstances (Texas Attorney General 2007a; Texas Secretary of State 2006). The prosperity experienced in the Texas–Mexico region is often characterized as economic growth, while the poverty that plagues colonias is associated with the lack of economic development.

At first glance, these differences are intuitively clear. But understanding the constraints that colonias face requires a more careful definition of economic growth versus economic development. *Economic growth* is a widely used concept that refers to positive gains in the production of goods and services and overall standard of living. It is traditionally measured by numerical increases in production, exports, income, and savings. These variables can be measured at the neighborhood, city, regional, or national scale and are used by economists and like-minded analysts. *Economic development,* on the other hand, is defined as the enhancement of opportunities that enable people to conduct meaningful lives without fear and in a more socially integrated environment (United Nations 2007). It includes qualitative variables such as equity, equality, safety, and security, as well as access to education, political participation, sanitation facilities, and health care. Economic development, therefore, involves a more complex set of factors that reference both monetary and nonmonetary objectives. The definition of economic development is enhanced by adding the spatial dimension. By this I mean that locally based economic development is rooted in the potential of human and physical resources to create new employment opportunities and to stimulate new, locally based economic activity (Blakely 1994). Since many colonias lack employment opportunities locally, economic development should focus on communities. Microbusinesses are ideally suited for local entrepreneurship because, in addition to creating jobs, they contribute to broader-based development by taking stock of community resources.

Given these definitions, it is clear that Texas colonias deal with a range of problems that inhibit economic development. Many of these problems are rooted in age-old conflicts of equity and equality that, over time, have limited access to life's basic needs such as safe infrastructure, housing, education, and jobs. The absence of these, in turn, has hampered economic growth.

A summary of programs that respond to the colonias "problem" in Texas demonstrates the nearly singular focus on physical infrastructure in economic development policy. Aware of the extreme difficulties posed by colonias, in 1989 the Texas legislature initiated a number of long-overdue programs that were designed specifically for colonias. The provision of clean water, electricity, and wastewater treatment facilities, and the legal conversion of property contracts, were identified as the most pressing needs (Giusti et al. 2006; Ward et al. 2003). Some of the largest and more significant programs were (and still are) the Economically Distressed Areas Program (EDAP), the Colonias Wastewater Treatment Assistance

Program, the Colonia Self-Help Program, the Colonia Plumbing Loan Program, and the Colonia Areas and Management Support Program. Since 1989, more than $250 million has been allocated for water and wastewater infrastructure, and $175 million for road paving in Texas colonias (Texas Secretary of State 2006).

Over the years, these programs have met with some success, although several obstacles have hindered implementation, and funding has not nearly equaled need. Basic infrastructure has improved in many colonias, especially access to potable water and electricity. Even though many colonias have not benefited from these programs, it is important to acknowledge that progress has been made.

Even so, programs and initiatives have responded to a narrow definition of what economic development entails. For example, basic infrastructure is important to improving quality of life, but physical needs are only part of the problem. Economic development requires a far more comprehensive approach that enhances the capacity to obtain jobs locally, earn higher incomes, become more productive citizens, and be active in charting future growth and development. This broader approach to economic development has been largely ignored, which may well explain the marginal success of policies and programs thus far.

Microbusiness and Economic Development

Despite the difficulties that colonia dwellers face, their creativity is reflected in the many resources drawn upon to make a living. More than anything, economic development should acknowledge the rich resources that people bring to the table, and implement approaches that take stock of their potential. The entrepreneurial spirit that underlies the microbusiness phenomenon is a prime example. Residents are creating sources of income locally through self-employment and microbusinesses that ignite diverse, active, and livable communities. Such activities capture the essence of economic development as defined above.

While the growing popularity of microbusinesses is clearly evident in colonias, how they emerge, their performance, and the challenges they face are uncertain. This applies to the microbusinesses in colonias of Texas and across the nation (Edgcomb and Klein 2005).

Defining Microbusinesses

In simple terms, microbusiness refers to "very small" firms. But the question remains, what is a "very small" firm? Very small businesses are defined by the characteristics of each economic sector. According to the Small Business Administration (SBA), a small business is independently owned and does not dominate its industrial sector (Pollinger and Cordero-Guzmán 2007; Small Business Administration 2007). Moving from this general definition, the Aspen Institute defines a microbusiness as a firm with five or fewer employees that requires $35,000 or less to start up and does not have access to the traditional commercial banking sector (Edgcomb and Klein 2005). The institute's definition is broadened by *The Directory of Microenterprise Programs,* which indicates that a microenterprise is a sole proprietorship, partnership, or family business with fewer than 10 employees and without access to the commercial banking sector, and which requires loans of under $15,000 for start-up (Clark and Huston 1992). Consumer Action (2005) defines microbusinesses as very small companies run by their owners with the assistance of few employees. They are often home-based and have annual sales of under $250,000 and few assets.

Identifying the number of microbusinesses locally and nationally is difficult because of their unique characteristics. For this reason, researchers most often rely on estimates. The Aspen Institute, for example, estimates that 22 million Americans are small business owners, including approximately 20 million who own very small microbusinesses. As the institute points out, however, these estimates do not include businesses in the "informal" sector (Edgcomb and Klein 2005). Since many microbusinesses are informal enterprises, this estimate likely undercounts the actual number substantially.

In Texas colonias, data from the U.S. Census Bureau (2002) suggest that microbusinesses are likely owned by Hispanics. According to the Census Bureau, for example, Hispanics owned 16 percent of businesses across the state, more than double the national percentage. In Webb County, located on the Texas–Mexico border, Hispanic-owned businesses reach 60 percent. While these data are somewhat dated, it is unlikely that ownership trends have changed in recent years. If anything, they undercount Hispanic ownership, as my research demonstrates. I found that nearly all businesses in Texas colonias are owned by Hispanics.

Because the bulk of microbusinesses in Texas colonias are owned and operated by Hispanics, a more careful definition is required. For present purposes, I define microbusinesses as firms with five or fewer employees that are owned by a disadvantaged minority. Disadvantaged minorities are low-income persons of an ethnic or racial minority group. In contrast to the definitions presented by the SBA and other organizations, this definition responds to the characteristics of Texas colonias.

Programs and Policies that Promote Microbusiness in Texas

There are several programs and policies that support small firms and microbusinesses because they have enormous potential for generating local employment (Servon and Bates 1998; Light and Rosenstein 1995; Raheim 1996; Robles and Cordero-Guzmán 2007). Policies aimed at reducing poverty and increasing wealth are especially well suited for colonias, because they convert low-paying jobs into independent businesses and provide opportunities for low-income segments of the population that otherwise might remain unemployed, especially in Hispanic communities (Fairlie 2001; Jurik, Cavender, and Cowgill 2006). Not all small and microbusinesses require the same type of policies, and ideally they should be tailored to the specific needs of entrepreneurs (Hall 1996; Harrison 1995; Headd 2000). For example, there are currently over 500 different funding agencies that lend support to microbusinesses (Pollinger and Cordero-Guzmán 2007). Given the variability of local programs and initiatives across the country, I focus on programs and policies that can assist colonias in all four border states. Many of these are sponsored by the Small Business Administration (SBA), and discussion draws upon select SBA publications that describe the nature of policies and programs, as well as applicant qualifications and procedures (Small Business Administration 1998, 2007, 2008).

The SBA's Microenterprise Program targets microbusinesses explicitly through a set of policies and functions that encourage microbusiness formation and longer-term operation. The SBA establishes agreements with local organizations or institutions—called Small Business Development Centers (SBDCs)—that serve as intermediaries and manage federally supported money to promote microbusinesses. Nationwide, there are sixty-three SBDCs, with at least one in every state (six in California; four in

Texas). Each state has a lead organization that sponsors the SBDC, manages the program, and coordinates services offered to small businesses through a network of 110 subcenters and satellite locations. Subcenters are located at colleges, universities, community colleges, vocational schools, chambers of commerce, and economic development corporations in order to take advantage of academic resources and better funding opportunities. The Texas centers located in San Antonio, Lubbock, Houston, and Dallas/Fort Worth serve 49 service locations. The San Antonio Center serves most of the border area.

The office of Women's Business Ownership, which works within the SBA, has established a national network of 103 Women's Business Centers (WBC). The WBCs assist women business owners, with special emphasis on low-income/socially disadvantaged women. The program seeks to level the playing field for women entrepreneurs who face unique obstacles in the business world. In Texas, there are four WBCs, located in Fort Worth, McAllen, El Paso, and Austin. As I describe below, women claim a sizable share of the colonias microbusiness ownership, and the Women's Business Ownership program may well be a fruitful source of support.

The Disadvantaged Entrepreneur program, also sponsored by the SBA, is geared to the needs of entrepreneurs who are attempting to launch microbusinesses. To qualify for assistance, entrepreneurs must be considered "low-income" and must be the owner, majority owner, or developer of a microenterprise that lacks access to capital or other resources essential for business start-up and success. In other cases, entrepreneurs must demonstrate that their ability to compete in the free enterprise system has been impaired due to diminished capital and credit opportunities, compared to other firms in the same industry. Through the Microloan Demonstration Program (MDP), the SBA contracts with local lenders (intermediaries) and local institutions to provide funding and technical support for microbusinesses. Two such organizations, ACCIÓN Texas and the Rural Development and Finance Corporation (RDFC), both nongovernmental organizations (NGOs), serve the needs of Texas colonias. RDFC provides technical support and small loans to microbusinesses that have been in operation for at least two years and have an established tax record. ACCIÓN Texas is more likely to benefit entrepreneurs in colonias because it has fewer requirements for loan eligibility and is willing to approve loans for start-up businesses.

Other organizations and agencies contribute to local economic development by encouraging microbusinesses, such as those sponsored by NGOs, but the SBA provides the widest range of policies and programs. Their federal funding base, coupled with networks of national, state, and local agencies and offices offers entrepreneurs and microbusiness owners the broadest base of support. Entrepreneurs, therefore, should investigate the range of programs sponsored by the SBA.

Microbusiness in Texas Colonias

Even though microenterprises are well suited for local economic development in Texas colonias, they have received little attention in the research literature. Responding to this deficiency, I launched an exploratory study of microbusinesses in Texas colonias. The research was conducted in 2002 and was funded by the U.S. Department of Housing and Urban Development's Young Scholars Program. It included 200 colonias in Webb, Hidalgo, and Cameron counties, some close to cities like Laredo and Brownsville, and others farther from urban areas. The survey included four sections that explored many dimensions of microbusinesses in colonias. The sections covered the general characteristics of microbusinesses and their owners, operation and financing status, contributions to local development, and business owners' opinions and expectations. Four promotoras conducted all surveys (in Spanish or English) face-to-face with business owners. Promotoras(es) are colonia residents trained as outreach workers and are trusted members of their communities. In total, 200 responses were collected, but after we checked for consistency and reliability, 155 valid survey responses were used for the analysis.

For present purposes, I report findings on four pivotal issues. First, I sought to identify principal characteristics of microbusiness owners, including gender, educational attainment, and income level. This information is useful in understanding which segments of the colonia population are most likely to engage in local business activities. Second, microbusiness owners were asked to indicate the reasons why they opened their businesses. This gets at the issue of factors that define entrepreneurship. Third, I sought to flesh out differences between male and female business owners. In this case, gender may well explain differing motives and attitudes toward entrepreneurship and business operation. Finally,

I sought to understand whether business owners take advantage of the many programs designed to encourage microbusiness start-up and operation in colonias.

The Characteristics of Business Owners

The survey revealed well-defined characteristics among microbusiness owners in Texas colonias. Foremost, women own most businesses. Of the total 155 valid responses, 71 percent (110) were women. There are also distinguishable patterns according to age of respondents. Fifty-nine percent of business owners were between 31 and 49 years of age. Finally, business owners had higher levels of educational attainment than other colonia residents. The study found that 46 percent of survey respondents had not completed high school, while the remaining 54 percent had a high school diploma or college-level education. In contrast, in Rio Bravo, a relatively wealthy and more established colonia located in Webb County, only 22 percent of the population had completed high school. Only 2 percent of Rio Bravo residents had a bachelor's or postgraduate degree, compared to 7 percent in the sample of business owners. Even though pairing colonia residents in a single colonia (Rio Bravo) with business owners in three counties allows only a rough comparison, these findings suggest that higher levels of educational attainment are positively correlated with entrepreneurship and microbusiness ownership.

In addition to personal attributes, the survey also queried respondents about the extent of local versus nonlocal business ties. The results indicate that microenterprises rely heavily on the local community for customers and suppliers. Seventy percent of their clients live in colonias, mainly in the same colonia as the business owner. These close-knit business relationships form networks of consumption and production and bring much-needed development to communities.

Reasons for Business Formation

Understanding the reasons for business formation is important for promoting microbusinesses in Texas colonias and the entire borderlands region. Risk taking is often associated with the entrepreneurial spirit, but what underlies this spirit? To get at this issue, respondents were asked to explain why they opened their own business versus taking a paid job working for someone else.

The reasons for starting a business were many and varied. Over 70 percent of respondents—both women and men—indicated that businesses were opened in order to earn a profit. This is to be expected, but beyond the profit motive, there are striking differences between men and women. For example, child care is an important issue for women but is not at all important to men. Over 36 percent of women indicated that being self-employed enabled them to care for children while working. Women also reported that supplementing the household's income was important (17 percent), while only 2 percent of men felt the same. On the other hand, men, more than women, viewed their microbusiness as the fulfillment of a long-term dream. Over 74 percent of men versus 44 percent of women indicated that owning their business emerged from longer-term aspirations.

In sum, the motives for entering the business world center on making a living for both men and women. Beyond this, the impetus of starting businesses varies considerably between men and women. Women indicate more practical, problem-based reasons, such as facilitating child care and supplementing household income, while men seek to realize longer-term ambitions of business ownership.

Microbusinesses and Gender

The survey results indicate that businesses vary significantly according to gender. First, the number of hours spent at work differs between men and women. The survey indicated that 54 percent of men work more than 40 hours a week, compared to only 20 percent of women. A little more than half the women (56 percent) spend 10 to 20 hours per week at the microbusiness, compared to only 23 percent of men. These differences arise from cultural forces that define the division of household labor. In Mexican society, women are primarily responsible for housework, so they devote fewer "free" hours to businesses. Even when women work full-time (40 hours per week), they bear the bulk of responsibility for child and elder care.

Second, business success also differs according to gender. In my sample, 40 percent of all the businesses had been in operation for less than a year, and 30 percent were six years or older. But gender says much about longevity. Over 65 percent of males had operated their business for more than three years; a significant survival rate for a small business. On the other hand, only 37 percent of women had owned their business for the same three-year period. At the same time, 49 percent of female owners indicated that their business was less than one year old, compared to 16 percent of male owners. These results suggest that male-owned businesses survive longer than those owned by women. This is to be expected, because women are typically responsible for domestic tasks (child care, housekeeping) in addition to running a business.

Finally, the size of microbusinesses varies between male and female business owners. Although quantitative data are not available, woman-owned businesses in general are smaller and have fewer paid employees. This, coupled with the comparatively lower likelihood of business survival, means that women-owned businesses are not as well established.

These results indicate distinctive differences between male and female business owners. Men devote more time to the business, mainly because women bear the responsibility for household duties, especially child and elder care. Nevertheless, women are undeterred; they open and run more microbusiness than men, with the majority in operation for less than one year.

Support for Microbusinesses

Despite the numerous policies and programs tailored to the needs of microbusinesses, few colonia business owners have taken advantage of them. This occurs largely because microbusiness owners are unaware of programs. The survey found that over 90 percent of respondents had no knowledge of loans or programs. Even more troubling, only one of the business owners who were aware of programs and policies had applied for and received a loan. Instead of seeking assistance from formal agencies and organizations, colonia microbusiness owners are self-reliant. Seventy-nine percent of respondents indicated that they financed start-up costs with personal or family resources, and subsequent improvements and operating costs are paid out of pocket. While this self-reliance is admirable, business owners forgo valuable resources that potentially promote greater success. But the limited participation witnessed among business owners suggests the need to adjust policies and programs aimed at microbusiness assistance.

Policy Recommendations

In recent years economic development policies and programs are moving from the narrow focus on physical infrastructure and, instead, target local grassroots initiatives that foster community-wide involvement. Microbusinesses play a critical role in this approach because of the many benefits they offer. Through its numerous policies and programs, the SBA contributes to this type of economic development by assisting the creation and growth of microbusinesses. The SBA's programs are well suited for Texas colonias, because they are low-income communities with high rates of unemployment, low educational attainment, limited English language skills, and a large concentration of Hispanic minorities. Even so, my research shows that these programs have met with limited success. Only a handful of entrepreneurs are even aware of these programs, and fewer still take advantage of them.

For this reason, program reforms should focus on the providers and receivers of assistance. In the first case, the SBA and other federal and state agencies need to make their programs more accessible to entrepreneurs in colonias. While this seems obvious, language barriers, low self-esteem, mistrust of government, and the informal nature of many microbusinesses impose limitations that are difficult to surmount. Chapter 4 of this book describes how similar problems hamper economic development in Arizona colonias. Thus, making program announcements available in Spanish, reaching out to colonias more aggressively, and easing application requirements will do much to improve participation. Nearly all agencies and organizations, for example, have offices in large cities located far from colonias. My research found that few of these agencies have taken their services out to colonias, where they are desperately needed. At the same time, the entrepreneurs who need financial and technical support cannot get to cities where agency offices are located. This calls for improved outreach, especially using the Spanish language, if the goal is to foster broader-based economic development in colonias.

In the second case, entrepreneurs lack many of the basic skills needed to apply for financial and technical support. Few know how to develop a business plan, and basic requirements for requesting a loan are rarely understood. This suggests that programs should bundle basic business education with other types of support. To overcome the language barrier, education should be bilingual.

Finally, policies and programs need to acknowledge and respond to the overwhelming presence of woman-owned microbusinesses in Texas colonias. The research reported above indicates that women own the majority of businesses, but, even so, their failure rates exceed those of men. The SBA sponsors WBCs (described above), but this does not go far enough, because women in colonias have special needs. First, they often are the least-educated segment of the colonias population, which hampers their ability to apply for financial assistance. Second, women typically have less work experience. This limits their ability to demonstrate the know-how needed to run businesses. Finally, women are most often saddled with the household's child- and elder-care responsibilities. This lessens the time available for work, which increases the likelihood of business failure. Programs, therefore, should be geared to the special needs of women by emphasizing basic education, especially in English language skills and business practices and procedures. Assistance with child and elder care will go a long way in improving the success of woman-owned microbusinesses (Sanders 2004). It may well be that promoting self-employment among women is the first step toward longer-term success. This approach responds to the demands placed on women by providing flexibility. Self-employment builds women's personal confidence, and running a business improves their ability to handle money and perform better in the business world as they gain experience.

These policy and program reforms build on the understanding that a broader approach to economic development is called for. While improvements to physical infrastructure are certainly needed, taking stock of a broader definition of economic development will likely lead to greater success. Such efforts must acknowledge cultural, social, and political underpinnings so that development extends throughout colonias by strengthening families, building community cohesion and participation, and providing jobs locally.

Summary

Colonias in Texas are plagued with high levels of poverty and unemployment, as well as social, economic, and political isolation. Like colonias throughout the borderlands, they struggle with the fundamental problem of encouraging economic growth and development. This chapter responded to these circumstances by examining the role of microbusinesses in promoting economic development. The chapter began by distinguishing economic growth from economic development. I argued that conventional approaches to economic development have often met with limited success because of their nearly singular focus on physical infrastructure. While infrastructure improvements are clearly needed and have proven beneficial, economic development should respond to the complex interdependencies that broach both human and physical dimensions. Development, therefore, should also address issues such as equity, equality, safety, and social and political justice, by providing education, strengthening families, and building identity, self-esteem, and community pride. Pursuing this comprehensive approach will more likely lead to sustained local economic development and, ultimately, economic growth.

The chapter then turned to microbusinesses, or microenterprises, because they are well suited to the needs of colonias. Microbusinesses are very small firms, typically privately owned, that embody the entrepreneurial spirit of our country. My research explored the reasons why they emerge, some of the characteristics of colonia owners, success rates, and their use of external sources of support. I found that women own and operate the majority of microbusinesses, even though they shoulder the burden of family care. These findings dramatize the social inequalities that are even more pronounced in Hispanic society. Finally, despite the numerous policies and programs geared to the needs of microbusinesses, they are seldom used by colonia microbusiness owners. This suggests the need to revise policies and programs so that they are more accessible and effective.

All agree that poverty and unemployment are perhaps the most recognizable characteristics of Texas colonias. This has led to the perception of colonia residents as hapless victims who struggle to survive. But a deeper inspection finds an enormous reserve of creativity, resilience, and desire for self-sufficiency. Microbusinesses are the visible expression of these characteristics, because success depends on risk taking, long hours of work, and the desire for something better. Efforts aimed at economic development will gain much by encouraging and supporting this entrepreneurial spirit.

3

Economic Development in New Mexico's Colonias

Robert Czerniak and David Hohstadt

THERE ARE MANY REASONS to be optimistic about New Mexico's colonias, but economic development is not among them. In recent years, for example, the quality of infrastructure and housing has improved, and health services are available to a growing number of people. Targeted programs and initiatives, coupled with increased scrutiny of land development practices, are largely responsible for these gains. But the pressing problems of high unemployment and the general lack of business development continue to plague these struggling communities. Colonias in Texas suffer a similar fate (see chapter 2): the lack of local jobs and economic growth.

Esparza and Donelson (2008) demonstrate the need for economic development in New Mexico's colonias. They estimate that as of 2005, New Mexico's colonias housed about 139,000 people. The median household income for colonia residents was $30,393, well below the statewide average of $39,156. In unincorporated colonias, which account for about 90 percent of all colonias in the state, over 23 percent of the population lived in poverty. This compares with a poverty rate of 17 percent for the state. Per capita incomes in unincorporated colonias also lag well behind the state average: $16,361 versus $20,269. More telling, 71 percent of the people living in incorporated colonias commuted to jobs located outside their place of residence.

The lack of local jobs brings economic development to center stage because it has a long history of bolstering economies. There is every reason to believe that economic development will benefit New Mexico colonias if development strategies and techniques are targeted to specific needs. This type of alignment enables the efficient use of development resources (financial and technical) and raises the likelihood of successful outcomes (Weisbrod and Piercy 2007). But tailoring strategies is difficult in New Mexico because, to date, there are few (if any) systematic studies of colonia economies or economic development efforts.

This chapter discusses the targeting of economic development strategies to the needs of New Mexico's colonias. We begin by summarizing the strategies available for colonia economic development. Strategies range from business attraction to education and entrepreneurial leadership and training. Next, we explore the needs and development potential of colonias. A fivefold typology of colonias is used to classify critical needs. The typology is based on a quantitative analysis of 24 New Mexico colonias. Development potential is examined by identifying the composition of businesses in colonias. The assessment is based on "windshield" surveys that identified principal businesses and employers in 16 colonias. The chapter concludes by targeting economic development strategies to colonias.

Economic Development Policies and Programs

We know little about the successes and failures of economic development in border colonias, because until recently they were largely ignored. Federal legislation aimed at colonias first appeared in 1990, with agencies such as the Department of Housing and Urban Development (HUD), the Environmental Protection Agency (EPA), and the Department of Agriculture's Rural Development program (USDA-RD) taking the lead. Funding for development programs was slow in coming in the years that followed, with the bulk of assistance funneled into the Texas–Mexico border region. Nongovernmental agencies (NGOs) have increased their outreach to colonias over the years, but with budgets stretched thin, they were forced to narrow the scope to basic problems such as infrastructure, housing and health care (Esparza and Donelson 2008; Pagán 2004; Ward 1999). Economic development in New Mexico, therefore, was far removed from many targeted programs and initiatives.

Even so, we can summarize commonly used economic development policies that hold the greatest potential for New Mexico's colonias. These policies and strategies have evolved over many years as scholars, analysts, and practitioners fine-tuned approaches and linked them to theories of economic growth and community development (Shaffer, Deller, and Marcouiller 2006). It is now widely understood, for example, that a "one-size-fits-all" approach to economic development is often doomed to failure, because it does not link strategies to specific needs and potential (Weisbrod and Piercy 2007). For this reason, strategies aimed at central cities or suburban communities may not work well in smaller and more remote colonias, which are prevalent in New Mexico. Thus, instead of rushing to popular economic development approaches, such as business expansion or recruitment, communities should consider a range of policies that seek to enhance local employment (Crowe 2006; Shaffer 1989). From this broad set of policies, five are most applicable to colonias: (1) business attraction, (2) expansion of existing businesses, (3) improving the community's capture of dollars (e.g., keeping consumer expenditures within the community), (4) the formation of new businesses, and (5) increasing financial assistance from external sources.

Of the five strategies, new business formation and attracting external financial assistance are best suited to colonia economic development. The formation of new businesses means that strategies should encourage business start-ups. Fostering business start-ups meets the needs of colonias because there are few businesses to begin with, a common feature of smaller and more remote communities (Crowe 2006; Lenzi 1996; Markley and McNamara 1995). Small businesses, in particular, play a valuable role in local job creation, because they invest in entrepreneurs (Bee 2004; Lenzi 1996; Servon 2006). Giusti, for example (see chapter 2), found that microbusinesses are popular in Texas colonias and contribute significantly to local employment. Strategies that encourage small business formation include business incubators, entrepreneurial education, facilitating access to capital, and encouraging microenterprise formation (Markley and McNamara 1995; Raheim 1996; Servon 2006; Shaffer 1989; Weisbrod and Piercy 2007).

In the second instance, attracting external financing is vital to economic development in colonias, because there are few local funding sources. This applies especially to unincorporated colonias, which have a limited ability to raise funds locally and must compete for scarce resources with other communities in the same county jurisdiction. In simple terms, attracting external funding involves bringing tax dollars from government agencies to the local community. This requires that economic development specialists encourage the full use of public assistance programs, such as those sponsored by HUD, the EPA, the USDA-RD, and the

Small Business Administration (SBA), and facilitate networking in the political arena (Esparza and Donelson 2008; Shaffer 1989). Such efforts have proven successful in funding community development in Arizona's colonias, where local leaders and organizers have formed alliances with county, state, and federal agencies. These networks are often facilitated by NGOs, but outreach efforts by federal agencies (HUD in particular) have also proven valuable. Local leaders and organizers in Arizona's colonias were instrumental in ensuring that federal dollars targeted the specific needs of colonias (Esparza and Donelson 2008).

Even though few studies document the success or failure of economic development in New Mexico's colonias, a range of approaches have been used. Regardless of which strategy is used, effective economic development requires that the needs of specific colonias are assessed so that programs and strategies complement needs and development potential. This requires an understanding of local problems and constraints; issues that are not widely known in New Mexico's colonias.

Assessing Development Needs and Potential

The colonias of New Mexico are varied on many levels, and treating them as a homogeneous group may well move economic development in the wrong direction. Differences can be described in terms of the regions in which they are located, historic heritage, and social, cultural, and economic makeup. Ideally, economic development strategies should be tailored to these characteristics. But such efforts require enormous budgets that fund primary data collection and analysis, public forums, and high-priced consultants, all of which are unavailable to nearly all colonias.

A Typology of New Mexico Colonias

We pursued an alternative approach that classifies communities according to characteristics that define local needs. The methodology used cluster analysis to classify a sample of 24 of New Mexico's 99 colonias (Czerniak and Esparza 2004). The 24 colonias were selected based on their location and population size so that they represent a broad range of communities.[1] For each of the 24 colonias, data were collected for six variables. The first two variables identify whether the colonia is incorporated or unincorporated, urban or rural. The third variable is population size, while the fourth approximates the level of local economic development. The fifth and sixth variables represent the status of infrastructure and accessibility respectively. Variables such as household income were excluded because of the absence of reliable data or difficulty in making reliable estimates.

For the first variable, unincorporated colonias were assigned a value of 1, while incorporated communities were assigned a value of 2. The second variable, urban to rural, was identified using distance to the nearest larger urban center. The road network was placed on a GIS platform so that "Manhattan" travel times could be measured. Distances were converted to commute times so that the urban-to-rural characteristic specified whether a colonia was within a 30-minute commute time, a 31- to 60-minute commute time, or more than 60 minutes to an urbanized area. Colonias farther than 60 minutes from an urban area centroid were considered rural and assigned a numerical value of 1. Those between 31 to 60 minutes were given a value of 2. The colonias within 30 minutes received a 3 and were considered urban. The third variable, population size, used census data when available (U.S. Census Bureau 2000a). Data for many rural colonias, however, are not available due to their small size. We estimated populations for these colonias using the number of housing units and average persons per household (U.S. Census Bureau 2000a). Population data were classified by assigning the values 1 through 67 to categories, each representing 200 persons (e.g., 1 = 0–200; 2 = 201–400; 3 = 401–600 . . .). The fourth variable, level of economic development, was estimated by using the number of local businesses in each of the 24 colonias. Businesses were identified from field observations taken during the period January–March 2004. The number of businesses was converted to 27 categories using increments of five businesses (1 = 0–5; 2 = 6–10; 3 = 11–15 . . .). The quality of infrastructure, the fifth variable, was estimated by determining whether a colonia had a community water system, a community wastewater system, and/or paved roads. For present purposes, the community was considered to have each type of infrastructure if it serviced over 60 percent of the community. For example, if over 60 percent of the streets were paved, the colonia was considered to have paved streets. These data were obtained from field surveys of each of the 24 colonias. Communities with all three types of infrastructure were assigned the number 4. Colonias lacking one of the infrastructure types were assigned the number 3; those lacking two components of infrastructure were assigned the number 2, and colonias lacking all three were assigned the number 1. The final variable, access, considers the location of colonias relative to roads with higher speeds and capacities. Colonias located within one-half mile of an interstate highway were given a value of 3. Communities farther from interstates, but within a half-mile of a state highway, were given a value of 2. Remaining colonias received a value of 1. To ensure consistency, the values for population size (the third variable) and level of economic development (the fourth variable) were standardized relative to other variables.

A cluster analysis was performed on the 24 sample colonias to identify groupings (clusters) according to the six variables described above.[2] Cluster analysis is an analytical tool that groups colonias together based on the strength of association among characteristics (the six variables). This enables the classification of colonias such that those in a particular class, or cluster, are associated more with one another than with colonias in different clusters.

The analysis defined a fivefold classification of New Mexico's colonias. We labeled categories in order to ease discussion and emphasize differences in the fivefold typology.[3] The first classification, *Small Unincorporated Rural,* is the largest and most cohesive of all the colonia groupings, with 13 of the 24 colonias included in this category. The colonias in this group cluster together because of similarities across all six characteristics. They are uniformly rural and unincorporated, and all have highway access. Of all the five groupings, they score the lowest on infrastructure. This indicates fewer paved streets and roads, and less extensive (or no) community-wide potable water and sanitary delivery systems. On average, they lack two of the three infrastructure elements. Colonias in this classification are small in size, an average of 400–600 persons. This means that they comprise the smallest average population size among all five groups. They also score much lower than the other groups in the level of local economic development, with an average of six businesses. Riverside, Dungan, La Luz, and Boles Acres form a subgroup within this classification, because they have better infrastructure scores, larger populations (La Luz and Boles Acres), and more businesses (Riverside,

La Luz, and Boles Acres). With further growth, this subset of colonias may well shift to one of the other classifications. In sum, the *Small Unincorporated Rural* group is indicative of many New Mexico colonias, which tend to be small, unincorporated places that are easily accessed by highways but often lack infrastructure and local businesses.

The second group, *Small–Medium Unincorporated Urban*, captures similarities among 5 of the 24 colonias in the sample set. The characteristics of this category differ from the first group in many ways. Foremost, it consists of a less cohesive set of colonias and was distinguished by a different set of variables. The colonias in this group are uniformly unincorporated and urban. This means that even though they do not have a formal political designation (e.g., formal town or city government), they are located closer to urban centers. Their access to transportation routes is mixed, with Berino and Vado/Del Cerro having interstate access, and the rest only highway access. They also have a higher infrastructure rating compared to the first group. On average, colonias in this classification lack one of the three infrastructure elements—a community water system, a community wastewater system, or paved roads. Colonias in this group are much larger, with average population ranging 2,400–2,600 persons. Colonias in this group also have a much higher economic development rating, with an average of nearly 21 businesses per colonia. This exceeds the average number of businesses in the first group, indicating that local jobs are more abundant. This also improves the chances for successful local economic development.

Several characteristics distinguish the third classification, *Incorporated Rural,* from the two previous groups. To begin, only 4 of the 24 colonias are included in this cluster. The smaller number results from their legal status as incorporated colonias, yet they are considered rural according to our criteria. Next, access is mixed for colonias in this category. Lordsburg is the only colonia located near an interstate highway (I-10); the other three colonias have highway access only. Colonias in this category have more local infrastructure than the previous two groups. On average, most residents in these colonias are served by all infrastructure elements: water, wastewater, and paved roads. The larger average population size, 2,600–2,800 persons, also sets this category apart from previous categories. The most significant difference is found in the level of local economic development, where colonias housed, on average,

69 businesses. This exceeds previous groups by a wide margin and indicates a far greater diversity of local jobs. Thus, economic development strategies confront a different set of needs, compared to the two colonia classifications described above.

The fourth category, *Large Unincorporated Urban,* consists of a single colonia: Anthony. Even though Anthony is unincorporated, it stands apart from other colonias because of its large size and high level of economic development. With a population that falls within the 7,800–8,000 range, Anthony is the second-largest colonia in the sample set, trailing only Sunland Park. It has interstate access, and nearly all residents are served by basic infrastructure (water, sanitation, paved streets and roads). It also has a comparatively high level of economic development, with 75 businesses operating locally. Anthony's character suggests that economic development strategies should be targeted to its unique needs.

The fifth classification, *Large Incorporated Urban,* consists only of Sunland Park. Many characteristics set it apart from all other New Mexico colonias. Sunland Park is an incorporated city that is bordered by El Paso, Texas, to the east and Mexico to the south. Its population is in the 13,200–13,400 range, which makes it by far the largest New Mexico colonia. It has interstate access, and infrastructure is available to nearly all residents. With 133 local businesses, Sunland Park also has the highest level of economic development. Even so, if businesses are paired with the local population (per capita), it trails well behind Anthony (*Large Unincorporated Urban*), and slightly behind the *Small Unincorporated Rural* category. Thus, economic development in Sunland Park requires a set of strategies that respond to circumstances far different from other New Mexico colonias.

In concluding this discussion, it is worth noting that we tested the robustness of the typology by exploring relationships between variables. We were particularly interested in investigating whether variables are highly correlated, because if so, they may overemphasize similar characteristics and bias results. A correlation analysis found that two variables, population size and level of economic development, are highly correlated (a coefficient of +.8). We responded by testing alternative data-weighting schemes but found that they did not alter outcomes. Thus, we are confident that the fivefold typology captures differences among New Mexico's colonias.

Assessing Development Potential

The fivefold typology described above goes a long way in classifying colonias according to development needs. We found substantive differences between categories in terms of size, accessibility, the availability of basic infrastructure, and level of economic development. But the typology says nothing about the types of businesses found in colonias. Such information eases targeting by identifying development potential. Strategies that focus on new business formation, for example, may target industrial sectors that complement existing businesses, or they may pursue an entirely new industrial sector that uses available resources such as a low-skilled labor force or an abandoned building. To the best of our knowledge, however, there are few, if any, published studies that profile the businesses found in New Mexico's colonias. This is understandable, because most colonias, and the agencies and organizations that work on their behalf, do not have the resources needed for developing detailed business inventories.

For this reason, we conducted "windshield" surveys of businesses and industries in 10 New Mexico colonias. The colonias were selected to represent the five classifications discussed in the previous section.[4] The surveys were conducted from January through March of 2004. Windshield surveys are admittedly less comprehensive than more formal business inventories, but they provide a reasonable assessment of local economies at a single point in time. We also acknowledge that the small sample size may not be representative of all New Mexico's colonias. Nevertheless, we selected colonias that represent all categories of the fivefold typology, and in this regard the results are indicative of the types of businesses found in colonias. The businesses identified by the survey fall within 19 classifications as defined by the North American Industrial Classification System (NAICS).

We begin by summarizing the industries found in all 10 colonias, then examine the distribution across the fivefold typology. A total of 489 businesses were identified across the 10 colonias, an average of 49 businesses per colonia. Three industries account for 55 percent of the total number. Retail trade is the single largest industry, claiming 25 percent of the total 489 businesses. "Other services" claims an additional 17 percent; accommodation and food services trails behind with 14 percent. The "other services" classification includes businesses involved in activities such as equipment and machinery repair, dry cleaning and laundry, and other personal services. The accommodation and food services industry provides lodging (hotels, motels, RV parks), full-service restaurants and bars, and other food and beverage outlets. The remaining 44 percent of businesses are spread across all other industrial sectors, with no industry claiming a significant percentage of the total.

The three major business types (retail trade, accommodation/food services, and other services) are not evenly distributed across the fivefold typology. Retail trade is most pronounced in the *Incorporated Rural* category, with 31 percent of the total number of businesses in this sector. Colonias in the *Small–Medium Unincorporated Urban* category have 26 percent of their businesses in retail trade, despite their very small populations. Retail trade is less prevalent in the *Large Unincorporated Urban* and *Large Incorporated Urban* categories, with 17 percent and 14 percent of total businesses falling within this business sector respectively.

The second business type, accommodation/food services, is found mainly in larger colonias. These businesses appear in the *Incorporated Rural* and *Large Unincorporated Urban* categories, which claim 16 percent and 15 percent of total businesses respectively. In contrast, the *Small Unincorporated Rural* classification accounted for only 5 percent of all businesses, and the *Small–Medium Unincorporated Urban* category housed 9 percent. Finally, only 10 percent of all businesses are related to accommodation/food services in the *Large Incorporated Urban* category.

The third principal category, other services, is related closely to colonia size. According to our fivefold typology, *Small Unincorporated Rural* colonias define one end of the spectrum. No "other services" businesses were found in these smaller colonias. This is understandable, because there are few people to support these types of businesses. At the other end of the spectrum, 19 percent of the total 489 businesses were located in the *Large Incorporated Urban* classification. Thus, the presence of other services increases with the size of colonias. This relationship applies to many of the businesses and colonias we surveyed and is captured in theories of spatial markets.

The distribution of businesses across the fivefold typology adheres to normative theories that explain the spatial arrangement of cities and the goods and services they provide. Economic theory argues that the types of businesses found in a community are associated with the community's size and location relative to other towns and cities (Esparza and

Krmenec 1999a, 1999b; Krmenec and Esparza 1993). In our case, smaller and more remote colonias have fewer local businesses than larger cities because local demand (population size) is sufficient to support only goods and services that are consumed regularly. Stated otherwise, even a remote colonia, such as Hope, New Mexico, with a population of about 100 persons, has a general store where local residents can buy goods that are consumed often. The people living in Hope must travel to the nearest larger town or city, Artesia, New Mexico, to purchase goods and services that are not available locally. With a population of about 14,000, Artesia offers a far wider range of goods and services. Even so, more specialized items, such as high-end automobiles or boutique restaurants, are not available in Artesia, which means that its residents must travel to a larger city to find them. Thus, there is a relationship between city size and the types of goods and services that are locally available. In general, therefore, smaller-sized colonias are expected to have more businesses in retailing and services industries compared to the total number of businesses.

Economic Development Strategies for Colonias

Targeting economic development strategies to local needs and development potential is never easy. Like communities everywhere, colonias differ in terms of constraints (needs), local resources, and the types and diversity of businesses that provide local jobs. But unlike many other communities, little attention has been placed on promoting economic development in New Mexico's colonias.

As a first step in this direction, we discuss the targeting of economic development strategies to local needs and development potential by integrating strategies with the fivefold typology and principal business types described above. Of the five strategies mentioned, new business formation and attracting external funding can be used effectively by any of the five categories of colonias. These two strategies are especially well suited for colonias in the *Small Unincorporated Rural* and *Small Unincorporated Urban* categories, because they have few local businesses and funding for economic development is scarce. In the first instance, most small colonias have businesses in retail trade but often lack businesses in basic industries that can employ local populations. Self-employment, small firms, and microbusinesses may well generate local employment in industries such as light manufacturing, agricultural food processing, and warehousing. In the second instance, unincorporated colonias do not have local governments or chambers of commerce, agencies and organizations that can provide funding for business start-ups and economic development programs. This means that attracting external funding from agencies such as HUD, the EPA, USAD-RD, and the SBA is pivotal to local job creation. These agencies support a variety of programs and initiatives that target basic infrastructure, especially potable water and waste delivery systems, and provide financial and technical support aimed at small business formation.

A different set of strategies is better suited for larger colonias. These include colonias in the remaining three categories: *Incorporated Rural, Large Unincorporated Urban,* and *Large Incorporated Urban.* For colonias in these categories, the capture-of-dollars strategy may well prove most successful. This strategy attempts to build the local economy by keeping consumer dollars within the community. This means that businesses in the retail, service, and accommodation and food service industries should be expanded so that they offer a broader range of goods and services locally. New business formation will also promote the capture of dollars by offering services that consumers purchase from more distant towns and cities. Larger, urban colonias such as Lordsburg, Anthony, and Sunland Park may well benefit from this strategy, because their populations are sufficient to support a range of businesses.

Finally, the largest colonia, Sunland Park, can implement all five strategies. Sunland Park has a large consumer base and a sizable reserve of labor to support a range of businesses in all industrial sectors. Thus, business attraction and retention, the capture of dollars, new firm formation, and attracting external funding are all appropriate strategies. Sunland Park also stands to benefit from paid professional staff who work for the city government and chamber of commerce.

Summary

New Mexico's colonias have witnessed improvements to infrastructure, housing, and health care in recent years, but economic growth and development remain vexing problems. The lack of economic development is troubling, because most observers agree that community-wide development is hinged to the economic foundation of communities. Locally owned and operated businesses employ the local population, build community identity, and foster community pride and participation while providing a range of sorely needed goods and services. Thus, economic development is pivotal to the longer-term sustainability of New Mexico's colonias. Most colonias, however, lack the resources needed to launch economic development campaigns.

Our research is motivated by the need to advance economic development in New Mexico's colonias. We sought to enable the targeting of development strategies to the needs and development potential of colonias. We accomplished this by generating a fivefold typology that classified colonias according to needs. This was buttressed by identifying development potential and linking specific strategies to colonias. While our efforts are more exploratory than definitive, we provide a first step to encouraging economic growth and development in colonias.

Notes

1. The 24 colonias used in the analysis include Anthony, Bent, Berino, Boles Acres, Chaparral, City of Bayard, Columbus, Dungan, Dwyer (Faywood), Hanover, Keeler Farm Road, La Luz, Lordsburg, Malaga, Mayhill, Riverside, Salem, San Miguel, Sunland Park, Sunshine, Tularosa, Turnerville, Vado/Del Cerro, Vanadium.

2. The software used for the cluster analysis was Webgrid III. Webgrid III arranges the input data in a repertory grid and uses Shaw's FOCUS, a hierarchical clustering method, to create the cluster dendrogram. It also provides a second clustering technique, which creates a cluster plot on *n* axes using Euclidean distance. This allows a verification of the clusters provided by the first method. Webgrid has a user-friendly interface and allows weighting of variables. Webgrid III was chosen also for its availability, without cost, as an interactive Internet application provided by the University of Calgary.

3. The assignment of colonias to categories is as follows: (1) *Small Unincorporated Rural:* Bent, Boles Acres, Dungan, Dwyer (Faywood), Hanover, Keeler Farm Road, La Luz, Malaga, Mayhill, Riverside, Sunshine, Turnerville, Vanadium; (2) *Small–Medium Unincorporated Urban:* Berino, Chaparral, Salem, San Miguel, Vado/Del Cerro; (3) *Incorporated Rural:* City of Bayard, Columbus, Lordsburg, Tularosa; (4) *Large Unincorporated Urban:* Anthony; (5) *Large Incorporated Urban:* Sunland Park.

4. The colonias selected for the "windshield" business survey and mapping included: *Small Unincorporated Rural:* Riverside; *Small–Medium Unincorporated Urban:* Berino, Chapparal, Salem, San Miguel, Vado/Del Cerro; *Incorporated Rural:* Columbus, Lordsburg; *Large Unincorporated Urban:* Anthony; *Large Incorporated Urban:* Sunland Park.

4

Arizona's Evolving Colonias Economy

Vera Pavlakovich-Kochi and Adrian X. Esparza

COLONIAS IN THE SOUTHWEST BORDER REGION confront a host of problems that affect quality of life. While health care, housing, and environmental degradation pose numerous challenges, many observers argue that economic constraints underscore the broader range of problems as the absence of jobs and economic opportunities spills over to all facets of community life. But economic problems themselves are tied to an array of factors, including labor force skills, educational attainment, the transborder economy, and impediments to local economic development (Donelson and Esparza 2007). Understanding current and future economic conditions in colonias requires that we address these deeper issues.

This chapter examines the economies of Arizona's colonias by pursuing three objectives. First, we summarize key economic indicators, including unemployment, educational attainment, and wages for colonia counties and selected colonias. The small size of many colonias (fewer than 2,000 persons) and the absence of a formal "colonias" census designation (e.g., there is no equivalent to the "county" or "census tract") narrows our investigation, because data are unavailable. Nevertheless, the summary of key indicators provides ample evidence of economic conditions in colonias. Second, we investigate the role of the transborder economy, because it is critical to the economic vitality of colonias (see chapter 1 for a historical discussion of the transborder economy). We show how formal and informal economic sectors affect cross-border trade, and we summarize employment and unemployment trends in industries affected by the transborder economy. We also present a case study of Santa Cruz County that details the interplay of cross-border trade, employment change in key sectors, and educational attainment. Finally, the chapter evaluates the critical role of economic development in Arizona's colonias. This analysis draws on research funded by the U.S. Department of Housing and Urban Development (HUD) that sought to identify factors that hinder and promote economic development in the region's colonias. Issues explored include microcredit, entrepreneurship, and local government regulations.

Economic Characteristics of Border Counties and Colonias

The federal government has designated 87 colonias in southern Arizona. Seven of these are located on tribal lands, 26 are incorporated towns and cities, and the remaining 54 are small and remote unincorporated towns and villages (Esparza and Donelson 2008). These colonias are located near the U.S.–Mexico border, with the majority found in Cochise, Santa Cruz, and Yuma counties. With the exception of Sierra Vista (Cochise County) and the city of Yuma (Yuma County), these counties are largely unpopulated, with cities such as Douglas (Cochise County), Nogales (Santa Cruz County), and San Luis (Yuma County) serving as major points of entry to Mexico.

A few basic statistics say much about economic conditions in southern border counties and selected colonias. Foremost, unemployment rates in border counties surpass the statewide average by a wide margin. The 2007 average annual unemployment rate for Cochise County equals 5.1 percent; unemployment rates for Santa Cruz and Yuma counties are 7.6 percent and 11.1 percent respectively (Arizona Department of Commerce 2008a). This compares with an unemployment rate of 4.1 percent across the state. Second, for selected colonias the lack of jobs may be linked to lower levels of educational attainment and poor English-language skills. Esparza and Donelson's (2008) study of the 54 unincorporated colonias of southern Arizona finds that as of 2005, only 65 percent of residents 25 years and older had completed high school. This compares with a high school graduation rate of 82 percent for the state. Across the 54 unincorporated colonias, estimates show that Spanish is the primary language of 40 percent of the population, compared to 22 percent across the state. These data point to critical constraints, because high school graduation and English-language proficiency are needed for many jobs as well as for advanced education. Finally, data provided by the

Arizona Department of Commerce (2008b) enable comparison of wage rates in selected colonias. Their estimates indicate that as of 2004, average annual wages trailed well behind the state average. For example, wages in Benson equaled $22,300, in Eloy $23,900, in Mammoth $12,200, and in San Luis/Somerton $20,300—all are formally designated colonias. These compare with an average annual wage across Arizona of $36,646 in the same year.

The data described above indicate that colonias face a tough economic future. Unemployment remains a critical problem in colonia counties, and low levels of educational attainment and poor English-language skills hamper job mobility and suppress wages in colonias. Regretfully, there is little indication that these trends will change in the near future. But these problems are complicated by the transborder economy, which is critical in Arizona's colonias. The next section looks more closely at cross-border trade, especially the formal and informal economies, employment trends, and the role of educational attainment.

The Transborder Economy

The term *transborder economy* refers to economic activities that take place across the international borderline. They include the physical flow of goods, people, and capital, as well as the virtual exchange of data and information. The transborder economy also includes economic activities on one side of the border that are influenced or affected by economic activities on the other side. Some activities may originate in faraway places: the majority of auto parts are shipped from Detroit-based parent companies to Mexico's assembly plants, known as maquiladoras. Other economic activities originate closer to the border, such as out-shopping by border residents in search of better or cheaper goods on the other side of the border. The former is an example of a globally induced transborder economy, while the later is primarily a locally stimulated transborder economy.

Another way of looking at the transborder economy is by determining whether it takes place within formal or informal frameworks. Formal transborder flows such as exports and imports follow from formal agreements and practices, and thus, at least in theory, can be recorded or documented. In contrast, informal exchanges and linkages, although

an important component of the transborder economy, are mostly unde-
tected. Staudt (1998) and others argue that the informal dimension of the
transborder economy receives little attention in the research literature or
in practice.

In the last four decades, two major economic policies have driven
the U.S.–Mexico transborder economy: the maquiladora sector, initiated
under the Mexican Border Industrialization Program in 1965, and the
North American Free Trade Agreement (NAFTA) initiated in 1994. Both
led to intended increases in cross-border trade and traffic (Clement 2003;
Esparza, Waldorf, and Chavez 2004; Gruben and Kiser 2001; Pavlakovich-
Kochi 2006; Vargas 2001). The number of people crossing the border
grew as well, reflecting the importance of cross-border economic ties.

Studies indicate that in past years, U.S. border states benefited from
the growth of maquiladora employment in northern Mexico. The loss
of manufacturing jobs to assembly plants in Mexico, a major concern
of traditional manufacturing states, was not a concern in border states,
because they had little manufacturing in the first place. In fact, the relo-
cation of manufacturing from the "Rust Belt" proved beneficial. Hopkins (1988), for example, found that in the late 1980s, Arizona's border
counties experienced an increase in non-farm employment as a result of
Mexico's expanding maquiladora economy.

Trade statistics indicate that exports to Mexico from U.S. border
states have grown continuously (with the exception of the 2001–2 recession, combined with the impact of terrorist attacks in 2001), although
at different growth rates. More importantly, export activities have been
overwhelmingly concentrated in metropolitan areas. Consequently, the
employment gains associated with export activity also accrued primarily
to metropolitan areas. In Arizona's case, Phoenix and Tucson are the
major exporters to global and Mexican markets.

Among six border ports of entry along the Arizona–Sonora border,
Nogales, San Luis, and Douglas account for the majority of cross-border
trade.[1] All three ports of entry experienced expansion of port facilities
and customs personnel as the volume of trade and number of trucks
grew. These investments were mostly funded by a combination of federal
and state monies.

The warehousing and transportation sector has expanded in Arizona's
border communities as a direct result of the participation in the global

economy. But for the most part, the economic structure of Arizona's border counties reflects more traditional, local cross-border ties. This is reflected in larger-than-state-average shares of employment in the retail trade sector and restaurants and bars. As elsewhere in the U.S. border region, a nearly constant 30 percent of the labor force remains in the category of sales, entertainment, hotels, and restaurants, always above the national average. It comes as no surprise, therefore, that low-wage service-sector jobs make up a larger share of the labor force than across Arizona and the United States (Anderson and Gerber 2007). All border communities struggle with how to get a larger share of the benefits from global economic flows as they pass through their communities to larger metropolitan areas.

Unemployment, Self-Employment, and the Informal Economy

As mentioned previously, the unemployment rate in U.S. border counties has consistently been above state and national averages (Taylor 2001). This coincides with relatively low labor participation rates for both men and women, but particularly for men. There are probably a number of explanations, but two stand out (Anderson and Gerber 2007). First, due to high unemployment rates some workers may become discouraged and drop out of the labor force altogether.[2] Second, the informal economy is decidedly larger in the border region than in other parts of Arizona and the country. Consequently, there may be more people working in an unrecorded cash economy, where they appear to be out of the labor force but, in fact, are not reporting their income and employment (Anderson and Gerber 2007).

In her in-depth study of the informal economy along the Texas–Mexico border, Staudt (1998) focused on low- and middle-income segments of the population and found that many of them had at least one foot in the informal economy. She reported that "informals" ranged from self-sufficient home- and street-based workers to employees of companies that cut costs below the basement of state-imposed protections and benefits to people engaged in labor-intensive, income-substituting activities. Furthermore, she concluded that ethnic enclaves and ethnic economies offered considerable self-employment and contracted labor opportunities. Historically, migrants have used self-employment and unpaid family labor as stepping-stones toward economic security. The concluding section of this chapter shows that similar trends hold in Arizona's colonias.

Staudt (1998) found no clear and simple relationship among poverty, migration, and informal work in the border region. However, she concluded, informal work serves as a cushion that protects people from absolute poverty. The informal economy has traditionally helped people stretch their incomes (Anderson and de la Rosa 1991).

Recently, Anderson and Gerber (2007) argued that the large concentration of immigrants and the importance of tourism in many areas along the U.S.–Mexico border ensure that the informal economy is more important in the border region than in many other parts of the United States. The border region has an informal economy in construction, tourism, and domestic services such as cleaning, gardening, and handiwork.

For some Mexican immigrants the border region offers an opportunity for entrepreneurial activity. Mexican immigrants in the border region tend to have higher self-employed rates than those in the U.S. interior (Mora 2006; Mora and Dávila 1998). One explanation for this higher self-employed propensity is the relatively strong opportunity to cater to Mexican consumers who frequently enter U.S. cities for shopping and trade. Also, the ability to directly interact with Mexican consumers in Mexico provides U.S.-resident Mexican immigrants more profitable opportunities compared to those businesses who operate solely on the U.S. side of the border (Mora 2006).

Both formal and informal sectors in the border region depend upon the ability to cross between the United States and Mexico to take advantage of better or cheaper resources. In light of recent policies toward strengthening border security, there is a growing concern that the disruption of border crossings could disproportionately affect border residents whose incomes and survival depend on cross-border economic ties. To better understand these processes on a local scale, Santa Cruz County, Arizona, is selected as an example of trends in the transborder economy.

Case Study: Santa Cruz County

Santa Cruz County is the smallest (by size) of Arizona border counties, and the least populous, although Nogales, its major city, is Arizona's principal border port-of-entry and is also an officially designated colonia. It handles the majority of import-export trade between Arizona and Mexico and is also used by the largest number of border crossers by car or foot. Our focus is on the kinds of job opportunities that a border economy offers, especially for residents of colonias who are known to have lower educational attainment and job skills.

According to County Business Pattern (CBP) data (U.S. Census Bureau 2005), which provides the most detailed employment by industry sector (albeit government and self-employed are excluded), the economy of Santa Cruz County has been dominated by four industries—retail trade, wholesale trade, transportation and warehousing, and accommodation and food services. In each of these industries, the percentage of employed was much higher than the state average. This reflects economic specialization in the border region, where international trade and the cross-border movement of people are visible components of the local economy.

In 2005, the retail trade sector was the major source of jobs, accounting for 24 percent of total employment, compared to Arizona's average of 14 percent. Wholesale trade claimed 16 percent of local employment (Arizona averaged 4 percent in 2005), while accommodation and food services and transportation and warehousing trailed behind with 13 percent and 12 percent respectively. Arizona averaged 11 percent employment in accommodation and food services, and 3 percent in transportation and warehousing.

As in other border communities, the retail trade sector has been dependent largely on out-shopping by Mexicans from south of the border. This means that retailing is subject to rapid growth and decline as border policies ease or restrict the flow of Mexican nationals. Exacerbating the problem, border retailing has been traditionally more sensitive to changes in exchange rates and devaluations. For example, Mexico's 1994 devaluation lowered the peso's value by 40 percent and sent shock waves throughout U.S. border towns (Esparza and Donelson 2008; Gerber 1999; Patrick and Renforth 1996). Increased waiting times at border ports of entry (due to more rigorous restrictions and inspections) also discourage shoppers from venturing northward across the border. Like the retail trade sector, accommodation and food services sectors localized, serving primarily the local population on both sides of the border.

On the other hand, wholesale trade and transportation and warehousing are linked to trends in the broader global economy. For example, the majority of manufacturing imports/exports passing through the Nogales port of entry are tied to Sonora's maquiladoras. Increases or decreases in trade flows depend primarily upon the expansion or contraction of Mexico's maquiladora sector, which in turn reflects business cycles in the U.S. economy. This dependency was apparent during the 2001–2 recession, which, combined with the September 11, 2001, terrorist attacks as well as increased competition from China, led to a 30 percent decrease in Sonora's maquiladora employment (Pavlakovich-Kochi 2006).

Warehousing, distribution services, and transportation services are also associated with the imports of Mexican fresh produce destined primarily for U.S. Pacific Coast markets and Canada. Unlike maquiladora-related trade flows, the shipment of fresh produce is seasonal. During the winter months, from November to April, demand for fresh produce rises and, in turn, employment grows.

The manufacturing sector, which is also tied to the maquiladora industry south of the border, accounted for 5 percent of employment (compared to Arizona's average of 7.8 percent).

The most important implication of these trends is that a large percentage of Santa Cruz County's employment is concentrated in volatile sectors such as retail trade or in seasonal industries, such as transportation and warehousing, which are connected to the shipment of fresh produce. A comparison with the year 2000 reveals that these two sectors became even more important in the county's employment picture. Employment in retail trade increased from 22 percent in 2000 to 24 percent in 2005; transportation and warehousing grew from 9 percent to 12 percent during the same period.

In absolute numbers, there were 11,127 jobs in Santa Cruz County in 2005, excluding government and self-employment (U.S. Census Bureau 2005). This represented a net increase of 1,047 jobs from 2000, indicating a recovery (albeit a slow one) from the economic slowdown in the early 2000s.

Comparison by sectors also indicates that certain shifts occurred during the economic recovery. The manufacturing sector declined by more than 300 jobs (a 36 percent decrease from 2000). Most of this loss in Santa Cruz County appears to be directly related to the decline in maquiladora production south of the border. County business pattern data reveal that, indeed, the decline in manufacturing was primarily due to a drastic decline in musical-instrument manufacturing and surgical appliances and supplies, both of which were linked to maquiladoras south of the border. The same forces might have affected employment in the wholesale trade sector, which fell by 78 jobs (a 4.2 percent decrease). Some of these jobs might have shifted to transportation and warehousing, and retail trade sectors that experienced net gains of 450 (a 50 percent increase) and 430 (a 19 percent increase) jobs respectively.

Educational services together with arts, entertainment, and recreational services experienced declines of 267 jobs. In the meantime, the administrative, support, and waste management services gained a net of 354 jobs, the highest relative (270 percent) increase from 2000.

The question remains: how have these employment shifts affected wages? Based on job losses and gains, we conclude that, overall, a major shift occurred from better-paid jobs in manufacturing toward lower average wages in retail trade and in transportation and warehousing (the latter due to the seasonal nature of employment).

We looked more carefully at how job gains and losses likely affect colonia residents by using a Santa Cruz County input-output model.[3] The model produces an occupational profile of estimated jobs associated with a given economic activity. We analyzed the occupational profile in terms of associated educational/skill levels. Five occupational categories were considered: (1) no high school diploma required, (2) only a high school diploma required, (3) some college or advance training required, (4) a university degree usually required, and (5) a graduate degree normally required. We focus our analysis on the first two categories, because of their prevalence among colonia residents.

First, we assessed the occupational mix of lost jobs by industry sector. The major decline of manufacturing jobs occurred in maquiladora-related surgical appliances and supplies (a net loss of 200 jobs), musical instruments (a net loss of 80 jobs), and computer and electronic product manufacturing (a net loss of 70 jobs).[4] The share of occupations that do not require a high school diploma equaled nearly 12 percent, or one out of every eight jobs in the region. The largest loss was in jobs requiring only a high school diploma. Such occupations comprised 46 percent of all lost jobs, or almost every second job.

Some of these jobs might have been absorbed by a few manufacturing industries that experienced growth since 2000, such as plastic and rubber products manufacturing (a net gain of about 100 jobs), fabricated metal (a net gain of more than 20 jobs), and electrical equipment manufacturing (more than 20 jobs). However, the total net gain in these manufacturing industries was substantially smaller than the total net loss in declining manufacturing industries. This means that some manufacturing jobs were lost for good. This is particularly important, because manufacturing jobs typically pay better.

On average, transportation and warehousing jobs are better paid than those in retail trade but less than those in manufacturing or wholesale trade. Moreover, average pay in this sector grew at the slowest pace between 2000 and 2005, by some 6 percent, compared to 14 percent in manufacturing and 16 percent in wholesale trade wages (not accounting for inflation). More than 60 percent of the total net gain of 441 jobs included occupations for which a high school diploma was not required. An additional 24 percent was in occupations that require a high school diploma only (no college).

In the retail trade sector, 10 percent of the total net gain of 440 jobs was in occupations for the lowest skill level (no high school diploma). In contrast, the lion's share of jobs, 83 percent, required only a high school diploma. Average wages in the retail sector are the lowest of the four main industry sectors: $17,957 annualized, compared to $24,614 in transportation and warehousing, $28,813 in manufacturing, and $35,037 in wholesale trade (U.S. Census Bureau 2005).

On the one hand, the large number of new jobs that required minimal skills/educational attainment might be seen as an opportunity for colonia residents to find jobs locally. On the other hand, this trend indicates a reduction of jobs requiring higher skills/educational attainment. As a consequence, workers with a high school diploma compete more frequently for the same job positions with workers with no high school diploma.

Many of the issues discussed above are explored in the next section as we look more closely at business owners and economic development specialists working in the border region. We will see that the informal sector, microbusiness, entrepreneurship, the cross-border economy, and educational attainment all play a critical role in economic development in Arizona's colonias.

Economic Development in Arizona Colonias

The discussion thus far indicates that Arizona's colonias face a tough future because of consistently high unemployment/underemployment, the prevalence of unskilled/low-skilled jobs, and the concentration of employment in larger cities at the expense of smaller and more remote colonias. The transborder economy adds another layer of complexity, because it is constantly in flux in response to changes in border security policy, the global economy, and seasonal demands. These limitations mean that economic development will play an important role in improving colonias' quality of life in the years ahead. Even so, there is little published research that looks firsthand at the types of businesses found in Arizona's colonias, the obstacles they face, and what can be done to promote greater economic success.

This section uses primary data to explore the nature of businesses in colonias, what is being done to meet their needs, and what can be done to encourage broad-based economic development. The analysis draws on interviews with 11 businesses active in Arizona colonias. Business owners shared information about their background and history, challenges, and future needs. We also report findings from interviews with 10 agencies that provide a range of services for colonia businesses and work to promote economic development in colonia communities. In both cases, interviews were conducted in 2003–4 and provide the most current and comprehensive information available. The study was funded by the U.S. Department of Housing and Urban Development (HUD) as part of a larger project that inventoried businesses in colonias of Arizona and New Mexico. Information obtained from interviews is summarized without specific reference to businesses or agencies, because confidentiality restrictions prohibit the identification of participants.

Local Businesses

The businesses operating in colonias of southern Arizona cover a narrow range of small-scale manufacturing, retailing and business, and personal services. The scope and scale of manufacturing are limited and most often tied to basic industries of the region, especially agriculture. Other types of manufacturing are characterized best as cottage industries—the informal sector—in which individuals, families, or small groups of individuals produce goods for personal use, such as apparel, decorative items, and foodstuffs. Retailing claims by far the largest number of businesses, which range from convenience grocery stores to food stands, restaurants, and video and hardware stores. Retailing relies almost exclusively on local demand and cross-border trade. In the latter case, many businesses indicate that Mexican nationals comprise a significant share of their clients. This means that the income and earning capacity of colonia residents, along with border security and immigration policies, largely determines the longer-term viability of local retailing. This corresponds with the data we reported for Santa Cruz County, where government policies affected trade and restricted the cross-border movement of Mexicans through the Nogales port of entry. Business and personal services such as bookkeeping and tax preparation, hair stylists/barber shops, and repair services for automobiles and homes are available in larger colonias, but less so in remote colonias. In the latter case, their availability is determined largely by the training and skills of individual colonia residents. For example, in one small and remote colonia, an auto mechanic may open a shop or work out of his home, but trained mechanics may not reside in other colonias. Thus, no auto repair services will be available.

As discussed in the preceding section, many local businesses in remote colonias are informal microenterprises. This means that, at times, they do not follow conventions found in the formal economy such as securing a business license, establishing a bookkeeping/tax accounting system, or seeking financing from conventional sources. Our interviews indicate that business owners do not turn to the informal sector to circumvent the system. Rather, these microenterprises simply cannot afford to follow standard business conventions. In nearly all cases, local businesses arose from an entrepreneurial spirit in which financing came from personal or family savings; friends and families came together to start the business; and, above all, long hours of work are the critical ingredients to longer-term success. In short, working outside the formal system is more a matter of necessity than of choice.

Business Constraints

Local businesses share a common set of constraints that hamper day-to-day functions and longer-term growth. Interviews with business owners and economic development specialists point to these constraints with overwhelming regularity. For one, the informal nature of microenterprises imposes problems. For example, government agencies that aim to promote business development cannot open the door to sponsored programs (e.g., financing and training), because clients (businesses) must be registered and follow formal business practices. The exclusion of informal microenterprises is understandable, given the mandates of government agencies, but this means that many colonia businesses are excluded from development assistance. Second, nongovernmental organizations (NGOs) that target business development have more leeway in that they can reach out to many microenterprises, but even they report numerous constraints. These include the lack of formal education and training among entrepreneurs in areas such as accounting, analysis, writing reports and business plans, conducting market research, and English language skills. Third, colonia businesses echo the need for these types of education and training, but issues such as child care, time constraints, and the lack of awareness prohibit taking advantage of opportunities. To make matters worse, government and nongovernmental organizations acknowledge that staffing shortages (limited budgets) often prohibit more aggressive outreach, especially to remotely located colonias. Fourth, some local businesses indicate that county regulations such as building and zoning codes impose another layer of obstacles. These are difficult to surmount, because regulations bring added costs and often require attendance at hearings and public meetings, which means time away from the business. Finally, business growth in colonias located near larger urban centers is constrained by market competition. In this case, they cannot compete with the lower prices available at "big box" outlets, nor can they offer the variety of goods and services available in larger nearby towns and cities. In sum, the plight of colonia microenterprises is rife with issues ranging from the need for financing, to training and education, to awareness of the types of assistance that is available, to government regulations, to market competition.

Summary

Economic stability and growth are matters of concern to villages, towns, and cities across the country. Everyone, it seems, is concerned with the implications of globalization, the shift to an information economy, and federal, state, and local policies that affect job retention and employer training. In the U.S.–Mexico border region, however, economic solvency is especially important, because it is pivotal to improving overall quality of life, especially basic health care, housing and infrastructure, and education. While some of these deficiencies are found in other regions as well (especially in inner cities), they are widespread in the border region's colonias.

This chapter examined the economic situation of Arizona's colonias. We began by summarizing basic indicators such as unemployment, educational attainment, and wages and found that colonias lag well behind Arizona and the nation. We then turned to a closer inspection of the transborder economy, because it is integral to communities in the border region, especially colonias. We showed how employment is tied to transborder trade in the formal economy, and that the informal economy is dependent on the ease of crossing the border. The case study of Santa Cruz County tied many of these issues together by showing how the interdependency of industrial and occupational sectors affects job gains/losses and places demands on educational attainment. The final section used primary data to investigate businesses in colonias. We found that many work in the informal sector that serves local communities, rely on individual and family financing, and manage to stay afloat by long hours of work. They face many constraints, including exclusion from formal avenues of assistance (because they work in the informal sector), the lack of basic business skills and English-language proficiency, and local regulations.

At a deeper level, however, the absence of a unified and coordinated border policy underscores the struggle for economic development in Arizona's colonias. As Esparza and Donelson (2008) indicate, the federal government's border policies are fragmented, inconsistent, and, at times, contradictory. There are several programs that target economic and community development in the border region, but more often than not they are piecemeal and subject to the whims of political expediency. Above all, a comprehensive and long-range approach to solving colonia problems will most likely provide the framework needed to improve quality of life. But the likelihood of such a program is contingent on political will.

Notes

1. From west to east: San Luis/San Luis Rio Colorado, Lukeville/Sonoyta, Sasabe/Sasabe, Nogales/Nogales, Naco/Naco, and Douglas/Agua Prieta.

2. Persons who have stopped looking for work (so-called discouraged workers) are classified as out of the labor force and therefore neither employed nor unemployed.

3. The IMPLAN Input-Output model has been developed by Minnesota IMPLAN Group, Inc. We acknowledge the permission of Eller College's Economic and Business Research Center at the University of Arizona to use the model in this study.

4. In the absence of real data, we assumed that the job loss occurred proportionally across all occupations; in reality, it might have been that the lower-skilled occupations were more affected, but we don't know.

5

Agricultural Prosperity, Rural Poverty, and California's Colonias

Vinit Mukhija

CALIFORNIA, THE GOLDEN STATE, is the country's richest state. According to the U.S. Bureau of Economic Analysis, California's gross domestic product is over $1.7 trillion (Bureau of Economic Affairs 2007). If the state were an independent nation, it would have the eighth-largest economy in the world. But California is also in the vanguard of growing income inequality and disparities in the country. Almost five million Californians live in poverty. According to federal measures, California's poverty rate of 13.3 percent is the fifteenth-highest in the nation. Critics, however, argue that if the federal measure of poverty were adjusted for the high cost of housing in the state, the poverty rate would rise to 16 percent, the third-highest in the country (Reed 2006). Either way, California, in part because of its large population, has the unfortunate distinction of having more poor residents than any other state.

Many of the poor are farmworkers or former farmworkers who have moved up marginally to more stable, but still low-wage, service sector jobs. Critics worry that the business of agriculture in California, although flourishing, constantly attracts desperate, low-skill workers, but its penurious working and living conditions fail to retain them. Many former farmworkers, however, find it difficult to escape from poverty and the state's burgeoning underclass, their ranks perpetually swollen by others trying to leave the hard life of toil on farms. While mechanization of agriculture has helped reduce the demand for seasonal labor, the state's farmers now focus more on labor-intensive crops, including fresh vegetables, fruits and nuts, berries, and nurseries (Mines 2006).[1] The shift to labor-intensive crops has resulted in an overall increase in year-round demand for labor, as some of the state's leading agricultural economists note (Taylor, Martin, and Fix 1997).

A recent consulting report, based on the National Agricultural Workers Survey—NAWS—indicates that almost 36 percent of the country's farmworkers are employed in California (Aguirre International 2005). In contrast, 10 years ago, the state accounted for around a quarter of the nation's agricultural employment. But amidst this growing industry and farming prosperity in the state, rural destitution is increasing. California challenges the conventional wisdom of failing farms and rural poverty. It has the contrarian reality of flourishing farms and rural distress. As Aguirre International's report also indicates, about 43 percent of the farmworkers earn less than $10,000 per year, and three-quarters make less than $15,000 a year (Aguirre International 2005).[2] With such low wages, it is not surprising that California's farmworkers inhabit some of the worst housing in the state. A recent study indicates that almost 30 percent of farmworker dwellings are recognized by neither the U.S. Postal Service nor the local county assessor's office (Villarejo and Schenker 2007). These unorthodox, substandard dwellings include sheds, barns, trailers, and garages. The poor private housing conditions are matched and exacerbated by the deficient and deteriorating public infrastructure. It is unfortunate and appalling that some of the contemporary living conditions are reminiscent of the Depression era accounts of agricultural workers and their exploitation fictionalized in John Steinbeck's *The Grapes of Wrath* (1939) and documented in Carey McWilliams's seminal *Factories in the Field,* which followed Steinbeck's classic by a few months (1939).[3] Remarkably, some of the modern living circumstances, such as the condition of farmworkers squatting in the canyons of northern San Diego County (Chavez 1991; Frey 2006), can be even worse.

This chapter discusses colonias as one of the key housing options for farmworkers and other low-wage, rural residents of California. First, I describe designated colonias in the state and compare them with the archetypal colonias of Texas. Second, I detail colonias that are not formally recognized but are discerned and acknowledged due to their demographic characteristics. I also contrast the demographic colonias with the designated colonias. Finally, I discuss some examples of the progress achieved in improving housing and living conditions in the colonias, and some of the remaining challenges and potential policy avenues.

California's Designated Colonias

Most of the formally recognized colonias—subdivisions with poor housing conditions and inadequate physical infrastructure—are along Texas's
southern border with Mexico. Recent evidence suggests that there are
over 1,800 colonias in Texas, with almost half a million residents. Colonia developers took advantage of the absence of effective subdivision
regulations in peri-urban areas of Texas to subdivide and sell modest-
sized lots without basic services to the state's poor. Because there were
no statutory requirements to provide minimum infrastructure such as
water, sewers, and roads in rural subdivisions, these settlements were
not illegal (Ward 1999). Many settlements were developed in hazardous
floodplains, but they were still legal. Numerous public health and epidemiological studies, however, have documented the higher health risk
and incidence of disease in colonias due to the unsanitary living conditions because of deficient water and wastewater infrastructure (Doyle
and Bryan 2000; Ortiz, Arizmendi, and Llewellyn 2004; Redlinger,
O'Rourke, and VanDerslice 1997).

As a response to the phenomenal growth in colonias during the 1970s
and 1980s, land development regulations in the state were revised in 1989
and 1995 to require more demanding standards, including the provision of infrastructure (Ward 1999). At the federal level, the key response
was the Cranston-Gonzalez National Affordable Housing Act of 1990,
which stipulated that in the border states—Texas, New Mexico, Arizona, and California—a portion of the U.S. Department of Housing and
Urban Development's (HUD's) Community Development Block Grant
(CDBG) funds be reserved for improving infrastructure and living conditions in colonias. The underlying assumption behind the federal response
was that such settlements had more to do with the proximity to Mexico
than with poverty and weak subdivision regulations in Texas. As a result,
federal funding was earmarked for the four border states but was limited
to their rural, border areas. Thus in California, HUD CDBG funding was
confined to Imperial County, because its other border counties are metropolitan statistical areas (MSAs), with a population that exceeds a million,
and are thus regarded as urban (Mukhija and Monkkonen 2006).

Imperial County has 15 designated colonias (table 5.1). The first colonias
were named in 1991, soon after the Cranston-Gonzalez Act was legislated,

TABLE 5.1 HUD-recognized Colonias in Imperial County, California.

Colonia Name	Jurisdiction
1. Bombay Beach	County of Imperial
2. Brawley County Water District	City of Brawley, Imperial County
3. C. N. Perry	City of Calexico, Imperial County
4. East Colonia	City of Imperial, Imperial County
5. El Dorado	City of El Centro, Imperial County
6. Heber	County of Imperial
7. Kloke Tract	City of Calexico, Imperial County
8. Niland	County of Imperial
9. Ocotillo	County of Imperial
10. Palo Verde	County of Imperial
11. Poe	County of Imperial
12. Salton Sea Beach	County of Imperial
13. Seeley	County of Imperial
14. South Colonia	City of Imperial, Imperial County
15. Winterhaven	County of Imperial

Source: State of California, 2002.

the most recent in 2002. But these designated communities differ from the conventional colonias of Texas. For more than 75 years, California has had demanding land development regulations through the state's Subdivision Map Act of 1929 and its subsequent revisions.[4] Consequently, unlike Texas, California cannot have legal subdivisions without the basic physical infrastructure unless the settlements are significantly older and were developed prior to 1929. As expected, California's designated colonias are not recent subdivisions but much older settlements.[5] For example, records from the Imperial County assessor's office indicate that both South and East Colonias were laid out in 1901 (Mukhija and Monkkonen 2006). Similarly, C. N. Perry, Kloke, and East Colonia were subdivided in 1902. Salton Sea Beach, founded in 1928, is the most recent.

The age and history of these settlements can also affect their demographic composition. In Texas, colonias are relatively recent and uniformly Latino. But in Imperial County, many of the designated colonias have less than a quarter Latino residents. The same colonias have a proportionately higher percentage of elderly residents. Many of these residents are seasonal and are known as "snowbirds." Typically, they are modest-income retirees who spend their winter months in California. There is an institutional and

TABLE 5.2 Housing Conditions in Imperial County's Designated Colonias.

Colonia	Sound (%)	Minor Repairs (%)	Moderate Repairs (%)	Substantial Rehabilitation (%)	Dilapidated (%)
Bombay Beach	16.0	11.5	23.0	17.9	31.6
Heber	50.0	5.0	40.0	2.1	2.9
Niland	22.1	12.5	51.9	4.8	8.7
Ocotillo	35.4	5.6	46.1	2.5	10.3
Palo Verde	9.2	4.6	32.4	16.0	37.8
Poe	26.7	13.3	30.0	10.0	20.0
Salton Sea Beach	19.0	3.8	65.1	3.6	8.5
Seeley	66.6	13.3	16.9	1.7	1.5
Winterhaven	9.7	10.3	22.9	9.7	47.4

Source: Imperial County Community and Economic Development, 2003.

spatial contrast with Texas too. Texas's colonias are unincorporated and under the jurisdiction of various county governments. Spatially, they tend to be independent sites, away from other established towns. In Imperial County, 6 of the 15 colonias are incorporated under the jurisdiction of local municipalities (table 5.1), and spatially they are at the periphery of these cities, contiguous with their boundaries.

California's communities designated as colonias nonetheless share the key characteristics of inadequate infrastructure and substandard housing with their Texas counterparts. Infrastructure conditions vary in Imperial County's colonias, but typically both water supply and wastewater systems are deficient. In some of the communities such public infrastructure was never provided. They were developed a long time ago and have survived on water delivery trucks and septic tanks. Others have had rudimentary systems installed, but these are below current standards, and decaying. In some communities, population growth is another problem, as it has over-burdened the barely adequate and fraying infrastructure. HUD's colonia funding through the CDBG program has helped improve infrastructure conditions in many of these settlements, although further improvements are necessary. Similarly, housing conditions in the colonias vary.[6] Some units need immediate or substantial attention, but others are sound. As table 5.2 indicates, most of the housing needs repairs or rehabilitation. In some of the colonias (Bombay Beach, Palo Verde, and Winterhaven), housing is so deteriorated that more than 50 percent of the stock needs substantial rehabilitation or complete replacement. HUD funds are also being leveraged for housing rehabilitation in many of the colonias (Imperial County Community and Economic Development 2003).

In addition to the 15 colonias of Imperial County, there are 8 designated colonias in Riverside County and 9 in San Diego County.[7] These communities, however, do not qualify for colonia grants from HUD, as the counties are MSAs. The communities have been designated by their local governments, but their classification is not formally recognized by the state government's Department of Housing and Community Development (HCD), which follows HUD's criteria. Fortunately, funding for upgrading colonias is also available from the U.S. Department of Agriculture (USDA) and the U.S. Environmental Protection Agency (EPA), and the two agencies follow a slightly different set of criteria.[8]

As in Imperial County, the settlements are older communities with subdivision maps drawn before 1929. For example, Mecca (Riverside County) was laid out in 1915, and Jacumba (San Diego County) in 1919. Similarly, living conditions vary in the designated colonias, but in all of them infrastructure is inadequate and housing is substandard. The USDA has been the most aggressive and active agency in upgrading infrastructure in colonias of both counties. In Riverside County some of these funds are disbursed through the county's agency for economic development, Riverside County Economic Development Agency, and the Desert Alliance for Community Empowerment (DACE), a nonprofit organization established in connection with the federal designation of a Rural Empowerment Zone in the county. In San Diego County, seven of the nine colonias are tribal colonias on sovereign land, and their tribes play a key role in the project management and implementation of infrastructure improvements.

California's Demographic Colonias

Similar living conditions, characterized by substandard private housing and inadequate public infrastructure, are often found beyond California's border region. But because of their distance from the U.S.–Mexico border, the communities cannot be formally designated as colonias. Such deficient conditions are particularly prevalent in the Central Valley (which dominates the middle part of California and includes the Sacramento Valley in the north and the San Joaquin Valley in the south), the heart of farming in the state and commonly referred to as the "fruit basket of the world." Although such communities do not meet the key criterion of border proximity for formal colonia designation, academic literature in anthropology, Chicano(a) studies, and sociology refers to many of these places as colonias (Allensworth and Rochin 1996; Galarza 1977; Martin and Taylor 1995; Rochin 1989; Rochin et al. 1998). Interestingly, some of the usage predates the academic literature that follows the more common, policy-oriented practice motivated by communities in Texas.

Ernesto Galarza (1977), the Bracero Program's historian and labor organizer, may have been the first to use the term *colonias* in California, in 1977. He referred to rural towns and communities with immigrant Mexican and Mexican American farmworkers as colonias. He described these colonias with their unique cultural and ethnic attributes as ideal ports of entry for new immigrants from Mexico. Subsequently, Refugio Rochin has been at the intellectual forefront of building on Galarza's insight and constructing the term more formally and operationally (Rochin 1989; Rochin and Castillo 1993). He and his coauthor Monica Castillo define colonias as demographic constructs, rural communities undergoing a transition in population, where the new Latino majority exceeds more than half of the total population. Housing and infrastructure conditions are not variables in this definition. The definition also builds on Juan Vicente Palerm's seminal insight on the dramatic demographic transitions in rural California (1991).

Based on their analysis of 1980 census data, Rochin and Castillo (1993) found 49 colonias, or rural communities (places with less than 20,000 residents) with over 50 percent Latinos. They also noted:

> No community of our study had more than 23 percent Latinos in 1950 (i.e., 0.1 percent to 22.6 percent), the proportion of Latinos ranged from 15.1 percent to 98.2 percent in 1980. We also found that from 1950 to 1980, all rural communities of our study had significant and dramatic growth in Latino settlers. Moreover, we found that the proportion and absolute numbers of non-Latinos in several communities declined significantly between 1980 and 1990, while the Latinos increased by large amounts. (Rochin and Castillo 1993, x)

Their analysis also suggested that by 1990, in almost 70 out of 148 rural communities, more than half of the residents were Latinos. These colonias, however, do not exhibit the characteristics of prosperous ethnic enclaves. On the contrary, Rochin and Castillo (1993) found that typical socioeconomic indicators, including educational achievement, poverty levels, and government expenditure, in most colonias were worse than the indicators in non-colonia–non-Latino majority communities.

Not surprisingly, the increasing poverty of colonias also corresponds with overcrowding and a deteriorating housing stock. The situation is exacerbated by local governments that are likely to be fiscally poor and unable, or in some instances unwilling, to maintain public investments in infrastructure, public safety, and community development programs. In colonias with heavy in-migration, both housing and infrastructure conditions can be far worse. A consequence is that these low-cost but substandard housing and living conditions are an implicit subsidy to agribusiness, as they help lower the economic pressure on farmers and the agriculture industry to increase farming wages. The poor living conditions, however, substantially reduce the prospects of upward social mobility for farmworkers and their children and are a key policy challenge for the state.

Parlier, in Fresno County, almost in the center of the state, illustrates the social and population transformations. In 1921 it was 95 percent non-Hispanic. In almost 50 years, by 1970, it became 70 percent Hispanic or Latino. The 2000 census indicates that Parlier's population is almost 97 percent Latino.[9] In parallel to the demographic changes in rural California, Runsten, Kissam, and Intili (1995) have concluded that there is a growing polarization of settlement patterns in the state. They argue that some rural communities are ethnically diverse with varied economic activities and businesses. Others, like Parlier, predominantly cater to low-wage Latinos and farmworkers. In such communities, or colonias according to the demographic definition, both housing and infrastructure are hardpressed for private and public investments and continue to deteriorate.

The larger demographic changes and growing Latino majority, however, can conceal an increasing social and economic stratification within the demographic colonias. As Runsten, Kissam, and Intili note:

We were therefore surprised to discover the extent to which the people who are "residents" of Parlier are not farmworkers and are not interested in doing farm work. The ethnic uniformity of Parlier hides a highly stratified community that mirrors in many respects the job structure of the surrounding agriculture and related businesses. Anglo and Japanese growers continue to control the economy of the Parlier area, while Mexican migrant workers, at the bottom, do most of the seasonal farm work. In between the growers and farmworkers are the year-round, Mexican American residents of Parlier, who control the community's political infrastructure and public institutions. (1995, quoted in Taylor, Martin, and Fix 1997, 45)

Such stratification within communities can make public infrastructure outlays and programs by local governments less likely and more challenging. State and federal levels of government might have to play a more active role in funding and ensuring the requisite investments. Thus, there is an overlap between the designated colonias and the demographic colonias. But there are a few designated colonias that do not have a clear Latino majority and therefore do not meet the demographic definition of colonias established by Refugio Rochin and his colleagues. Similarly, there are many demographic colonias beyond the border region that do not meet the current policy criteria for designation as colonias.[10]

The Future of California's Colonias

The poor living conditions in colonias represent significant economic and social challenges that are much larger than housing rehabilitation and infrastructure upgrading. Ultimately, higher and more sustainable living wages in the farming sector are likely to be linked to profound changes in the operations of agribusiness, including intractable immigration reforms. In a similar vein, continuous and adequate investments in physical and social infrastructure are likely to depend on a complete revamp of existing institutions of local governance, including the prevailing structure of public finance. In the absence of wide-ranging reforms, worse housing and living conditions, like some of the recently documented trailer parks for migrant workers on sovereign tribal land (Kelly 2007), are liable to expand.

Nonetheless, more modestly, policy efforts to increase the supply of affordable housing, improve existing housing, and augment current infrastructure need to continue and are the most promising. At least three diverse and existing housing endeavors in the state are noteworthy. First is an initiative of the Napa Valley Vintners (NVV), a trade association representing the Napa Valley wineries and vineyard owners. In 2002, members of the NVV voted to tax themselves and created a permanent assessment of $7.76/acre to fund housing for migrant workers. The assessment monies, along with funding from the state and county governments, have been used to build farmworker housing centers operated by the Napa Valley Housing Authority. Earlier the association supported an amendment—Measure L—to the county's general plan to allow for the building of farm labor camps in agriculture zones.

A second undertaking, similarly guided by self-interest, is afloat in Ventura County. This endeavor is led by the Ventura County Ag Futures Alliance, a citizens' group keen on keeping agriculture viable in the county. According to the group, if "agriculture is to survive in Ventura County it must have farmworkers and they need clean, safe, affordable housing. Supporting its provision is in the interest of every resident of Ventura County. It is a matter of economic common sense and the right thing to do!" (Ventura County Ag Futures Alliance 2002, 2). The group's members are concerned about the possibility of losing agricultural land to the pressures of urbanization from neighboring Los Angeles County. Urban sprawl threatens to change the idyllic, more pastoral quality of life in Ventura County, and the citizens' group is trying to mobilize to support the construction of affordable housing for farmworkers.

The third initiative is a much older example. Self-Help Enterprises is a nonprofit that started working on farmworker and rural housing in 1965. Since then it has been responsible for the development of over 5,000 new houses, and also the rehabilitation of over 5,000 homes in eight counties of the San Joaquin Valley. It follows and advocates a model of self-help, in which potential beneficiaries actively participate in the construction and rehabilitation of housing. A pledge of sweat equity is accepted and encouraged as the down payment for ownership-based new homes. The mortgage loans are secured through funding support from the USDA and the California Housing Finance Agency, the state's affordable housing bank.

In addition to such housing-focused endeavors, funding and initiatives for upgrading deficient infrastructure in colonias also need to continue.

The existing programs of HUD, EPA, and USDA have benefited a number of settlements and communities with inadequate services. The extent and scope of their work, however, must expand. This includes a more active and meaningful involvement of community groups in upgrading efforts (Donelson 2004). One strategy for California to access additional funding for infrastructure improvements is the expansion of the current HUD program for colonias. Such an effort will require lobbying from the state government and should include a discussion on whether to continue calling infrastructure-poor places colonias or something else (Mukhija and Monkkonen 2007). But at the other extreme is the risk that public funding for infrastructure in poor communities may continue to dwindle. Recent developments in California suggest a new forceful push for the privatization of infrastructure delivery (Rothfeld 2007). This can adversely affect the prospects for improving living conditions in colonias and needs to be closely monitored, and if necessary resisted, by residents, activists, and housing and civil rights groups.

Summary

California's agriculture economy continues to reap enormous profits, but farmworkers have not shared this prosperity. Instead, their lives are colored by long hours of hard work, deplorable living conditions, and exclusion from the state's power base. Many farmworkers live in colonias, but impoverishment is not confined to these formally designated districts. Unlike colonias in Texas that house large Latino populations in recently built subdivisions, California's colonias are older and many are occupied by white retirees who seek refuge from inclement weather in other parts of the country. At the same time, there are dozens of rural towns in California that reflect the deeper historical and cultural roots that define colonias in demographic terms. In this case, Latinos often represent over 50 percent of the population and also struggle with poverty and dilapidated housing in much the same way as do residents of Texas colonias. In California, therefore, federal and state programs are disconnected from the deeper demographic realities that define colonias. This disconnect suggests the need to revisit federal and state policies, because, well intentioned or not, the one-size-fits-all approach ignores much of California's underclass. Ultimately, the farmworker population shoulders the weight of exclusion as inequities deepen.

Notes

1. There are still seasonal differences in farm labor employment. The peak season, September, accounts for almost one-and-a-half times more farmworkers than the regular months.

2. The data suggest that more than half of California's farmworkers are unauthorized to work (Aguirre International 2005).

3. Also see Richard Steven Street's noteworthy *Beasts of the Field* for detailed accounts of earlier farmworkers' housing and work conditions (2004), and Ernesto Galarza's (1977) *Farm Workers and Agribusiness in California* for an account of farming and the Bracero Program in the state.

4. The original Subdivision Map Act of California was approved by the state legislature in 1907. This act, however, did not impose regulatory requirements on land subdivisions. It only required developers to file subdivision maps to maintain robust records of property transactions. But the significant revision of 1929, and subsequent amendments through the 1930s, imposed demanding infrastructure requirements on developers.

5. This suggests that the development trajectory of California's colonias more closely resembles the logic of most colonias in New Mexico (Koerner 2002) and Arizona (Donelson and Holguin 2001).

6. The housing conditions assessment is based on criteria established by California Housing and Community Development (HCD). According to the criteria, housing conditions are defined on the basis of the number of minor or major repairs needed in five areas: foundation, roofing, siding, windows, and electrical wiring. If no repairs or only one minor repair is needed, the unit is defined as "sound"; two minor repairs or one major leads to the "minor repairs needed" classification; three minor repairs, two major, or a combination thereof defines "moderate"; if repairs are needed in all five areas, then needs are defined as "substantial"; and if the estimated cost of repair exceeds the replacement cost of the structure, then the house is classified as "dilapidated."

7. The designated colonias in Riverside County include the city of Coachella, Mecca, Mesa Verde, North Shore, Oasis, Ripley, Thermal, and Torres Martinez. San Diego County's colonias are Campo, Jacumba, La Jolla, La Posta, Los Coyotes, Pala, Rincon, San Pasqual, and Tecate.

8. The EPA limits its colonia funding to the border region as defined in the North American Free Trade Agreement (NAFTA): 62 miles, or 100 kilometers, north of the border. USDA funds are disbursed through its Rural Development (RD) program and are confined to rural areas with fewer than 20,000 residents.

9. Even this is likely to be an undercount because of the difficulties in correctly accounting for poor Latinos that live in unorthodox and undocumented housing.

See Jennifer Sherman and her colleagues' *Finding Invisible Farm Workers: The Parlier Survey* (1997).

10. Another recent, although less common, use of the terminology *colonia* has been for Latino-majority, unincorporated islands in the Central Valley (Romney 2005). These pockets have deficient infrastructure and are left unincorporated by cities keen to avoid the public expense of upgrading their services. Many of these neighborhoods are not census designated places and are missed in the typical accounting of demographic colonias. While designated and demographic colonias are spatially either independent sites or at the periphery of other municipalities, these unincorporated colonias are islands surrounded by incorporated cities and represent a unique spatial arrangement.

PART II

Housing and Community Development

Colonia Housing and Community Development

Lydia Arizmendi, David Arizmendi, and Angela Donelson

COMMUNITY DEVELOPMENT APPROACHES in colonias are either place-based or people-centered. Place-based solutions, typical of legislative and regulatory schemes that address colonia problems, fall short of achieving effective community development, because they focus exclusively on the physical or structural aspects of colonia conditions. People-centered approaches implicitly consider the realities of the people directly affected by the problems. They employ a value system that respects the fundamental right of people to determine their own well-being and competence to craft solutions to their problems.

This chapter examines both approaches in the four states bordering Mexico. However, we focus mostly on Texas, because advocates in this state have the longest and most established track record in addressing colonias' concerns. First, we show how most Texas legislation has been targeted toward halting the growth of colonias, and how it has hindered residents from attempting to move out of poverty. We then compare the Texas experience with regulatory approaches in New Mexico, Arizona, and California. Next, we explore why resident-driven approaches are better at addressing the imminent needs of colonias as well as the underlying conditions that perpetuate their development. We share examples of how successful resident-led efforts have impacted change at both the community and state levels. Finally, we conclude with recommendations as to how colonia-serving organizations can better support local residents in their efforts to enhance colonia conditions and capacity for self-determination.

Place-Based Solutions in Texas Colonias

Texas colonias have grown steadily for the past 50 years, since migrant farmworkers first immigrated to Texas to fill agricultural labor shortages during the Bracero Program (Lorey 1999; Ward 1999; Weaver 2001).[1] Because farmworkers could not find affordable housing in south Texas cities and towns, many built their own homes in rural areas and unincorporated areas on the fringes of urban areas (Chapa and Eaton 1997; Davies and Holz 1992; Ward 1999).

During the 1980s, colonias underwent a population explosion.[2] The Industrial Areas Foundation (IAF) of south Texas sponsored several organizations, including the El Paso Interreligious Sponsoring Organization (EPISO) in El Paso County, and Valley Interfaith in the Rio Grande Valley, to draw attention to the plight of these residents. They called for state and federal action. But it was not until the *New York Times* ran a story in 1989 describing these Texas settlements as "one of the nation's most wrenching public health problems" (Applebome 1989) that Texas officials conceded that something had to be done about the "colonia problem."

Previous attempts of IAF groups to get the attention of policy makers had been met with the same refrain: the growth of colonias is the result of unauthorized immigration, and therefore a concern of the federal government. Many, therefore, presumed that colonias were inhabited solely by undocumented Mexican immigrants. They were wrong. The Texas Department of Human Services conducted a formal survey that revealed that two-thirds of colonia residents were U.S. citizens (Texas Department of Human Services 1998). University of Texas at Austin researchers later put that number higher, at 85 percent (Chapa and Eaton 1997). Not surprisingly, colonias figured prominently in the 1989 legislative session.

Taking a place-based approach, the Texas legislature defined the colonias as a public health and safety crisis. Senate Bill 2, dubbed the "Colonias Water Bill," created the Economically Distressed Areas Program (EDAP) to assist local governments in addressing the immediate health and safety threat posed by colonias in their jurisdictions (Texas Senate 1989). EDAP funded water and wastewater systems in border counties with income and unemployment rates at least 25 percent below the state average. Specifically, the state authorized the Texas Water Development Board (TWDB) to issue general obligation bonds for investment in local bonds issued by counties, cities, and water supply corporations (Texas Senate 1989). By 2001, EDAP had received nearly $600 million for water and sewer projects.

While EDAP has represented an important source of financial investment, it has failed to meet many colonias' needs. A majority of residents have continued to live without adequate water and wastewater services (Texas Secretary of State 2006). In response to criticism of the slow pace of infrastructure development, the TWDB has declared that it is not ultimately responsible, but rather: "it is local utilities . . . cities, districts and water supply corporations. . . . that actually build and operate TWDB-funded projects. The TWDB is proud and honored to do its part to address the important public health issue of the colonias" (Texas Water Development Board 2000, 1).

Today, the fate of thousands of colonia residents without water and sewer services in Texas is unclear. In October 2001, the TWDB admitted available funds would not be able to pay for all of the EDAP projects currently engaged in facility planning, estimating that an additional $80 million would be required (Texas Water Development Board 2001, 3).

Most other Texas legislation has similarly intended to regulate, and eventually eliminate, the proliferation of colonias. Provisions of the 1989 law, Senate Bill 2, required the promulgation of model subdivision rules with strict safety and sanitation standards for new rural subdivision developments. Counties and cities applying for EDAP funding were required to formally adopt the rules. The state law also required developers to plat and subdivide new properties, and to provide bonds or other financial guarantees ensuring water and wastewater services were available in new subdivisions. However, colonias platted before 1989 were "grandfathered," or exempted from the rules. This allowed some of the worst-case conditions to persist.

House Bill 1001 had a similar law enforcement–oriented approach. In 1995, Texas attorney general Dan Morales introduced the bill in an endeavor to get tough on colonia developers. The bill passed and gave affected counties unprecedented authority to enforce strict subdivision rules. It also gave the attorney general greater power to enforce the model subdivision rules and subdivision standards. Violations triggered hefty civil and criminal penalties for land sales in unregistered subdivisions and noncompliance with platting requirements (Texas House 1995a). Soon after its enactment, in a highly publicized campaign designed to deter colonia development, the attorney general filed numerous lawsuits against colonia developers.

Local governments supported the new laws because they blamed the "colonia problem" on unscrupulous developers who evaded subdivision laws. They did not assume responsibility for failing to provide access to affordable housing. In fact, local governments attempted to make the laws even tougher by imposing building codes for colonias housing without providing families resources for compliance. In 2001, a press release about one such bill, Senate Bill 517, indicated local authorities had tried to secure ordinance-making authority to impose building codes in colonias for the past 10 years (Texas Senate 2001). A renewed attempt was made during the 2003 legislative session (Texas Senate 2003). The proposed laws—which failed as a result of opposition from land developers and builders—would have made it impossible for many colonias homeowners to improve their housing conditions, since families do so incrementally, as finances permit.

New land use laws and infrastructure requirements penalized colonia residents in other ways. Many were treated as culprits when they could not afford to meet minimum infrastructure standards. Some were forced to pay fines for using faulty septic systems that they could not repair (County Attorney of El Paso, Texas, pers. com. with D. Arizmendi 1995; Sparks Housing Development Corporation Board, pers. comm. with D. Arizmendi 1995). Others could not afford the rising prices of housing. With increased regulation, lot prices tripled within a few years of the passage of the 1995 law, House Bill 1001.[3] Lot payments in new rural subdivision lot sales were averaging $250 per month, with typically 14 to 18 percent interest. Yet the typical colonia resident served by Proyecto Azteca, a Hidalgo County housing development corporation with a waiting list at the time of 3,000 families, could not afford more than $125 a month for housing. To cope, colonia residents increasingly began living with relatives in overcrowded conditions and moved multiple dwellings onto single lots (Hidalgo County's Urban Counties Program representative, pers. comm. with D. Arizmendi 1999).

Place-Centered Approaches in New Mexico, Arizona, and California

Compared with Texas, state lawmakers in the three remaining U.S.–Mexico border states have enacted few laws directed at colonias. This is largely because the three states have far fewer such settlements. The U.S. Department of Housing and Urban Development reports there are 140 colonias in New Mexico and 87 colonias in Arizona (U.S. Department of Housing and Urban Development 2004). Researchers Mukhija and Monkkonen have identified 32 in California (2006).

Fewer colonia settlements exist in these states because their nonmetropolitan border counties are more sparsely populated, with less private land than in Texas, and because their counties have had more land use enforcement authority over unincorporated areas than in Texas. Texas counties could not enforce subdivision rules until 2001, when House Bill 1445 granted them authority to approve subdivision plats in peri-urban areas next to cities and towns (Koerner 2002).

California counties have had the strongest subdivision laws of the four border states. Because counties have required infrastructure of subdividers since 1929, most California colonias are very old settlements (Mukhija and Monkkonen 2006). However, some newer colonia-type settlements in California have grown up more recently. Most of these are home to farmworkers living in "cartolandias," or small complexes of cardboard and scrap-material huts, sited on agricultural land. Chapter 10 describes how substandard living conditions in these settlements have proliferated in southern California over the past decade, since a 1992 California law intended to protect farmworkers has been misused by opportunistic developers.

In New Mexico and Arizona, regulatory approaches have fallen somewhere between the formerly lax Texas county laws and the more strict California regulations. Since the 1990s, county land use authority has become weaker in Arizona, but stronger in New Mexico. In 1994, Arizona rural interests and farmers convinced the state legislature to loosen county subdivision regulations: they now can split lots up to five times—up from four previously—and sell them without providing basic services (Davis 2000). The law has had the effect of enabling property owners to sell lots to others who can split property indefinitely (Esparza and Donelson 2008). Some of this so-called wildcat development has contributed to new colonia settlements in Arizona since the mid-1990s (Carroll 2006; Davis 2000). Yuma and Cochise County have responded by creating area-specific land use plans, which regulate the density of development in some of these places. However, county-level efforts are limited, because border counties lack the staff, and sometimes the political will, to enforce land use laws (Esparza and Donelson 2008).

New Mexico has more regulatory policies toward colonias. Until 1996, property owners in New Mexico were able to split their property into four parcels without triggering subdivision laws. After waiting two years, property owners could split their land again, indefinitely (Donelson and Holguin 2001). In an effort to eliminate unplanned, colonia-style growth, state legislators passed an amendment to New Mexico subdivision law. It required developers in the southern part of the state to comply with subdivision regulations, in effect banning the development of new colonias (Esparza and Donelson 2008). Since the law was passed, the state of New Mexico has recognized the need to improve colonia infrastructure. Under the tenure of Governor Bill Richardson, the state invested $15.8 million from 2005 through 2007 in colonia infrastructure projects prioritized by local governments (New Mexico Department of Finance and Administration 2008). This represents the first time a dedicated funding source for colonia infrastructure and housing needs has been allocated by the state.

The Value of People-Centered Approaches

Though federal resources and some state funding in Texas and New Mexico are earmarked for colonia infrastructure, residents have had to fend for themselves in tackling most problems. Their tenacity has helped them develop creative solutions to surmount very difficult conditions. For this reason, resident-centered approaches are best suited for making long-term change in colonia conditions. Such strategies draw upon the knowledge and self-determination of residents who see their colonias not as poor slums, but as viable, even dynamic communities where they are building homes and raising families.

Our experience working with colonia residents who carry out community-improvement strategies gives us great respect for their skill, humility, and commitment. Most leaders are women who are inclined to give of their time and energy to improve their communities. Women, in particular, have been effective because tending to their communities is a natural extension of tending to their families. They take responsibility for major aspects of community projects and activities. Most do not identify themselves as leaders, nor do they necessarily exhibit attributes associated with traditional leadership. Words like *understanding, nurturance, cooperation,* and *service* are more descriptive of their approaches.

They are motivated by confidence in their fellow residents' abilities and potential for growth. Their leadership style is relational; they build trust through respecting, supporting, and befriending those in their community. As such, they embody the essence of Paolo Freire's characterization of revolutionary leaders in Latin America who had discovered the art of working in communion and solidarity with the people.[4] They capture the humanism that Freire (1970) believes is essential for community: they have love for their neighbors, faith in their ability to understand the issues and make decisions, humility about their own roles and contributions, and a shared hope that they can succeed in their efforts. They exemplify what Friere (1970) terms "dialogical action," or action that is precipitated by dialogue, rooted in direct understanding and personal experience of the issues at hand.

Colonia leaders are effective when they respect and yield to the capacity of the community to define its own problems and decide how it will resolve them, tapping the self-help motivation of residents. Their experience has taught them that when people are not involved in making decisions, they cannot be expected to follow along blindly. They accept a nonlinear development process based on purpose rather than plan, recognizing the inextricable nature of social and personal change.

In a practical context, these women operate much like *promotores(as),* or lay community educators/outreach workers. Over time, they visit with residents in their own homes and in this way build trust. Lay community educators are widely used throughout the U.S.–Mexico border, Latin America, and Asia to deliver health care to hard-to-reach populations (May and Contreras 2007; May et al. 2003). Lay workers are increasingly common in the U.S.–Mexico border region, active in community organizing, development, and research. They bring five types of resources to their communities: information and referral services, education in specialized areas, capacity building to build leadership and connect residents, emotional support, and local empowerment (May et al. 2003). While their skills are invaluable, most colonia leaders do what they do without compensation; rarely do organizations pay them for their outreach services.[5]

The Impact of People-Centered Approaches

Resident-centered work has fundamentally changed the character of some colonias of the border region. The impact is particularly true in Texas, where the strongest, and longest-standing, advocacy work on colonias has been advanced. Therefore, this section discusses how Texas residents have spearheaded numerous victories, expanding beyond local boundaries to create statewide impacts. Resident-led organizing efforts in other states are discussed in chapters 8, 9, and 10 and have been covered in other research (Esparza and Donelson 2008).

Most Texas grassroots organizing began in the early 1990s, when colonia residents launched neighborhood associations and small nonprofits to provide a collective voice for their communities and to help them to access resources. Local efforts that succeeded were mostly based on a locally driven promotor(a) approach integrating Freire's (1970) concepts of community action.

In colonias such as Las Lomas in Starr County, residents shaped dramatic quality-of-life changes. The leaders in Las Lomas, mostly women, began to act in 1995 when they fought the proposed siting of an animal transfer station on the periphery of their community (Blanca Juarez, interview with D. and L. Arizmendi 1997). Over the next four years, they worked with community organizer David Arizmendi and a newly formed advocacy organization—Initiativa Frontera, or Border Initiative—intended to assist in organizing efforts. Their organizational structure changed from one reflecting traditional, hierarchical notions of leadership to one that built consensus and distributed leadership among those who had the trust and respect of the community. Leaders turned their dormant community organization, which had previously experienced only short-lived, small successes, into one that effectively mobilized the community.

Through a mutual process of education, David Arizmendi and Initiativa Frontera provided support to help the community identify its leaders, define its problems, implement decisions, and choose effective strategies to accomplish its objectives. In a matter of months, residents constructed a small community center to house its organization, Colonias Unidas, or United Colonias. Residents paid $20 annual membership fees, used to maintain center operations. Using self-help methods, leaders and volunteers organized and offered classes in English as a Second Language, general education (GED), citizenship, parenting, nutrition, sewing, cake decorating, first aid, and home improvement.

Teaming up with such unlikely partners as the U.S. Immigration and Naturalization Service and the state's environmental agency, Las Lomas won widespread respect. In 1998, Colonias Unidas secured the Texas Governor's Environmental Excellence award for its community environmental campaign: the nonprofit recruited 250 volunteers to stop garbage burning and illegal dumping. Later, the organization launched a program that produced 3,000 U.S. citizens within two years. Moreover, Colonias Unidas helped land a state-funded nutrition program that has served 1,300 children, who also benefit from informal child-care arrangements. These, among other accomplishments, helped Las Lomas develop a stronger voice and an improved quality of life.

Similar community-based organizing efforts in other Texas colonias have brought local improvements and state-level policy changes. Advocacy efforts in Colonia B&E serve to illustrate this point. For decades, most homes in this colonia, located not far from Las Lomas in Starr County, lacked electricity. Residents ran long electrical extension cords from the homes of their neighbors, some the length of several city blocks, across makeshift ditches built in response to drainage problems. The situation was dangerous and unhealthy, especially for the children who played outside.

Desperate to remedy these conditions after several years of attempting to find help, a frustrated resident leader of B&E Colonia contacted Texas Rural Legal Aid in the fall of 1996. She already had called and written letter to numerous state and federal agencies, including the White House. Those who bothered to respond let her know she could not get electricity because she lived in an illegal subdivision. When Texas Rural Legal Aid gave a similar response, she knew the law had to change. She was referred to Colonias Unidas in Las Lomas, which had just succeeded in some of its organizing efforts. With the help of Colonias Unidas and other Border Coalition partners, including two Hispanic legislators, Colonia B&E residents changed the law (Colonia B&E residents, pers. comm. w. D. Arizmendi 1996–97). By the end of 1997, thousands more colonia residents had obtained electricity.

But the fight was not over. Residents wanted a blanket exemption for all existing colonias. They wanted to cover all colonia lot owners, because they knew future residents would move in soon, given they had no other housing alternatives. State legislative experts thought the proposed exemption could cover only households already living in the affected colonias.

The legal experts and authors of the bill were frustrated. They believed the proposed exemption would alienate the attorney general and a majority of legislators. The colonia leader asked what residents could do. She was told that they would have to win the necessary support themselves. Without a second thought, the residents prepared for the work ahead. They selected representatives, raised funds, and organized their three-day visit to Austin. The trip included a press conference, in which they read a poem asking legislators to imagine life without electricity. They also held a seven-hour, media-covered "stand-in" on the premises of the attorney general and scheduled a final day of visits with legislators to relate the heart-wrenching realities of their need for electricity service (Colonia B&E residents, pers. comm. with D. Arizmendi 1996–97).

Before returning home, the residents had won the support of the attorney general, key legislators, and the governor's office. They gathered in front of the capitol, tired but happy that they had accomplished what they set out to do. The legislative expert told the residents she had misjudged them. They had taught her an important lesson: the will of the people really counts. She thanked them for having allowed her to be a part of their struggle. Texas Senate Bill 1512 passed, allowing colonia residents to access utility hookups in unplatted subdivisions. Five months later, Colonia B&E had water and electricity services. A few days before Christmas in 1997, the community celebrated its victory at the leader's home.

These cases illustrate how grassroots activists essentially have become "squeaky wheels" in their communities. In carrying out their work, they have drawn the attention of community-based organizations and service providers. Organizations like the Border Low Income Housing Coalition have helped residents "scale up" their local initiatives to influence state policy. Through the work of the Border Low Income Housing Coalition (whose activities are described in greater depth in chapter 7), residents forged effective partnerships with nonprofit advocates and government (Border Low Income Housing Coalition 1993).

Between 1995 and 2001, partnerships launched through the work of this coalition produced more humane, people-centered legislation. Residents gained greater protections from developer abuses and greater access to self-help resources through a number of resident-driven legislative measures. The Colonia Fair Land Sales Act required developers in EDAP counties to make contract for deed land sales more transparent and ensured greater buyer protections (Texas Senate 1995a). Texas House Bill 2726 directed the Texas Department of Housing and Community Affairs to develop a $20 million, tax-exempt bond program to convert contracts for deed into mortgages, enabling residents to earn equity on their properties, obtain lower interest rates, and protect their homes (Texas House 1995b). Senate Bill 1509 provided resources for one-stop centers in the five major border counties to offer construction education, a revolving loan fund, home financing assistance, homeownership counseling, a tool lending library, and technical assistance with septic tank installation (Texas Senate 1995c). This bill has brought more resources to the colonias, even if the one-stop centers have not been as locally self-managed as originally intended. (Chapter 7 critiques the state's method of implementing it). Texas Senate Bill 1421 gave EDAP counties authority to issue waivers to colonias established prior to 1995, thereby providing residents in unplatted colonias a mechanism to receive water and electricity services previously prohibited under Texas House Bill 1001 regulations (Texas Senate 1999). In 2001, the Texas Bootstrap Loan Program began providing mortgage loans for low-income colonia families (Texas Senate 2001). It has since appropriated funding for the colonia model subdivision revolving loan program and the contract-for-deed conversion program. All of these programs have assisted residents in meeting subdivision standards to convert their contracts into mortgages.

Supporting Colonia Residents

The stories of Las Lomas, Colonia B&E, and others in the following chapters of this section illustrate how colonias have effectively organized for change. Residents have adopted consensus-based forms of leadership, based on Freire's (1970) concepts of dialogical action, successfully operating on a promotor(a) method of outreach. People-centered approaches work because they come from the conviction that the people themselves, with the proper support from public and private resources, can succeed in designing policies and programs that meet their needs. They require that colonia residents be treated not as beneficiaries or recipients of service, but as equal partners in the process of developing and implementing solutions. Organizations assisting colonias should attempt to internalize these principles and reflect on them in their work, engaging in what Freire (1970) refers to as courageous dialogue. This kind of dialogue elicits the wisdom and knowledge of the people and presents the knowledge of the capacity builder in a way that creates new knowledge needed to properly assess issues and develop appropriate strategies. This process of cultural synthesis, as Freire calls it, enables both capacity builders and residents to engage in community action and self-development activities not possible through place-based approaches.

As discussed later in the book, successful colonia improvement efforts in other U.S.–Mexico border states also draw upon these principles. Chapter 10 highlights the experience of California organizations that have engaged residents, faith-based groups, nonprofits, and government institutions to address deplorable farmworker living conditions in the Coachella Valley. Chapter 8 explores how faith-based organizations have advocated with residents to bring about change in New Mexico colonias.

As nonprofit organizations carry out their work, they must remain grounded in community priorities. At times, residents say their main concerns have been displaced by those of policy networks that have provided little help to local associations (Donelson 2004; Esparza and Donelson 2008). Similarly, nonprofit organizations have sometimes subverted the intent of promotores(as) outreach programs (May and Contreras 2007). When funders use the promotor(a) model solely as a vehicle to market their programs with contract workers, they misuse local leaders and hinder local efforts to build sustainable communities. As May and Contreras (2007) observe, funders can foster more effective community building by funding colonias-based promotores(as) who are far more familiar with immediate and longer-term needs.

Summary

Colonia residents are working people demonstrating a remarkable ability to use even meager resources for maximum benefit, essentially doing very much with very little. Against all odds, colonia residents have clung to the dream of a better life for themselves and their children. They have refused to concede to a life of poverty and have never waited for someone to come to save them. Despite their daily struggle, they have persevered, sometimes for decades, under conditions that would have exhausted most of us. Their unrelenting capacity for self-help remains the single most valuable and available resource in colonia community development.

Self-help is the cornerstone of their lives. As we have shown—through stories of community work and resident-directed legislative efforts in Texas—residents have demonstrated their capabilities for improving their quality of life. These stand in stark contrast to the place-based, regulatory efforts that have hindered the self-development of colonias residents.

Clearly, colonias residents must participate as equal partners with community builders to effect legislative changes and to make improvements in their communities. Helping organizations from outside the community must employ the kind of humanism found in the leadership of the women on the front lines of colonia change efforts. And they must catalyze residents' talents, motivation, determination, and willingness to use self-help by continuing to create the types of structures and support systems shown to be effective.

Notes

1. The Bracero Program imported millions of Mexican guest workers into the United States between 1942 and 1964, so as to fill labor shortages brought about by World War II.

2. Colonias populations probably grew rapidly for at least two reasons. For one, demands for labor increased in the United States and in the border region due to growth of the maquiladora, or binational twin plant manufacturing program (Henneberger 2000; Herzog 1990). Second, Mexican workers in the United States were granted immigration amnesty under the Immigration Reform Control Act of 1986, enabling previously migrant families to permanently settle in the United States.

3. David and Lydia Arizmendi identified that lot costs tripled during a two- to four-year period after the passage of HB 100 by tracking the cost of unimproved land sales in their local newspaper and by talking extensively over this time period with colonia housing clients of Proyecto Azteca.

4. Paolo Freire was a Brazilian educator whose path-breaking work *A Pedagogy of the Oppressed* (1970) has influenced educational and social movements around the world, especially among the poor.

5. By retaining independence from outside organizations—rather than serving as contract promotor(a) employees—leaders can avoid the danger of becoming what May and Contreras (2007) refer to as solely the "labor for hire" for outside organizations. Independence enables colonia residents to retain local control of their priorities, rather than marketing and promoting a particular service for external agencies.

7

Housing in Texas Colonias

John Henneberger, Kristin Carlisle, and Karen Paup

COLONIAS IN TEXAS have attracted considerable attention in recent years for their "Third World" characteristics. Poverty is widespread, housing is often substandard and lacks basic infrastructure, and the incidence of infectious disease is abnormally high. Even so, residents of Texas colonias embody the same aspirations held by middle-class Americans everywhere: homeownership, rising housing values, and children growing up in safe and comfortable environments near friends and family. Yet these dreams did not materialize in the same way for colonia residents. Instead, they pieced together the means to improve their living conditions incrementally, largely in response to the housing affordability crisis in the Texas border region.

This chapter visits colonias in Texas with two aims in mind. We seek to document the impoverishment that characterizes colonias and to discuss how, and why, they emerged. We also discuss the positive efforts to improve colonia housing. Forward-thinking initiatives include some state and locally led efforts, but mostly involve nongovernmental organizations (NGOs) that have worked side by side with colonia residents to provide safe and decent housing. As this chapter will demonstrate, it is the firm resolve of residents themselves that overcomes disadvantage and social inequity.

The chapter is organized into four sections. First, we provide an overview of Texas colonias. To bring this picture to life, we describe how a typical family ended up in their colonia, and how they struggle to make ends meet. Next, we summarize how grassroots advocacy organizations like our own—the Texas Low Income Housing Information Service—have worked with colonia residents and the Texas legislature to resolve many challenges. We contrast grassroots efforts with state-led approaches that have proven to be less effective. We then move to conditions in a specific colonia: El Cenizo. We show how this colonia's residents have organized to improve their community despite many difficulties. Finally, we summarize the chapter and describe the needs that have yet to be addressed.

The Emergence of Texas Colonias

The First World and Third World meet along the 1,300-mile Texas–Mexico border. Colonias consisting of used trailers and scrap-metal shacks flourish in this vast region of mixed urban and rural landscapes. Texas is home to the largest colonia population and the largest number of colonias in the United States. An estimated 400,000 Texans live in some 2,333 colonias, many without basic necessities such as electricity, running water, wastewater, sewers, and paved roads (Texas Secretary of State 2006). In the six Texas counties that claim 90 percent of colonia residents, government-funded projects have brought water and wastewater infrastructure to 36 percent of the colonias, 22 percent have some level of service, and one-quarter remain without any service (Texas Secretary of State 2006).[1] Housing conditions are dire as well. Texas border colonias still comprise the largest concentration of people living without basic sanitation in the United States.

Approximately 15 to 20 percent of people living in the Texas–Mexico border region reside in colonias (Olmstead 2004). Belying popular stereotypes, 85 percent of colonia residents are U.S. citizens (Chapa and Eaton 1997). In their University of Texas study of colonias, Chapa and Eaton (1997, 3) summarized it well: "Colonias are not an immigration problem; they are a highly inadequate solution to a shortage of affordable housing in an impoverished region."

In Spanish, the term *colonia* simply means "neighborhood" or "community," but in Texas the term is synonymous with poverty. In fast-growing Texas border counties that have the highest concentrations of Hispanics—such as Starr, Maverick, and Hidalgo counties—statistics are grim. As of 2004, median household incomes in these places were half the national median income of $44,334: in Starr County, $19,775; in Maverick County, $24,786; and Hidalgo County, $26,375 (U.S. Census Bureau 2008). In 2000, the percentage of families with children living below the poverty level was more than double the state's rate of 17 percent: in Starr County, 54 percent; in Maverick County, 35 percent; and in Hidalgo County, 39 percent (U.S. Census Bureau 2000b).

Texas colonias arose in the border region mainly because of economic and political factors. Beginning in the 1950s, developers responded to the gap between extremely low wages and the lack of affordable housing by selling lots to low-income residents with the promise that utilities, sewers, and paved roads would soon follow (Belden and Wiener 1999; Davies and Holz 1992; Ward 1999). But developers rarely kept their promises. They sold the land—often located in ill-suited areas such as floodplains—at cheap prices and with low down payments, but with high interest rates. Using a predatory financing mechanism known as "contract for deed," developers transferred title to buyers only when loans were fully paid.

The number of colonias also grew because Texas counties—which lack ordinance-making powers—have traditionally had little regulatory authority over colonia development. This gave developers unrestrained ability to exploit thousands of poor families by carving out isolated communities beyond the reach of city codes.

Through the 1970s, Anglo politicians responded to the colonia phenomenon with a policy of willful neglect. In many communities, Anglo politicians isolated Mexican Americans outside of municipal voting boundaries (Henneberger 2000). This meant politicians bypassed federal resources that could have provided housing options to extremely low-income families within city limits. Instead, they let politically connected landowners amass profits from the development of colonias in exurban or rural areas.

With the growth of Texas colonias in the 1980s and 1990s, city governments could no longer ignore the issue. Cities could not grow to accommodate rising populations without annexing colonias and providing services. In contrast to the annexation of more affluent communities, where property owners can afford assessments for municipal infrastructure, colonia residents were too poor to follow suit.

The Velas: A Colonia Family

The story of the Velas, who live in a Texas border colonia, is emblematic of the trials facing thousands of similarly situated families. (We have given this family a fictional name and changed the name of their colonia of residence to conceal their personal information.) Efren Vela immigrated to California from Mexico in 1977, when the plight of farmworkers made headlines and had a place in the nation's consciousness. The nationwide grape boycott led by Cesar Chavez was under way, and the United Farm Workers Union (UFW) had just gained the sole right to organize workers. Efren and his father spent three years laboring in the grape vineyards before moving to the Texas border in 1979. Upon reaching Texas, he found that housing was unaffordable on a farmworker's wages. A dilapidated rental trailer was the only shelter he could manage. Efren also discovered that steady jobs were rare.

In 1984, he met and married Angelica, also a Mexican immigrant. Once married, and with newly gained status as legal residents, they started a family. This set in motion the Velas' decades-long pursuit of a stable home. They saved for several years to purchase their first piece of land, but their housing options were limited. Angelica worked as a *palomita* (home care provider) and seamstress, bringing home about $900 a month. Efren earned about $7,500 a year as a farmworker—far below the income needed to qualify for the nation's largest source of subsidized housing, the low-income housing tax credit program. Long waiting lists placed public housing or Section 8 Housing Choice vouchers out of reach. The Velas were limited to what the private housing market offered. After living in rented trailers, they decided to purchase a lot in a colonia called Sunset Village.

Originally planned as a middle-class retirement community, the barren lots in Sunset Village did not sell. The owner defaulted on the loan, the bank went insolvent, and the Federal Deposit Insurance Corporation (FDIC) placed a lien on the property. A land sales agent saw the potential for profit and began selling Sunset Village lots under contracts for deed. The Velas put $100 down on a 49-by-109-foot lot that cost $12,500. They paid a 12 percent interest rate, even though conventional mortgage rates stood at 8 percent.[2] Like other families who bought lots, the Velas were unaware of the $100,000 lien against Sunset Village. Their purchase was loaded with debt. Under threat from Texas Rio Grande Legal Aid (TRLA), the seller converted contracts for deed to traditional deeds of trust. The TRLA negotiated with the FDIC, which forgave the lien.

For $800, the Velas bought a used, two-bedroom trailer from a friend. Among other problems, the trailer's roof was rife with leaks, and the wiring was faulty. For a family of five, it was also severely overcrowded.[3] Yet it was their only option. Although Texas law prohibits manufactured-home dealers from selling substandard trailers, no laws regulate the sale of used manufactured homes between individuals.

Nonetheless, the Velas felt a sense of economic progress and freedom when they moved into their home. A strong community network supported the Velas as they repaired their home. Efren labored alongside his neighbors to mend the roof, stabilize the foundation, and repair the electrical system. The repairs cost $1,300. Efren installed a septic tank for $200, saving thousands of dollars over contractor prices.

In short order, the landscape of Sunset Village began to change. Water service nearly reached the Velas' lot but left neighbors up the street without water.[4] Shortly after, sewer service came to the Velas' property even though Efren had installed the septic tank. Along the dirt roads, half-built cinderblock homes slowly emerged on previously empty lots. Like his neighbors, Efren transformed his trailer into a permanent home. With each paycheck, he purchased cinderblocks and began building walls for a home next to the trailer.

But the Velas' aspirations were dimmed by a devastating financial blow. While working in the fields, Efren injured his foot. He lacked health insurance and what might have been a minor injury became debilitating. No longer able to work the fields, he landed a promising factory job, but the factory closed. Then Efren was hired to organize deer hunts at a private ranch. Shortly afterward, the owner of the ranch died, and once again Efren was unemployed.

The Velas were forced to sell the trailer, their only shelter. They made $1,800, a net loss of $500 in equity. The family spent the summer camped out next to the unfinished walls of their home. With money from the trailer and an income tax refund, Efren partially completed three cinderblock rooms. The home still lacks heat. A single sheet at the back door attempts to shield the family from the chill winter wind. A makeshift kitchen in the front room is testament to ingenuity and poverty—a school desk functions as a kitchen counter, a nonworking refrigerator is a pantry, and its crisper drawers function as a double sink.

Today, the Velas continue to improve the home, but financial strains threaten their future. Efran projects the lot will be paid off in five years, and the family will own the property outright. He takes out the mortgage papers, which reveal a remaining principal of $5,465. If they pay as planned, the Velas will have spent over $9,000 to service the interest.

Like tens of thousands of other families living in Texas colonias, the Velas live each day with a better life seemingly in reach. Yet low wages and a lack of affordable housing force them to navigate the fine line between poverty and security.

Grassroots Advocacy Efforts to Improve Colonias

Since the 1980s, the plight of the Velas family and those like them has driven community organizing efforts of faith-based community groups, such as Valley Interfaith, the Border Organization, and El Paso Inter-religious Sponsoring Organization (EPISO). In conjunction with Hispanics who now held elected offices, these organizations worked to obtain infrastructure, especially potable water for colonias (Ward 1999). National media attention amplified their organizing efforts. In 1986, the Texas Water Development Board (TWDB) committed $100 million to colonias from their low-interest infrastructure development program. However, the funding opportunity was of limited value, because colonia residents could not afford TWDB loans (Wilson and Menzies 1997).

Undeterred, grassroots organizations refocused their efforts, which met with greater success. In 1989, their advocacy prompted the Texas legislature to adopt a more comprehensive approach to servicing existing colonias with water and reining in new colonias development. Under Senate Bill 2, the state established the Economically Distressed Areas Program (EDAP), which provided more affordable infrastructure funding and developed subdivision rules compelling developers to provide potable water, sewer and infrastructure. State law required counties to adopt these rules in order to be eligible for EDAP money (Texas Senate 1989).

Buoyed by their accomplishments, NGOs set their sights on a larger agenda. A core group of grassroots border leaders convened quarterly meetings that drew together colonia leaders, state and local officials, and housing authority directors, with the aim of resolving broader border community development issues. By 1993, they released the Border Housing and Community Development Partnership Plan. Among other things, the plan called for new community-based organizations, numerous community development initiatives, job and literacy training, employment for 5,500 people in self-help and public works programs, and assistance for 300 people in retail business start-ups. Most of these programs were to benefit the extremely low-income population earning less than 30 percent of the state median income (Border Low Income Housing Coalition 1993).

Initially, Border Coalition members were optimistic. Henry Cisneros, the former mayor of San Antonio, and then-director of the U.S. Department of Housing and Urban Development (HUD), promised to bring their proposal to the federal government. In 1993, Cisneros prepared a $270 million package for colonia housing aid. The package included $70 million in funding from the AFL-CIO pension trust fund and the Federal National Mortgage Association, and $200 million in subsidies and credits to be appropriated by Congress. Yet congressional proponents of the "Contract with America" did not share Cisneros's vision. *Progressive* magazine wrote: "Cisneros' proposals were slashed, then slashed again, and finally bled to death on the Congressional floor" (True 1996, 3).

Grassroots advocates turned to state-level government. The Border Coalition drafted the Colonia Fair Land Sales Act (SB 336), sponsored by El Paso senator Peggy Rosson and Brownsville Representative Rene Oliviera. The legislation was adopted in 1995 (Texas Senate 1995a), largely because the Border Coalition brought in colonia residents who testified the bill would avoid predatory land sales. The act struck at contracts for deed—the dark underbelly of colonia lot sales. Senate Bill 336 required that sellers provide buyers with clear identification of utility services, a cooling-off period allowing cancellation of sales, an annual accounting of payments and contract balance, a mechanism for assuring payment of property taxes, improved protections against eviction, streamlined conversion to a warranty deed, and fines against sellers for noncompliance. The legislation induced colonia developers to convert to traditional deeds of trust, rather than risk running afoul of the new law and its aggressive penalties.

To sustain legislative progress, colonia residents continued developing a leadership base and leveraging power from the Border Coalition. In 1997, the Border Coalition and self-help homebuilders assisted Brownsville senator Eddie Lucio's introduction of the colonias Bootstrap Program legislation, which funds mortgages for border self-help homebuilders who agree to contribute at least 60 percent of the labor needed to build their home (Texas Department of Housing and Community Affairs 1997).

As they worked with the Texas legislature, the Border Coalition learned initiatives requiring no funding or funds from existing revenue sources were far more successful than those requiring new revenue. In 1995, the Border Coalition assisted Senator Lucio's unsuccessful attempt to finance the Texas Housing Trust Fund through interest earned on trust accounts of title insurance companies (Texas Senate 1995b). They then shifted to a more modest approach. In 2001, Senator Lucio secured $2.5 million from general revenue for the trust fund, including the colonias Bootstrap program. The resources enabled the state to institutionalize the Bootstrap program, which remains an extremely successful and efficient community-led response to substandard housing in colonias. Similar smaller-scale efforts have helped bring annual appropriations to colonias, such as Senator Lucio's 2001 success in bringing general obligation bonds for road improvement to colonias.[5]

Yet since 2001, grassroots organizations have faced new challenges; predatory lenders altered tactics and targeted new, more urban locales. Unfavorable court decisions, coupled with developers' ability to operate under the radar of city government, have threatened to undermine the principal enforcement mechanism of the Colonia Fair Land Sales Act: fines against sellers. The Association of Communities for Reform Now (ACORN), along with the Texas Low Income Housing Information Service (TxLIHIS) recently exposed widespread contract-for-deed abuses in inner-city Houston.[6] Bolstered by housing policy expertise from TxLIHIS, ACORN organized advocacy to outlaw predatory tactics used in contracts for deed and a new (but similar) sales tactic called rent-to-own. Legislation ended the worst abuses of both tactics in 2005 (Texas House 2005). In 2007, contract-for-deed sellers lobbied unsuccessfully to overturn these reforms.

State-Driven Colonia Strategies

In contrast to grassroots organizing, state agencies have attempted to resolve colonia concerns through two narrowly conceived strategies. These include clamping down on colonia developers and promoting a self-help program. In the first case, the Texas attorney general's office (AG) sought to rein in colonia developers in the early 1990s by strengthening the enforcement of laws and regulations. They filed countless lawsuits against developers who failed to provide water and wastewater services in colonias and increased efforts after House Bill 1001 in 1995 granted their office (and district and county attorneys) enforcement powers of 1989 Model Subdivision Rules. Remedies included the formal platting or replatting of land, connecting utilities to residential communities outside city limits, and pursuing substantial civil and criminal penalties against errant subdividers (Texas Attorney General 2007b). Yet the AG's Colonia Strike Force was staffed by three lawyers only, and their efforts failed to meet expectations. Most lawsuits were civil, and lawyers received little money from court decisions (Ward 1999). For example, the AG's lawsuit against the infamous colonia developer Cecil McDonald (discussed below) sought $19 million but settled for a fraction of that amount (Myerson 1995).

The state also tried to tighten control of developers by prohibiting substandard residential subdivisions. The outcome, however, has been disastrous. State-level legislation succeeded in stopping development of new colonias but failed to accommodate the housing needs of the border's fast-growing low-income population. The message is now clear: low-income border residents can find affordable housing only in existing colonias.

In the second case, state bureaucracy led a self-help center program away from its intended goals. The state established self-help centers in response to the Border Coalition's 1995 initiative. That initiative had intended self-help centers to function as community development corporations (CDCs), providing on-site technical assistance to low-income families building homes and making their own infrastructure improvements. CDCs were to be accountable to local communities through colonia-based boards of directors. But the state veered from this vision by turning to county governments for the administration of the self-help program. County governments—lacking the know-how and experience to develop grassroots CDCs—turned to large social service organizations to administer the centers. In the end, self-help centers became social service providers instead of the envisioned community-based problem-solving organizations.

Sustainable solutions to colonia problems most often arise from the dirt-floor living rooms of residents and the makeshift community centers found in colonias. They have rarely surfaced from city halls or the chambers of the Texas legislature. The next section describes how colonia residents have brought decent shelter and basic services to their communities through grassroots organizing.

Organizing and Self-Help Solutions in El Cenizo

Nowhere is the ingenuity and determination of colonia residents better illustrated than in the story of El Cenizo. We are intimately familiar with El Cenizo, because the Texas Low Income Housing Information Service has assisted the community for many years. During this time, we helped with community organizing, leadership development, and technical assistance in forming a nonprofit housing organization.

More than 3,500 people live in this colonia, hidden off a two-lane road from the Zapata Highway, 17 miles outside Laredo, Texas. Prickly pear cacti, mesquite trees, and the tough-stemmed cenizo sagebush, after which the town is named, surround the colonia. The community is typical of Texas colonias in many respects. Lots were sold on contract for deed, and the colonia initially lacked any utility service. El Cenizo is predominantly Hispanic, and its residents are extremely poor. Sixty-eight percent of residents have incomes below the poverty level, and about 90 percent of El Cenizo residents did not graduate from high school (U.S. Census Bureau 2000b).

Housing affordability is a primary reason why people choose to live in colonias like El Cenizo. As of 2000, for example, the median monthly mortgage in El Cenizo equaled $287, compared to $915 in Laredo and $1,088 nationwide (U.S. Census Bureau 2000b). More recent data are unavailable for El Cenizo, but the difference in mortgage costs demonstrates the financial advantage of living in colonias.

Like residents of other border colonias, many El Cenizo families are jammed into overcrowded, dilapidated dwellings ranging from used trailers to cinderblock and plywood structures. The average number of people per household (4.9) is almost double the national average (2.7), according to the most recent data available (U.S. Census Bureau 2000b). Although a few homes are contractor-built, El Cenizo residents built most homes themselves.

While El Cenizo's socioeconomic conditions are much the same as in other Texas border colonias, its unique formative process sets it apart. Its residents have fought and overcome some of the worst developer abuses in Texas. The community's history highlights the challenges that residents faced in establishing livable communities.

Cecil McDonald, a well-known developer in the area, established El Cenizo and many other colonias in Webb County. In 1983, McDonald purchased a remote patch of land on the high banks of the Rio Grande (City of El Cenizo n.d.). He divided the tract into 917 lots, which were sold for $50 down and $85 a month under 10-year contracts for deed. He sold the lots through an aggressive advertising campaign that targeted local news outlets (Chapa and Eaton 1997). At the same time, he avoided bank financing and contact with public officials. McDonald reaped huge profits from his colonias. In El Cenizo alone, his monthly colonia receipts usually ran $70,000 to $90,000, and up to $1 million per year (Myerson 1995).

McDonald made many promises to residents about infrastructure and loans to build homes once they purchased lots. When McDonald failed to deliver, residents sued with representation from Texas Rio Grande Legal Aid. The people of El Cenizo prevailed in the lawsuit, forcing McDonald to establish a trust fund to build a sewer plant. For a brief period, there was hope that residents would actually build a decent community. The sewer plant was completed in 1988, but it was built in a floodplain and failed to meet minimum standards. McDonald tried to avoid the reach of the county health department by persuading residents to do something few colonias have done: incorporate as a city. Residents voted to incorporate on August 29, 1989. Nonetheless, in the same year, McDonald found himself in court again for having constructed the plant illegally. In 1990, the sewage holding tank collapsed (Chapa and Eaton 1997).

El Cenizo's residents continued to insist on functional services and fair accounting for their payments. In 1992, McDonald sought refuge in bankruptcy. In contrast to a typical bankruptcy reorganization that would leave McDonald in control of his assets, the bankruptcy court asked buyers to vote on continuing to pay McDonald or allowing a state agency to take over. Residents overwhelmingly chose the state (Chapa and Eaton 1997). This enabled them to convert contracts for deed to traditional mortgages, eliminate overcharges, and establish a fund to make good on

McDonald's infrastructure and housing promises. When the state housing agency failed to reinvest lot payments into the community fund, El Cenizo leaders won a mediated settlement for street paving, rehabilitation of 45 homes, and a self-help housing and home repair program (Marianne Reat [Texas Rio Grande Legal Aid attorney], memorandum to Karen Paup, 27 March 1998). At $1.94 million, the ultimate settlement was a fraction of the creditors' $19 million in claims against McDonald. Nevertheless, the community's freedom from McDonald, coupled with the civic culture engendered by incorporation, created local leadership and municipal funds.

The democratic spirit and determination of this secluded town have not gone unnoticed. In 1999, El Cenizo gained international attention when it became the first U.S. municipality to hold city commission meetings in Spanish (Price 1999). Everyone in El Cenizo spoke Spanish anyway, so it seemed natural to hold city council meetings in their native tongue. The media took hold of the story, which incited a flow of hate mail from across the country. White supremacists threatened to burn El Cenizo to the ground (Garcia 1999). But, as Stuesse (2001, 81) observed, "El Cenizo's leaders choose to say 'We, like all other communities in the United States, have a right to understand the actions and words of our government and participate in the democratic process.'"

Residents have also taken the initiative in addressing specific infrastructure and housing concerns. They formed La Gloria Development Corporation (La Gloria), which is governed and administered completely by colonia residents. For its first project, the organization secured grants to install indoor plumbing in homes. Then, with funding from the bankruptcy settlement, La Gloria created a self-help, affordable housing construction program, which has since been supplemented by the state's Bootstrap Program. La Gloria's well-built homes, painted by future owners in vivid hues of red, blue, and yellow, average $35,000 in total costs ($250 in monthly Bootstrap mortgage costs), helping those with median incomes of $13,638. La Gloria is now planning a revolving loan program for home improvements.

Residents' efforts to build community go beyond housing and infrastructure. Over the years, El Cenizo's citizens have consistently made efforts to develop municipal services. The community has provided for weekly trash collection for several years. In 2004, the community organized a coalition called Agua Clara (Clean Water) to gain access to potable water.[7] In 2006, the community built a fire station manned by volunteer firefighters. Plans are under way for a library and a city park on the Rio Grande (Olsson 2006).

On a summer day in El Cenizo, the searing heat does not stifle the town's activity. La Gloria's offices are open early, children crowd the community center to participate in reading lessons prepared by local women, and there is a line at the grocery store. It is hard not to feel optimism for El Cenizo and other colonias. Yet the same forces that shaped El Cenizo are felt well outside the community, burdening working families who struggle to make ends meet.

Summary

The story of Texas colonias is often filled with poverty and exploitation. Families like the Velas struggle against great odds, facing setbacks that pull them deeper into poverty. In this chapter, we pointed to the lack of access to decent, affordable housing as the root of the problem. This has excluded many from legitimate means of acquiring wealth and stability.

Yet some communities are also making progress with limited government assistance. The situation in Texas underscores the pivotal role of NGOs that work hand in hand with colonia leaders to improve the standard of living, as in El Cenizo. Grassroots community organizing efforts—such as the region-wide Border Coalition, local movements such as Agua Clara, and community development corporations like La Gloria Community Development Corporation—have made headway in resolving some of the thorniest colonia problems. The Texas Low Income Housing Information Service and other grassroots organizations have also worked through the Border Coalition and the Texas legislature to address some of the needs. Even so, the state's approach to colonia development remains distorted, and there are at least three reasons this continues. For one, the Texas legislature has long refused to grant counties basic land use tools such as planning and zoning powers. The absence of these powers led to the propagation of unregulated subdivisions that are costly to retrofit with water and sewer infrastructure. Second, the Texas bureaucracy still lacks the institutional capacity to foster community-based solutions such as colonia self-help centers operated as

CDCs. Third, resources remain small compared to needs. While many programs merit funding, housing is perhaps the most basic need of all and deserves greater support.

Notes

1. In the 1980s, a minority of Texas colonia residents were connected to drinking water and wastewater treatment. As of 2006, at least 62,675 residents still lack water (Texas Secretary of State 2006).

2. Texas state law does not protect consumers against high interest rates. Language barriers and a lack of credit or steady income leave colonia families like the Velas vulnerable to predatory loans.

3. For families like the Velas, crowding rates are four times the national rate; 26 percent of Hispanic border households are overcrowded (Housing Assistance Council 2005).

4. In Texas colonias, residents often buy water from tanker trucks and store it in plastic storage tanks, paying $22 per 1,000 gallons—compared to $1.65 for the same amount in Texas municipalities (City of Pharr Water Billing 2007). Texas law makes it the responsibility of developers to provide services to colonias not located in a floodplain. However, developers have often been able to avoid that requirement because authorities have not properly regulated their activity (Ward 1999).

5. For those families who had purchased property under contract for deed prior to 1995, Brownsville senator Eddie Lucio took action in 1997 to ensure that they, too, benefited from the reforms. Senator Lucio secured an annual earmark of state funds to pay off old contracts for deed and refinance colonia lots with deeds of trust at favorable interest rates through the state housing agency.

6. ACORN, one of the nation's leading grassroots community-organizing nonprofits, discovered that a Houston developer who operated under 19 different registered companies had been selling property under contract for deed to immigrant families, keeping most of their 800 properties out of county records. A lawsuit filed against the developer alleged that he targeted native Spanish speakers who did not understand the language of a contract for deed (Plocek 2006).

7. In 2004, Webb County proposed to increase water rates. As El Cenizo residents organized, they decided to act not only on water rates, but also on their poor-quality drinking water. Colonia leaders formed Agua Clara, or Clear Water. As colonia leaders researched the source of their water, they found it seriously exceeded federal standards for chlorine-related carcinogens (Lopez 2004). Through Agua Clara, colonia leaders dogged county officials until they obtained service through a county state-of-the-art treatment plant that was under construction at the time. The plant now provides safe water to colonia residents.

8

Sustainable, Affordable Homeownership in Arizona and New Mexico Colonias

Angela Donelson and Esperanza Holguin

In Arizona and New Mexico, federally designated colonias are considerably different than their counterparts in Texas. There are fewer places: Arizona and New Mexico share fewer than 250 of these settlements between them, while Texas is home to more than 2,000. Arizona and New Mexico colonias also tend to be older, with a longer history of multigenerational residence than those in Texas (Donelson and Holguin 2001; Esparza and Donelson 2008).

Their established nature makes colonias in Arizona and New Mexico a logical choice for incorporating traditional, sustainable building methods and materials complementing the prevailing community character. Materials such as adobe, rammed earth, and straw bale are ideal, given their insulating qualities in the arid desert environments of Arizona and New Mexico. While custom and higher-end homebuilders have increasingly adopted native materials and energy-saving efficiencies, affordable home builders rarely do so. Only recently have some nonprofits around the country created more sustainable, or "green," housing, defined as using fewer resources, having reduced harmful impacts on the environment, and providing healthier living conditions than traditional mass-produced housing (Housing Assistance Council 2007). Few affordable housing builders build green housing, because they face many barriers: higher initial capital outlays, contracting challenges, and perceived risks (Bradshaw et al. 2005). These problems are compounded in rural areas, including colonias, because builders also tend to lack organizational capacity and have difficulties in achieving economies of scale in construction (Housing Assistance Council 2007).

The U.S. Department of Housing and Urban Development (HUD) has responded to these challenges by commissioning several reports on how to adapt energy-efficient building materials and methods to colonias in arid desert environments (Vint and Neumann 2005; Winter et al. 2004). Yet few organizations in Arizona and New Mexico colonias have since ventured into such projects. In this chapter, we explain why. First, we explore the benefits of traditional and energy-efficient building materials in colonias. Next, we discuss the cost, cultural, and regulatory impediments to using them. We conclude by sharing how two organizations are overcoming these obstacles—one that has adopted traditional materials and innovative energy-saving methods, and another that has integrated newer materials and methods in housing design and construction. Both organizations are creating homeownership opportunities that promote social equity and environmental sustainability.

Appropriate Traditional Building Materials

Traditional building materials—especially adobe, rammed earth, and straw bale—are the most appropriate sustainable materials for arid-weather colonias when they incorporate energy-efficient site and building design (U.S. Department of Housing and Urban Development 2003; Vint and Neumann 2005). Although most housing in the Southwest is built of wood or concrete block (Winter et al. 2004), adobe, rammed earth, and straw bale are better suited materials for several reasons.

For one, these materials have long been used for their insulating value in harsh environments. Adobe, or earthen brick, is appropriate for low-humidity desert environments experiencing significant swings in daytime temperatures, like most of Arizona and New Mexico. Adobe's thermal mass enables it to store coolness in the night to moderate the indoor temperature during the warmer months, and to store and release the sun's heat during winter months. Adobe is also sought after because of its ability to resist gravity loads, its abundance, and its low energy requirements for production (Vint and Neumann 2005). Rammed earth, an ancient building material used to build the Egyptian pyramids, is outstanding. Modern-day rammed earth construction uses high pressure and heavy equipment to compact sand and clay, often with a small amount of reinforced concrete. Its durability and thermal mass are superior to that of adobe (U.S. Department of Housing and Urban Development 2003; Vint and Neumann 2005). Straw bale is another excellent material; in fact, the first legally permitted, insured, and bank-financed of these homes were built in New Mexico and Arizona in the 1990s (Vint and Neumann 2005). Settlers of the Great Plains initially used straw as a building material when they found that this nonedible by-product of the harvest could be made into modular forms. Straw bales made excellent shelters, homes, and schools, offering extremely effective insulation in severe weather (Vint and Neumann 2005). When coated with stucco, they are weather-proof, fire-resistant, and pest-free (Global Green USA 2007).

Traditional materials also are well suited to Arizona and New Mexico colonias because they blend with the community character. Native materials complement the vernacular architecture of these established settlements—many settled in the 1800s or early 1900s (Donelson and Holguin 2001; Esparza and Donelson 2008).

Finally, traditional materials are often appropriate because they are less expensive than conventional ones. Although they tend to require more labor-intensive techniques, low-cost labor is typically abundant in colonias, especially among residents who want to build their own homes.

Challenges to Affordable Building with Traditional Materials

Few builders have incorporated traditional materials into colonias housing construction, but not for lack of interest or attention. The U.S. Department of Housing and Urban Development has encouraged the use of native building materials, for example, by issuing memoranda to its grantees and its field directors, sponsoring "green building" conferences, and commissioning two studies recommending traditional construction materials and techniques in the colonias (U.S. Department of Housing and Urban Development 2003; Vint and Neumann 2005; Winter et al. 2004). Yet three major impediments to their adoption remain: cost challenges, cultural impediments, and regulatory difficulties.

Cost Challenges

Costs often preclude sustainable housing construction in the colonias. Affordable-home builders commonly discover unexpected infrastructure problems that raise the costs of construction; they often must bury inadequate septic systems, install or improve water and sewer systems, secure easements, and replat illegally subdivided properties. Labor requirements also pose cost challenges. The time investment required for adobe building, for example, makes regional costs for this building type comparatively high (Vint and Neumann 2005).

Rammed earth construction presents technical challenges that can require costly, specialized expertise. The University of Arizona's College of Architecture and Landscape Architecture Design/Build Studio has created a lower-cost solution, by developing rammed earth in forms that can be reassembled into homes. Under the leadership of Professor Mary Hardin, the studio in 2001 developed a rammed earth home for the Gila Indian River Community, with construction costs for walls (not the entire structure) at $8.77/square foot when student labor was paid at minimum wage, compared with the industry average of $26/square foot (Hardin 2006).[1] However, the process took significant time to perfect—six years, requiring fine-tuning to properly level the rammed earth formwork, obtain a consistent soil, water, and cement mixture, and perfect the rammed earth compaction techniques (Hardin 2006). Although this expertise has since been applied to build a rammed earth residence for the Tucson affiliate of Habitat for Humanity, the demonstration has not yet translated into larger-scale affordable housing projects. Habitat for Humanity Tucson has pursued other collaborations in its more recent projects, and the Gila Indian River tribe has not yet built additional subdivisions using rammed earth construction (Mary Hardin, pers. comm. 23 November 2007).

Straw bale construction similarly requires special knowledge. While unskilled labor can be used to pour footings, place bales, and apply plaster, professional carpenters must frame roofs, assist with windows and doors, and install plumbing, electrical, heating, and cooling systems (Vint and Neumann 2005). Colonias rarely have skilled contractors experienced in this building process.

These challenges have impelled some nonprofit housing providers to opt for less labor-intensive, manmade building substitutes. For example, the Las Cruces/Doña Ana County Public Housing Authority in New Mexico is managing a self-help homeownership project (discussed later in this chapter) in the Vado/Del Cerro colonia using structural insulated panels (SIPs). SIPs—comprised of foam between two sheets of wood board—provide significantly more insulation and structural strength than does typical stick frame construction. The Yuma County, Arizona, non-profit Comité de Bienestar is considering an alternative product, insulating concrete forms (ICFs), in its next round of self-help homes (John McGrady, pers. comm. 13 November 2007). ICFs—produced by manufacturers under such names as RASTRA or PolySteel—are interlocking plastic foam forms typically made of polystyrene. They act as molds that hold concrete in place during and after construction and provide higher thermal insulation than traditional concrete walls. While SIPs and ICFs produce higher energy efficiency than conventional construction, those that do not use recycled foam can create their own negative environmental impacts.[2]

Cultural Resistance

Cultural resistance can stymie use of native building materials. Although traditional materials are increasingly popular among the affluent, colonia residents often perceive them to be for "poor people." Winter et al. (2004) explain:

> Many people in the rural Southwest might perceive cost-saving construction techniques and features as "cheap" or "low quality." These views usually stem from cultural experiences. For example, a number of housing providers will not use metal roofs because they are perceived as "cheap" and suggest the makeshift housing which many of the residents born in poor rural villages in Mexico remember. They've come to the United States in search of the American dream, and metal roofing is seen as a step in the wrong direction. (14)

Tom Hassell, the director of the Las Cruces/Doña Ana County Public Housing Authority, notes that many colonias residents of the area disapprove of earthen materials because most Mexican poor live in adobe housing. He says a manufactured home is typically the preferred starter home, since it is adaptable to family needs—it can eventually become an additional housing unit to rent out or can house extended family (Tom Hassell, pers. comm. 10 January 2008).

Some colonias residents fear traditional materials are unsafe. For example, Cesy Rodriguez, director of affordable straw bale housing builder

Tierra Madre (whose work is discussed later in this chapter), notes that many families in their self-help projects initially believed the straw bale buildings would blow away, become infested with termites, or burn down (Cesy Rodriguez, pers. comm. 17 January 2008).

One of the few colonia-serving organizations that has readily embraced traditional materials is the Gila Indian River Community. The tribe has long favored traditional wood-and-packed-mud housing, or so-called sandwich homes (Hardin 2006). They have long rejected government-sponsored efforts to build more conventional housing in order to retain tradition. Cultural preferences have made it much easier for the University of Arizona's Design/Build studio to work with the tribe.

Regulatory Barriers

Local, federal, and regulatory barriers also complicate efforts to incorporate traditional materials and energy-saving design, especially in rural areas. Yet this soon may be changing. Home builders and municipal governments are beginning to embrace sustainability, as organizations such as the National Association of Home Builders and the U.S. Green Building Council promote nationally recognized "green" building standards. Both organizations have voluntary guidelines, with the National Association of Home Builders promoting its "NAHB Model Green Home Building Guidelines" and the U.S. Green Building Council promoting its Leadership in Energy and Environmental Design (LEED) Green Building Rating System. The criteria enable assessment of the design, construction, and operation of sustainable buildings.

A thornier challenge is the lack of federal program incentives for producing more sustainable housing. The U.S. Department of Agriculture Rural Development (USDA/RD), the primary funder of self-help, or "sweat equity," housing programs in the United States since 1963, does not award grants based on energy-efficient criteria. Two of the largest Arizona self-help nonprofit housing providers—Comité de Bienestar and the City of Casa Grande, Arizona—say current regulations discourage them from building housing incorporating new materials and energy-efficient design (John McGrady, pers. comm. 13 November 2007; Rosa Bruce [director of the City of Casa Grande housing department], pers. comm. 12 November 2007). Both organizations say funding is not readily available to retrain their construction supervisors in new methods, and that new methods could raise contractual costs, making housing less affordable to low-income families.

Moreover, lending institutions are averse to financing homes built with unusual materials or methods. For example, the nonprofit straw bale builder Tierra Madre struggled to find lenders to finance their project, because lenders know little about the materials and self-help building methods; only one private lender, a community bank, financed the loans (Cesy Rodriguez, pers. comm. 17 January 2008b). Lenders also tend to avoid loans to low-income colonia homeowners, who are perceived as a risky group with little or no credit.

Fortunately, attitudes about lending in sustainable building may be changing, at least among nontraditional banks. In Arizona, a Phoenix-based nonprofit, the Arizona MultiBank Community Development Corporation, has given the Navajo Nation a low-interest loan for production of Navajo Flexcrete, an aerated concrete block composed of waste fly ash from the tribe's coal-generating electrical plants (ASU Stardust Center for Affordable Homes and the Family 2006a). The block, providing mass and insulation, has been used in two innovative affordable housing projects: the Nageezi House on the Navajo Nation in New Mexico (built in 2005), and a home on the predominantly Pascua Yaqui Indian and Mexican American community of Guadalupe, near Phoenix (built in 2006). The Nageezi House incorporates traditional Native American design elements, passive heating and cooling, rainwater harvesting, recycled windows, and use of native small-diameter timber. It uses 70 percent less energy in the winter than a conventional home, and 52 percent less energy in the summer (ASU Stardust Center for Affordable Homes and the Family 2006a; Global Green USA 2007). The Navajo Nation Housing Authority has since applied their technical expertise to build additional subdivisions on tribal land (Daniel Glenn, Associate Director for Design, ASU Stardust Center, pers. comm. 2007). The Guadalupe project incorporates culturally responsive components, including a courtyard, the ability to expand into a second floor, energy-efficient roofing and mechanical systems, photovoltaic panels, regionally culled materials, rainwater and graywater harvesting, and nontoxic building materials. The home has energy bills averaging $40 per month for the six warmest months of the year (Daniel Glenn, pers. comm. 2007).

The town of Guadalupe, Arizona, is replicating the prototype with funding from federal self-help housing programs and the U.S. Department
of Labor–funded Youthbuild program, which trains youth in housing
construction (ASU Stardust Center for Affordable Homes and the Family 2006b).

Two Case Studies of Sustainable Colonias Housing

Two organizations in Doña Ana County, New Mexico—the Doña Ana/
Las Cruces Public Housing Authority and Tierra Madre—have hurdled
numerous barriers to produce sustainable, affordable housing. This section describes the context and vision for each of the projects. It then
analyzes how both sponsoring organizations have surmounted cost, cultural, and regulatory challenges to develop sustainable affordable housing in colonias. This information is based on interviews with the executive directors of both organizations (Tom Hassell, interview 10 January
2008; Cesy Rodriguez, interview 17 January 2008), as well as background
information each organization has compiled about its projects.

Doña Ana County is the largest of New Mexico's 11 border counties, with the largest number of colonias in the state. While some efforts
are under way to develop affordable sustainable housing in Arizona, no
known projects are ongoing other than the University of Arizona's work
on the Gila Indian River Community (already documented by Hardin
2006), and Comité de Bienestar's emerging work in Yuma County, Arizona (Comité de Bienestar 2008).

Context and Vision

Tierra Madre. In 1995, three Catholic nuns serving in the Las Cruces/El
Paso area launched the nonprofit organization Tierra Madre, or Mother
Earth. They sought to provide affordable homeownership opportunities to
very low-income families, while preserving the desert's natural resources.
At the same time, they envisioned helping residents develop the skills and
resources to eventually manage and operate the development.

The nuns chose to anchor their dream to a single site: a 20-acre
parcel of state land located in Sunland Park, New Mexico. In 1996, the

FIGURE 8.1. Tierra Madre straw bale home, building in progress. *Source*: Photo by Tierra Madre

organization entered into a contract with the State of New Mexico Land Commission, signing a 99-year lease to create a community land trust whose proceeds benefit the state's education fund. After subdividing the property into 47 parcels, Tierra Madre organized its first group of six families to build their own homes in 2001. (See figures 8.1 and 8.2.) Seven phases have been completed; the remaining two phases will be completed in 2009.

Without this opportunity, Tierra Madre residents could not afford homeownership. Nearly two-thirds of families in Sunland Park—a Mexican American community with a 2006 population of 13,309 persons on the perimeter of El Paso—earn low incomes, even by regional standards. Tierra Madre enables families earning a median income of $12,500 to own a four-bedroom, two-bathroom (1,300-square-foot) home for $60,000 to $62,000, compared with regional, 2007 private market costs ranging between $85,000 and $130,000. Each homeowner's entire monthly mortgage and fees are $270. The mortgage is $250 per month, with an additional $10 per month covering the lease to the State of New Mexico

FIGURE 8.2 Tierra Madre completed straw bale home. *Source*: Photo by Tierra Madre

Land Commission, and an extra $10 per month for an escrow account. That account maintains the development's facilities and funds emergencies, such as coverage for families who miss a mortgage payment. When the account exceeds $10,000, funds are earmarked for future economic development pursuits.

Casas Del Quinto Sol. In 2003, HUD commissioned a study to select a needy New Mexico colonia as a quality-of-life demonstration project for intergovernmental agency efforts (Medius, Inc. 2005). The Vado/ Del Cerro community became known as the HUD "Model Colonias Initiative."

Vado/Del Cerro, with a 2005 estimated population of 4,000 to 5,000 persons, had a long history of poor infrastructure, improperly platted sites, substandard roads, and mostly substandard housing. Vado was settled as an African American farming settlement in 1886; the adjacent subdivision of Del Cerro grew up in the 1960s as a farmworker settlement (Medius, Inc. 2005). Soon after the community was selected for the federal initiative in 2004, Vado/Del Cerro experienced a massive flood that destroyed the earthen berms on the outskirts of the community, which had provided a barrier against the nearby dairy. The flood entered the homes and threatened the water quality of local wells.

During the flooding, Governor Bill Richardson declared Vado/Del Cerro a state disaster area. Richardson committed funds to address the flooding, and then assistance to address infrastructure problems. Soon after, in 2005, his office institutionalized a new state funding source for colonias infrastructure and housing needs (New Mexico Department of Finance and Administration, Local Government 2007).[3] The flood also provided the impetus for numerous state and federal agencies to become involved in upgrading water lines and capacity, improving emergency access roadways and easements, improving flood control, and securing a new elementary school.

The Doña Ana/Las Cruces Public Housing Authority also made a strong commitment. They purchased an 11.2-acre parcel of land and committed to construction of a self-help, 21-unit affordable housing project. In 2006, the housing authority ran a design competition for the project, subsidized with a $25,000 grant from the Fannie Mae Foundation. Multidisciplinary teams of students from seven universities created conceptual designs for energy-efficient homes, with the University of North Carolina at Charlotte submitting the winning design.

As of 2009, the project, Casas Del Quinto Sol (Houses of the Fifth Sun) is currently under construction. It is named after the legend of the rising of the fifth sun of the Aztec Empire, an era that provided inhabitants protection, growth, and prosperity (Medius, Inc. 2005). Each of the two- to three-bedroom, one-and-three-quarter- to two-bath homes is sited on one-third-acre lots. Although each unit has only 1,200 square feet, families can add a bedroom if they so choose.

Casas Del Quinto Sol serves a very needy population. More than one-third of residents are below the national poverty line, according to the 2000 census. New construction in the area for a three-bedroom, two-bath home currently averages $130,000 to $175,000. Although Casas Del Quinto Sol homes cost approximately $140,000 to build, grants, down-payment assistance, and sweat equity brought the mortgage down to $77,000. This translates to monthly mortgage costs of $500 without, and $650 with, private mortgage insurance.

Surmounting Barriers

Both the Casas Del Quinto Sol and Tierra Madre subdivisions incorporate a number of sustainable features, shown in table 8.1. Project developers

TABLE 8.1 Summary of Project Details: Tierra Madre and Casas Del Quinto Sol.

	Tierra Madre	Casas Del Quinto Sol
Site Design	Passive solar access maximized by building orientation	Passive solar access maximized by building orientation
	Community center	Community park
	Community gardens (in development)	Located near interstate/ school bus stop
	Greenhouse (in development)	
Materials and Resources	Straw bale (post and beam construction)	Structural Insulated Panels (SIPS)
Energy Efficiency	ENERGY STAR appliances, windows	ENERGY STAR appliances, windows
	Solar water heaters	Passive solar shading in summer, and passive solar heating in winter through thermal mass and glazing concrete walls
	Energy audits by University of Texas at El Paso	All-electric home with wiring for photovoltaics
		Tankless hot water heaters (in development; contingent upon funding)
		Energy audits (in development)
Water Conservation	Rainwater harvesting system	Low-water-use shower heads, faucets, toilets
	Low-water-use shower heads, faucets, toilets	Retain existing vegetation on the park site
	Graywater irrigation system	Xeriscaping
	Xeriscaping	
Ease of maintenance	Resident education: life skills, budgeting, nutrition, homeownership, environmental stewardship	Post-purchase homeownership education
	Development of a homeowners' association	Development of a homeowners' association

Source: Compiled from authors' January 2008 interviews with Tom Hassell, executive director of Las Cruces/Doña Ana Public Housing Authority, and Cesy Rodriguez, executive director of Tierra Madre.

have incorporated "green" features by overcoming a number of cost, cultural, and regulatory barriers, described below.

Cost Challenges. Both organizations have worked hard to attract pilot program financing from federal, state, and foundation sources to make their projects financially feasible. The Casas Del Quinto Sol project team found that costs easily spiraled above initial expectations, due to unexpected deficiencies in basic infrastructure. After the Las Cruces/Doña Ana County Public Housing Authority purchased the parcel of land in 2003, they found it lacked sufficient water pressure and capacity. This issue was resolved, in large part, through several federal and state grants that enabled the local water utility to expand.

Next, the housing authority found it had to develop legal road access to the site. The housing authority negotiated with the county to accept, pave, and maintain a heavily traveled, private dirt road where property is located. In the process, the housing authority assisted approximately 200 colonias families who lived in improperly subdivided parcels near the property by giving them access to a paved road, electricity, and a school bus stop at a previously dangerous intersection.

The high infrastructure costs associated with easements, access, and water infrastructure connections were covered by a $500,000 New Mexico Colonias Initiative grant from the governor's office. This grant provided $23,810 in subsidies per lot. Other partners also helped buy down the mortgage costs. As the state administrator of the HUD-funded HOME Investment Partnerships Program, the New Mexico Mortgage Finance Authority granted $14,999 in HUD-funded housing subsidies per lot. State housing tax credits for using energy-efficient SIPs provided an additional $4,700 in subsidies per home. The New Mexico Community Action Agency invested up to $8,000 per family through its individual development account program, which matches family savings on a 4:1 basis.[4] Each family's 1,200 hours of sweat equity buy down an additional $12,000 of the mortgage. Without this funding, the housing authority says it could not have created homeownership opportunities that are both sustainable and affordable.

Initially, the Las Cruces/Doña Ana County Public Housing Authority hoped to use adobe brick or rammed earth building materials. After investigating the highly intensive labor required, the project team decided upon an energy-efficient SIP produced at a plant, KC Panels, several hundred miles away. They reasoned that the process of fitting insulating panels would be faster and easier for the families, especially in very hot weather. They also wanted families to invest more of their sweat equity in the aesthetic features of their homes.

Tierra Madre was a more natural candidate for traditional materials. For one, the founders had a strong vision for them in their model of sustainability. Second, cost challenges were not as great. A HUD Self-help Homeownership Opportunity Program (SHOP) grant paid for road improvements and infrastructure. The nonprofit also negotiated a lease with the State of New Mexico, renewable at the end of the 99-year period, to develop a community land trust. These cost savings enabled the nonprofit to pour more resources into straw bale construction training and on-site amenities. Facilities include a community center, a playground, and social supports including an after-school tutoring program, periodic socials, a girls' club, and a monthly breakfast to discuss common issues, concerns, and plans. Several planned new amenities include a home vegetable-gardening program and a technology center. The home vegetable gardens, in development through a federal loan program, will enable grandparents to teach their grandchildren gardening skills, and grandchildren to teach their grandparents about computers. The technology center is made possible through a contract that Tierra Madre has negotiated with a California digital imaging company. The company is paying for the technology center's Internet connections, printers, and computer upgrades. In exchange, six senior citizens at Tierra Madre will perform digital scanning work for the company, earning $10 per hour for 20 hours of work per week.

Cultural Resistance. Both nonprofit housing organizations have surmounted cultural resistance by showing prospective homebuyers how more sustainable, well-designed housing can increase housing durability and safety, while decreasing monthly energy costs. Some of Tierra Madre's families learned firsthand about housing durability while building their homes. Staff had assured families their homes could not burn after being properly sealed with stucco. However, in the middle of construction, one of the builders used a blowtorch to complete some work, ignoring requests to wait until the homes were sealed. A fire ensued, burning the unfinished home and all wood structures on the site. Yet all finished straw bale homes were unscathed.

Public hearings and individual consultations with prospective homebuyers and project partners throughout the design process helped the Casas Del Quinto Sol design team respond to questions about safety. Concerns were addressed by building enclosed garages, adding a fenced property that separated the subdivision from the main highway, and installing a drainage pump to prevent flooding. The housing authority is working through the local YWCA—a HUD-approved housing counseling agency—to educate homeowners about the energy-saving features of the home.

Tierra Madre has also done much to educate homeowners since its first homes went up in 2001. All homebuyers are required to attend homeownership education classes, where they also learn about the utility savings, healthier living environment, and increased durability of straw bale homes. Today, the families are in the process of learning broader concepts of sustainability—not merely environmental management but also self-governance. Tierra Madre has gradually been in the process of turning governing authority over to the residents. When the subdivision is fully built out, Tierra Madre's three full-time staff will leave, and the homeowners association will assume full management of the property. The residents already have ideas to build a robust escrow account as insurance against emergencies or family mortgage troubles. They are also interested in using it to launch an economic development venture, where they will build and manage a 10–12-unit, straw bale apartment complex for senior citizens and individuals with special needs. Several investors have already agreed to finance the project.

Regulatory Barriers. Both Tierra Madre and Casas Del Quinto Sol have successfully hurdled regulatory barriers. By launching programs from scratch—instead of relying on federally subsidized self-help building programs—these builders have developed innovative projects. They have avoided the risk aversion and path dependency common to rural self-help building programs.

Tierra Madre is the only known organization in Arizona or New Mexico to pioneer a straw-bale affordable housing development among a very low-income population. The organization was successful, in large part, because they negotiated with the USDA/RD Las Cruces office to become their mortgage lender. In the late 1990s, USDA began to offer Tierra Madre its self-help housing financing for 33-year terms, with no down payment and interest as low as 1 percent, depending on family income. Since then, First National Bank has become a lender whose loans are guaranteed through USDA/RD's Las Cruces office. However, Tierra Madre has been unsuccessful in recruiting other lenders. Wells Fargo Bank did not participate because its mortgage lending regulations prohibit community land trust loans. Other banks have been reluctant to loan to families with very low incomes. Some are also unfamiliar with, and hesitant to finance, self-help housing, land trusts, and materials like straw bale.

Casas Del Quinto Sol has overcome potential local regulatory and planning and zoning barriers by enlisting the support of local and state elected officials. Although the project is not yet built, approvals are moving quickly because of its high profile. It is supported by a diverse alliance of federal, state, and local authorities.

Already, the Las Cruces/Doña Ana County Public Housing Authority has set its sights on developing a second self-help homeownership subdivision, in the agricultural valley of Hatch, New Mexico. The housing authority has purchased 15 acres of land and is in the process of identifying grants and loans to develop the project. Because the housing authority will be the developer, it can earn approximately 10 percent of the total development costs, probably about $300,000. Sources of funding like this are essential, given that Congress has progressively cut operating budgets for public housing authorities, forcing them to become increasingly financially self-sustaining.

Summary

Current research suggests that new housing construction in colonias could integrate traditional materials and energy-efficient design. However, cost, cultural, and regulatory barriers mostly have discouraged Arizona and New Mexico affordable-housing providers from doing so. In this chapter, we explored these challenges and assessed how two colonias-serving organizations have hurdled obstacles to produce more sustainable, affordable homeowner-occupied housing.

Successful nonprofits have cut costs by selecting building materials and processes with which families and construction supervisors can easily build. Innovative arrangements, including land trusts, funding for infrastructure, and subsidies for families, have lowered builders' costs and family mortgages. Passive and low-cost energy-saving improvements, with room for future energy-saving additions, have also enhanced long-term affordability.

Home builders have surmounted cultural resistance by implementing homeowner education programs. These have encouraged residents to embrace the safety, durability, and cost-effectiveness associated with more sustainable housing.

Colonias home builders have also overcome regulatory barriers by securing early "buy-in" and support from local and state elected officials. Accessible sources of mortgage loan financing, through programs such as USDA/RD's direct and guaranteed mortgages, have also guaranteed success.

We are encouraged by the growing number of support organizations that assist affordable-housing developers. Arizona State University's Stardust Center for Affordable Homes and the Family as well as the University of Arizona Design/Build Studio have provided innovative technical assistance and support for development of sustainable affordable housing. Nonprofit intermediary organizations such as the Enterprise Foundation and the Housing Assistance Council also now offer predevelopment grants and loans for "green" building. HUD's Partnership for Advancing Technology has sponsored an online affordable housing design advisor specifying low-cost ways to improve the energy efficiency and quality of affordable rental and homeowner-occupied housing. As "green" building goes mainstream, we hope that more colonia-serving organizations will avail themselves of assistance to pioneer healthier, more vibrant, and more environmentally sustainable housing suited to the region's arid desert environment.

Notes

1. The Gila River Indian Community—located approximately 40 miles south of Phoenix—is one of six Arizona tribes with federally recognized colonias. The U.S. Department of Agriculture Rural Development designated the area a colonia in February 1999.

2. SIP and ICF systems typically use virgin polystyrene or polyurethane foam core. Some use recycled materials such as wood fibers or composites of Portland cement (Boser, Ragsdale, and Duvel 2002). Well-known products such as RASTRA are made of cement and Thastyron, produced from 85 percent recycled post-consumer polystyrene waste.

3. Since 2005, the governor's New Mexico Colonias Initiative has funded colonia infrastructure projects through the New Mexico Department of Finance and Administration. From 2005 through 2007, $15.8 million was allocated to support projects prioritized by local governments (New Mexico Department of Finance and Administration, Local Government 2007).

4. Nationally, a number of community development corporations offer Individual Development Accounts (IDAs), or savings accounts that nonprofits match on a 2:1 to 4:1 basis. IDAs provide a means for historically unbanked populations to develop financial literacy and savings for home or business ownership or for higher education.

Faith and Development in the Colonias of New Mexico and Arizona

David S. Henkel Jr.

FAITH ORGANIZATIONS HAVE an important role in border communities, both as sources of relief and as partners in community development. In many cases, they are the only organizations operating in border
communities. They regularly provide advocacy, social services, and economic development unavailable through government-funded programs.
Yet little is known about faith organizations operating in colonias. This
chapter responds to the lack of knowledge about these organizations by
exploring their potential to mobilize border communities in Arizona and
New Mexico.

The chapter is organized as three sections. First, I examine the dimensions of the problem. That is, I discuss the needs of colonias residents
and describe why federal, state, and local government resources are
insufficient to meet them. Second, I make the case for why faith organizations have become essential partners in improving border colonias.
In this section, I explain how many faith-based nongovernmental organizations (NGOs) in the U.S.–Mexico border region grew out of the
Sanctuary Movement of the 1970s and 1980s. (It is important to note this
chapter excludes discussion of the borderlands activities of traditional,
evangelical churches, which often carry out work based on convictions
of spiritual and physical needs and tend to be less focused on social justice issues.) The unique history of the Sanctuary Movement has led a
number of faith-based NGOs to adopt a different take on border problems and solutions than secular, service-oriented NGOs. Third, I explore
the opportunities and challenges that faith-based NGOs currently confront in their work. I discuss how they have unique capabilities that set
them apart from government organizations and secular, service-oriented

NGOs. I also explore challenges they face in gaining the trust of colonia residents and developing an adequate resource base, and how they have the potential to make important and unique contributions in helping colonia residents improve their chances for a better future.

Dimensions of the Problem

Low-income people of color in the United States experience disproportionate social, economic, and physical needs that are difficult to meet. Chief among the basic needs for all people are shelter, employment, education, nutrition, health care, environmental health, and public safety. In the disadvantaged settlements of the U.S.–Mexico border region known as colonias, these needs are chronically unmet.

In Mexico the term *colonia* describes a primarily residential neighborhood located in an urban area or as a satellite community outside of it. It is a formal term of urban design denoting a structured human settlement. However, in the United States, the word *colonia* carries loaded meanings that color the discourse about living conditions, the worthiness of their residents, and what the appropriate responses might be.

U.S. colonias refer to settlements located in the four states along the U.S.–Mexico border that lack adequate infrastructure and services. They are primarily unincorporated and populated by low-income residents.[1] The U.S. Department of Housing and Urban Development (HUD) and the U.S. Department of Agriculture–Rural Development (USDA-RD) both describe colonias in terms of deficient physical infrastructure and proximity to the U.S.–Mexico international boundary (U.S. Department of Housing and Urban Development 2004). Such settlements commonly lack utilities, have numerous environmental health problems often contributing to respiratory and gastrointestinal illnesses, and are located in floodplains or locales unsuitable for housing. Colonias have long been present in this region (Donelson and Holguin 2001; Esparza and Donelson 2008; Mukhija and Monkkonen 2006). However, some grew from the 1950s onward, as old settlements and new unincorporated communities were increasingly populated by immigrants, primarily farmworkers. This was largely a legacy of the Bracero Program that had its origins in the labor substitution initiative initiated during World War II.

Due to their lack of disposable income, colonia residents are rarely able to obtain adequate resources to improve their living conditions. Official statistics on U.S.–Mexico border counties reveal that poverty and deprivation are widespread. In New Mexico and Arizona, for example, percentages of border county residents that are unemployed, in poverty, have children in poverty, and live in manufactured housing as a portion of the overall housing stock are all more than 20 percent higher than the state averages (U.S. Census Bureau 2000b). Percentages of those with a high school diploma and levels of median income are both 10 percent lower than the state averages. In some cases the figures are startlingly extreme. In New Mexico's border counties, 67 percent of the housing stock in the year 2000 was comprised of manufactured units. In Arizona border counties, manufactured units accounted for 63 percent of the housing stock, while unemployment was 84 percent higher than in the state as a whole (U.S. Census Bureau 2000b).

Furthermore, language barriers and lack of access to the political system make it difficult for colonia residents to obtain adequate physical infrastructure and social services. Most colonias are unincorporated, and government regulations prohibit unincorporated human settlements from acting as fiscal agents on behalf of their residents. This eliminates the possibility of deriving resources from local revenues. Most colonias are therefore dependent upon nonlocal political processes. In many cases, the settlements in the most desperate situations are ineligible for grants and loans because they are unincorporated. Because so many of these settlements are unincorporated, they frequently fall outside of the jurisdiction of conventional government programs and can even set up conflict between political jurisdictions over the nature and extent of the responses to social and environmental need.

The Role of Federal, State, and Local Government

While some budgetary resources are made available for social, economic, and physical needs in colonias from federal, state, and local government appropriations, the amounts are far outstripped by the needs.

The federal government has tried to directly respond to these issues primarily in terms of physical infrastructure, while allowing social services to be delivered as part of overall funding strategies. The National Affordable Housing Act of 1990 appropriated some resources for colonias through HUD and USDA-RD. More specifically, HUD provides special assistance through its colonias set-aside program to rural communities of less than 50,000 population, a portion of the Community Development Block Grant (CDBG) program. The amount of funding is determined on the basis of need as determined by the decennial U.S. census. In Arizona and New Mexico, a formula is used to determine the amount that goes to their state agencies, which, respectively, are the Arizona Department of Housing and the New Mexico Department of Finance and Administration. In Arizona, funds flow from the state through regional councils of governments and then on to rural local and county governments; nonprofit organizations must apply through rural local and county governments. In New Mexico, colonia CDBG set-aside applicants can include local counties, municipalities, and water associations; nonprofit organizations must similarly apply through counties or municipalities. However, in both states this CDBG set-aside funding has been insufficient to meet the many infrastructure and service needs. It amounts to approximately $1 million per year in Arizona for the state's 86 colonias, and $1.5 million in New Mexico for the state's 144 colonias (Esparza and Donelson 2008).

Other resources are similarly available, but colonias have difficulties in accessing them. The USDA-RD makes colonia priority funding available for water, sewer, and housing projects. However, these resources are often loans or complements to other sources of loan and grant funding, which are scarce in unincorporated places. The Environmental Protection Agency (EPA) participates in infrastructure development for wastewater and sanitation projects as well as the mitigation of air pollution. The agency does so through a series of programs related to the binational Border Environment Cooperation Commission (BECC), with projects funded by the North American Development Bank (NADBank). However, colonias are unlikely to use these loan programs unless they can leverage resources from local, state, or regional units of government.

It is clear that sources of funding and decision-making that govern the implementation of colonia public programs often come from distant places, such as Phoenix, Santa Fe, and, especially, Washington, D.C. Theoretically this requires at least some kind of collaboration, but it also assumes a degree of political mobilization and unity that is not always present at what is essentially a small-town or neighborhood level without elective representation.

The Response of Faith Organizations: Human Migration in the *Frontera*

In lieu of public revenues and adequate sources of government support, colonias have responded to the shortfall through social mobilization and building alliances with nonprofit organizations. Some of these non-profit organizations are rooted in faith traditions, including organized church service and spiritually grounded volunteerism by members of faith communities.

It would be misleading to make exclusive distinctions between faith-based community-development and service programs on the one hand, and service-oriented NGOs on the other, because there is a fair degree of overlap between the two. This is particularly true with respect to community outreach programs that address primary needs such as food, shelter, and clothing (Chaves 2004). Yet the response of the faith community often has been different from that of service-oriented NGOs. That is partly because of many faith groups' involvement and attention to issues involving human rights and migration. The American Friends Service Committee (AFSC) stands as an excellent example of a faith-based, social justice organization dedicated to support for immigrant rights and advocacy for proper respect and labor relations for industrial workers in the maquiladora industry. Since 1981, it has operated in the borderlands, and it has joined with other organizations and with other programs of the AFSC in advocating for the rights of residents and migrants and in monitoring abuses of those crossing the international boundary (Arizona American Friends Service Committee 2008).

The differing response of the faith community is also partly due to its independence from government funding, when that is indeed the case. Faith-based organizations have been more flexible in meeting the needs for services while at the same time recognizing the constraints of formal public policy, such as outreach to groups of migrants at risk of deportation. Justification for this approach is derived from broad, ethical concerns, as embodied in the United Nations Declaration of Human Rights, as well as from theologically based social witness (U.S. Conference of Catholic Bishops 2005).

In contrast to their faith-based counterparts, service-oriented NGOs have largely responded to the service and infrastructure provision needs alone in colonias, and less to policy and volunteer-based advocacy at a regional level. This is because secular programs require continuity and support of staff, so they may be less inclined to potentially jeopardize their funding from government sources.

Much of the faith community's active involvement in and support for border causes goes back to the 1970s, and even earlier in some cases. With the increase of hemispheric conflict and Central American genocide in the late 1970s and 1980s, the press of population across the international boundary increased. These immigrants were generally refugees fleeing civil conflict, and their presence prompted a response from religious groups and other humanitarian organizations concerned for their safety and welfare. One result of this increased activity was the Sanctuary Movement that grew out of the social ministry of Presbyterians, Roman Catholics, members of the United Church of Christ, Quakers, and others in Arizona, New Mexico, and states farther north (Corbett 1991).

Some of the organizations founded in the 1970s to provide safety and refuge to primarily Mexican immigrant workers were later compelled to divert their resources to cope with the acute needs of Central Americans fleeing religious and political persecution. The lack of a coherent and sympathetic immigration policy by the U.S. government during these years intensified the risks experienced by the refugees and complicated the economic migration patterns of seasonal Mexican workers. It also placed many religiously motivated people and congregations at odds with the U.S. government. This resulted in a new version of the Underground Railroad that had rescued slaves from the southern United States before the Civil War, to now move Central American refugees to safety away from the U.S.–Mexico border region and as far north as Canada.

As the genocidal conflicts in Central America subsided in the early 1990s, and as the North American Free Trade Agreement was concluded early in the first Clinton administration, shifts in global capital and labor became the forces for immigration into the United States from countries to the south, primarily Mexico. Fewer Central and South American migrants fled to the United States. Greater numbers of Mexicans took their place.

Initially, this new wave of Mexican immigrants resembled the historic migration patterns, because a large number consisted of seasonal agricultural workers. However, the migrant tide soon became different: it comprised a growing number of laborers skilled and semiskilled in manufacturing, agro-industrial work such as meatpacking, and construction trades.

The diversity of this labor force is significant. While the borderlands continued to host agricultural workers, larger numbers of workers seeking employment in agribusiness, manufacturing, and construction no longer settled in colonias. Many made their way into the interior of the United States. Large populations of Mexicans joined earlier pioneers in Los Angeles, Denver, and Chicago. Soon, noticeable numbers of Mexican workers were appearing in Iowa, Florida, North Carolina, Maine, and the Pacific Northwest (Zúñiga and Hernández-León 2005).

At this juncture, some organizations that had grown from earlier diocesan efforts of ministry to the refugee population of the 1970s and 1980s turned their attention and resources to this new, largely economic migrant population. However, the migrant phenomenon had changed much since the even earlier influx of the 1950s and 1960s, for at least two reasons. For one, a larger number of migrants were women and children who were either stranded or abandoned at the border as the male head of household went north in search of work. Second, a noticeably larger segment of the population of migrants was comprised of young women and single women heads of households who were desperately seeking ways to provide remittances to their young children and aging parents at home in Mexican cities, towns, and villages (Ruben Garcia, interview 2007). An indeterminate portion of these migrants ended up settling temporarily or semipermanently in the colonias of New Mexico and Arizona, as well as in the informal settlements on the periphery of Mexican border towns.

Some of these women traveled long distances at great risk. Some were seriously injured or crippled by transportation accidents involving rail transport. Others were cheated, robbed, or assaulted by the human traffickers called *coyotes* as they sought to cross the border. Still others fell victim to the grisly work of the sociopaths who preyed upon young female workers in the maquiladora industry, sometimes assaulting and dismembering them (Amnesty International 2007; Libertad Latina 2006).

Those victimized in Mexico often face a halfhearted response at best by police authorities; many of those exploited or injured in the United

States avoid contact with public safety officials, because they are afraid that they might be arrested or deported irrespective of their legal status. The current politics of hysteria and exaggeration about border and migrant issues in the United States marginalizes these people even further. It has created a furtive subculture in colonias, composed of people who try to live normal lives in normal domestic circumstances out of sight of the authorities. The subculture is visible to itself; it attempts to be invisible to the surrounding population. This is an adaptive strategy common to many immigrant groups in American history, but as with immigrants in the past these people are disproportionately vulnerable to disease, economic exploitation, threats to personal safety, and separation from family members.

Opportunities and Challenges for Faith-based NGOs

Faith-based NGOs can have a unique role in improving colonias. They make essential contributions that cannot be advanced by governments or traditional, service-oriented NGOs. Faith-based NGOs can more easily mobilize projects across physical borders and interorganizational jurisdictions than can governments. In the international border region—with its overlapping jurisdictions and intergovernmental relations at multiple levels—government organizations struggle to make joint decisions, even while cost-effective. As an official of the New Mexico Department of Health observed, it is far less expensive to treat tuberculosis in Chihuahua than in New Mexico, but the state's health plans do not account for their Mexican origin. It would be much easier and inexpensive to treat the causes of contracting tuberculosis than to respond to the disease at the cost of $250,000 a person per year for treatment of multi-drug-resistant cases (Paul Dulin, interview 2007). Government professionals are often hamstrung by their jurisdictional boundaries, even in unofficial capacities. For example, as one retired department official related (pers. comm. 1995), federal officials of the U.S. Department of Agriculture have been discouraged as a matter of policy from consulting with their Mexican counterparts in Mexico even on their own time.

It is in this context that nonprofit organizations, especially faith-based ones, have found they can be uniquely effective in supporting the needs of colonias residents. It is also a place where partnerships between non-profit organizations and units of local government can operate symbiotically. Big government bureaucracies are perhaps well suited to major investments in expensive infrastructure, such as water and sewer systems and moderately large-scale housing programs, but they have not proven to be as effective in dealing with smaller projects at the local level.

Faith-based NGOs have the potential for great social impact for several reasons. For one, they have a more flexible resource base: they can draw upon support of congregations, private foundations, and individuals. These sources are less fettered by the restrictions, rules, and regulations that narrow the scope and activities of most secular, service-oriented NGO programs. They enable faith organizations to come up with creative solutions not bound by the "silo orientation" of categorically funded federal programs. For example, DouglaPrieta Works, an NGO jointly based in Douglas, Arizona, and in Agua Prieta, Sonora, has created a joint binational microenterprise drawing upon financial capital from the United States and human capital from Mexico. A parallel case in Columbus, New Mexico, and Puerto Palomas, Chihuahua, mobilizes financial and technical resources from the United States to assist a production cooperative in Mexico. Both of these efforts are able to make progress, largely because of the lack of restrictions they face in moving resources across the international boundary.

Second, faith-based NGOs can have a pivotal role because some are incorporated in a legally unique way. Registering as 501(c)4 nonprofit organizations with the Internal Revenue Service—rather than the more ubiquitous 501(c)3 designation—they can engage in lobbying and political activities. Organizations such as the border-wide Industrial Areas Foundation's (IAF) Interfaith Sponsoring Committee, which works in Arizona, New Mexico, and California, have incorporated as such to mobilize voters and to engage in state-level policy advocacy on economic, social, and political concerns of importance to U.S.–Mexico border residents (Warren 2001; Buckwalter 2003; Esparza and Donelson 2008). In contrast, political activities are expressly prohibited for organizations with 501(c)3 nonprofit status; most federal funding and philanthropic giving is available only to these types of organizations.

But faith organizations also share some challenges familiar to their secular counterparts. Their faith-based status rarely offers them greater rapport with colonias than secular organizations have, unless they are connected with churches based in colonias themselves. That is because colonias, like other communities facing racial oppression and isolation, tend to have very high levels of distrust of "helping" organizations (Earle 1999; Milofsky 2003). As Esparza and Donelson (2008) find, colonias residents sometimes believe clergy ignore or manipulate leaders to serve church interests. In their case study research of five Arizona and New Mexico colonias, they found three communities where residents felt misled by their faith-based partners: in one, the church dismissed some residents' plans of introducing a bilingual mass, in their hopes to better unite an ethnically divided community; in another, the church used colonias resident volunteers to help renovate a church building, which was promised for a community center but later was restricted to church functions; in a third, the residents were upset when the new priest of their parish abandoned the church's prior efforts to improve the community. Yet broadly based church activities, such as Catholic Social Services, that draw upon diocesan resources can be uniquely effective working on the household, parish, and community levels, as is the case in southern New Mexico and southern Arizona.

While faith-based organizations often can tap their congregations and individual donors for funding, many may still come up short on financial resources. They may look to government funding, which has increasingly become "faith-based-friendly." In 2001 the administration of President George W. Bush introduced the "Faith-Based and Community Initiative," a program of formal federal support for the work of religious organizations providing services to needy communities. Ten federal agencies were tasked to respond to this incentive: the U.S. Departments of Labor, Health and Human Services, Justice, Housing and Urban Development, Commerce, Agriculture, Education, and Veterans Affairs, the Agency for International Development, and the Small Business Administration (Farris, Nathan, and Wright 2004). Each agency established offices of faith-based initiatives. They were staffed with individuals who some critics charge were selected more for their political allegiance to the administration than for their skills and experience in meeting the social service needs of needy communities.[2] This has given rise to some controversy about the mingling of church and state in American society, as well as some concern that the motivation for this approach includes partisan political gain along with social service provision. The Rockefeller Institute of Government's Roundtable on Religion and Social Welfare Policy points to five distinct areas in which the Bush administration's initiative conflicts with traditional separation of church and state in America (Farris, Nathan, and Wright 2004):

- The federal government now allows federally funded faith-based groups to consider religion when employing staff.
- The Department of Justice now permits religious organizations to convert government-forfeited property to religious purposes after five years, replacing the previous policy prohibiting such conversions.
- The federal government now allows federally funded faith-based groups to build and renovate structures used for both social services and religious worship.
- The Veterans Administration no longer requires faith-based social service providers to certify that they exert "no religious influence."
- The Department of Labor now allows students to use federal job-training vouchers to receive religious training leading to employment at a church, synagogue, or other faith-based organization.

Nathan and Wright (2003) point out, however, that President Bush's initiative was foreshadowed by the "charitable choice" provision in Section 104 of the welfare legislation sponsored by then-senator John Ashcroft, and signed into law by President Clinton in 1996. Thus, it is important to recognize the antecedents of current federal policy implemented by executive order, organizational realignment, and reinterpretation of existing regulations.

One of the marked changes since 2001 has been the degree to which some states have modified their operating procedures to induce faith-based organizations to enter into partnerships with the executive branches to provide services to needy communities. The modifications impacted 53 percent of states by 2005, up from 36 percent of the states in 2003 (Ragan and Wright 2005). However, only a minority of the states were considered "activist" in this regard, with the majority making only incremental changes.

Clearly, government resources are not a panacea. Government funding can hinder the activist work of faith-based NGOs by steering their work toward resource acquisition and "professionalization" (Dolhinow

2005; Lemos et al. 2002). As such, it can turn these organizations into mere pass-throughs of government funding (Wolch 1990). Faith-based NGOs that are mindful of the risks associated with accepting government funding can make significant impact.

Summary

This chapter has considered four themes: the circumstances of the need facing colonia residents, the unique role played by faith-based organizations providing social services not adequately addressed by government agencies, the capabilities and limitations experienced by faith-based NGOs, and the means by which they have gained the trust of the residents and also maintained their independence in the face of increased political pressure and the militarization of the borderlands. In lieu of securing public revenues and adequate sources of government support, colonias have responded to the shortfall through social mobilization and building alliances with nonprofit organizations. Some of these nonprofit organizations are rooted in faith traditions. They include organized church service and spiritually grounded volunteerism by members of faith communities. Their active involvement in and support for these communities goes back to the 1970s, and even earlier in some cases (Henkel 1979).

Although there can be a fair degree of overlap between faith-based community service organizations and secular social service organizations, the former often have a greater degree of independence in carrying out their chosen mission than do the latter, because they are less constrained by government prohibitions or the fear of alienating donors. At the same time, they face financial instability in the medium term unless they are associated with a larger institutional support network.

The current borderlands activities of those faith-based organizations rooted in the Sanctuary Movement are not large-scale, nor are they focused on the provision of basic needs, which is the most common kind of social outreach undertaken by church organizations (Chaves 2004). Instead, they fill a niche generally avoided by secular organizations, a niche concerned with social justice and institutional oppression of poor people. These organizations arise in response to particular conditions, such as those brought on by the increased militarization of the U.S.– Mexico borderlands, and persist as long as they are able to address the issues that have brought them into being. Because they are less constrained than their secular counterparts, they are sometimes capable of taking the lead on issues that are subsequently embraced by the society in general, including the championing of immigrant rights and the modification of harsh laws. They play a small but important role in helping the residents of the colonias to improve their living conditions and chances for a better future.

Notes

1. According to Esparza and Donelson (2008), in Arizona 30 percent of the colonias federally designated by the U.S. Department of Housing and Urban Development are incorporated (26 of the 87 colonias); in New Mexico, 10 percent are incorporated (13 of the 127 colonias). Although the Texas secretary of state (2006) lists the names and locations of Texas colonias, the state does not indicate how many are incorporated or unincorporated.

2. When writing (for the *American Baptist Press*) about the departure of Jim Towey from the White House directorship of the Faith-Based and Community Initiative, Marus (2006) notes, "Both his predecessor in the office, John DiIulio, and a former Towey aide, David Kuo, ended up criticizing the White House's handling of the issue following their departures. They and other former supporters of the plan have suggested Bush's political operatives have simply been using it to gain support among religious voters—without actually expanding funding for social services."

10

Farmworkers, Housing, and California's Colonias

John Mealey

AGRICULTURE IS BIG BUSINESS in California. The state's 76,000 farms earned more than $31 billion in 2006, twice the total of Texas, which ranked second in agricultural cash receipts in the country. California leads the nation in the production of more than 40 agricultural commodities ranging from almonds to plums and milk, and exports to more than 150 countries (California Department of Food and Agriculture 2007). Needless to say, farm labor is vital to California's agriculture economy, with more than 730,000 farmworkers in the fields. Exact figures are difficult to come by, but estimates place the number of undocumented farmworkers at about 50 percent, many of whom are migrant workers (Martin 2002; Martin and Taylor 1998). In 2005–6 farmworkers earned an average of $13,120, with about 30 percent living below the poverty line (Pacheco 2007).

Farmworkers face many problems, ranging from health to food security, but housing is perhaps the most pressing issue. Across the country, only 17 percent of farmworkers own their homes, which is not surprising in view of their low incomes. About 58 percent of farmworkers live in rental housing, while another 21 percent live in employer-provided housing (Strauss 2005). A study conducted by the Housing Assistance Council (2003) found that farmworkers live in deplorable conditions. About 52 percent live in crowded housing (more than one person per room), and about 33 percent of the dwelling units were moderately to severely substandard. Mobile homes, which provide shelter for about 15 percent of the farmworker population, were often found to have holes in roofs and walls, as well as insect and rodent infestation. Some farmworkers live in hotels, while others sleep in tents, in cars, or out in the open.

Housing conditions for California migrant and year-round farmworkers are among the worst in the United States. This is largely because the supply of farmworker housing has dwindled over the past three decades.

In 1976, privately owned employee housing licensed by the State of California sheltered an estimated 45,000 farmworkers and household members in 1,254 housing units. By 2000, only 1,000 privately owned licensed units remained, with capacity for half as many farmworkers and household members, or 23,000 persons (State of California 2005). Because decent housing is scarce, farmworkers are generally forced to choose affordable, yet substandard, options. Conditions are appalling not only in California's colonias along the border, but also in farm labor camps and communities throughout the agricultural areas of the southern and central parts of the state (Forbes 2007).

Although decent housing options are scarce, they are essential to the economic advancement of farmworkers and their families. Safe, sanitary housing is critical to the ability of migrant and seasonal farmworkers to find and hold a job, enroll in job training, and improve their earnings. Adequate housing promotes good health, which in turn reduces health-care costs and absenteeism. Access to secure housing also enables farmworker families to envision a future for themselves and their children through economic asset building.

California's strong network of active and creative rural nonprofit developers has made good use of local, state, and federal resources to fill at least part of this gap. They have placed many agricultural workers and their families in good-quality single-family homes, apartments, and manufactured housing parks (Bandy 2004; National Rural Housing Coalition 2005; Rural Community Assistance Corporation 2007). However, demand for housing far exceeds supply. Many rural working families continue to live in substandard and unsafe farm labor camps, or in rented shacks often lacking such basic services as clean drinking water, paved roads, and safe wiring.

In this chapter, I discuss California farmworkers' conditions and evaluate the role of nonprofit organizations in mitigating their housing problems. I focus on agricultural workers and their families who live in southern California's colonias.[1] Much of the discussion centers on Riverside County's Coachella Valley, because this is where my organization—the Coachella Valley Housing Coalition (CVHC)—is based and has worked extensively over the past 27+ years.

This chapter is organized in five sections. the first section provides a brief history of the living conditions confronting southern California's agricultural workers. It explains how California's 1992 Farm Labor Housing Protection Act had an unintended impact: the proliferation of substandard mobile home parks in the Coachella Valley, which in the 1990s and even today has subjected farmworkers to increasingly dangerous health and safety conditions. The second section explains how the CVHC and other nonprofits countered a county-driven regulatory approach that would have forced thousands of agricultural workers and their families out of their homes. The third section of the chapter takes a broader look at how some California nonprofits have developed effective approaches to meet farmworker housing needs. The fourth section analyzes why some well-meaning efforts led by local nonprofit organizations have failed in their attempts to provide decent housing for agricultural laborers and their families. Finally, the chapter concludes with a summary and a look at the challenges ahead in addressing the tremendous needs of farmworkers living in California's colonias.

Farmworker Conditions in the Coachella Valley: From Bad to Worse

For generations, industrious and desperate men and women have moved from Mexico and beyond to southern California's border communities of Imperial and Riverside counties in search of decent-paying work and a better life and future for their families. They were pushed out by poverty at home and drawn north by the promise of jobs picking oranges, lemons, dates, and grapes. The rich agricultural lands of the Imperial and Coachella valleys and the need for hands to harvest them have worked as a magnet drawing workers from Mexico since the Bracero Program of the Second World War (Martin 2002; McWilliams 1999; Nevins 2002). Hard workers could earn more in a day in "Gringolandia" than in a week in Mexico. Jobs were plentiful but the housing was often worse than at home, and the boss could fire you, keep the wages you had earned, and export you back home at will. The need for workers to pick crops grew after the Bracero Program ended in the 1960s; what little protection the workers once had disappeared (Rodriguez, Toller, and Downing 2004).

Historically, in southeastern California's Coachella Valley, many migrant workers found shelter in *cartolandias,* small complexes of cardboard and scrap-material huts on agricultural land. The better available homes were abandoned trailers, usually with no water or electricity hookups. The rent was cheap, and the locations close to work. Water for showers, cooking, and sometimes drinking came from nearby irrigation lines or ditches. Families and single migrant workers lived wherever there was available space. Extension cords ran hundreds of feet from nearby homes, usually the home of the landowner, precariously providing tenants with electric power. Some cartolandias grew to be sizable communities. Many included open-air restaurants that provided hot lunches for the workers to take to the fields, as well as places to congregate and swap stories. Some of these *campos*—operated by entrepreneurial farmworkers eager to join the capital-formation class—grew large enough to support not only restaurants, but also boxing rings and open-air dance halls, all made from discarded materials.

Cartolandias popped up to fill the need for housing that was affordable to farmworkers. But with this unregulated housing opportunity came tragedy. Poor wiring and shabby construction caused fires. People died. Cartolandias closed down in one place and opened the next day in another. No one seemed to care. Dilapidated mobile home parks began cropping up and replacing cartolandias throughout the valley. In 1990 the Riverside County Consolidated Plan reported that approximately 16 percent, or 79,086 units, of the county's existing housing stock was composed of mobile home parks, when only 9 percent of the California housing stock was mobile homes (Housing Authority of the County of Riverside 2008; U.S. Census Bureau 1990).

Finally, after years of neglect, in 1992 the California state legislature passed the Farm Labor Housing Protection Act, AB 3526, known as the "Polanco Bill" (California Housing Law Project 2001). The bill was designed to encourage development of farmworker housing on agricultural land. The act enabled owners of agricultural land to house up to 12 farmworkers without having to pay business taxes or local registration fees or to obtain conditional use permits. Unfortunately, the great need for decent farmworker housing attracted opportunistic developers and landowners in the Coachella Valley. Many of these entrepreneurs built small mobile home parks that not only bypassed local land use regulations but also ignored basic health and safety requirements concerning placement of wells and septic systems, and utilities such as electricity. Wells were dug, septic systems placed, and extension cords run without regard to safety. Up to 500 of these "parks" popped up in the Coachella Valley. In the summer of 1998, four children burned to death at four different locations due to faulty wiring (Henry 1999).

In 1999, Riverside County moved to close down more than 200 of these illegal trailer parks, declaring them to be subject to dangerous health and safety conditions caused by overcrowding and lack of adequate infrastructure, or substantial violations of health and safety standards. The county initially identified 86 parks (later almost 400 parks were identified, but more than 500 parks were believed to exist). Instead of proposing an approach that offered assistance to residents, the county initially chose a regulatory approach that made things worse. The county sent park owners legal notices in the form of lawsuits to shut them down. Instead of protecting tenants, they listed them as defendants (Kelly 1999).

These actions forced thousands of laborers and their families to move. A few members of the local Torres Martinez Desert Cahuilla Indian Tribe, along with some nonmembers, saw an opportunity to earn a few dollars (Villarejo and Schenker 2007). They rapidly developed trailer parks on land within tribal boundaries. The parks filled up quickly and continued to expand beyond original expectations; the results were disastrous, with conditions as bad or worse than those of the illegal "Polanco" parks. Once again, overcrowding, poor water and septic facilities, and serious illnesses were pervasive. Eventually the U.S. Environmental Protection Agency filed a lawsuit against one of the tribal park owners, Harvey Duro, and received a court order demanding that Duro close his park.

Harvey Duro, a member of the Torres Martinez Desert Cahuilla Indians, claimed that he saw an opportunity to help people and also make a profit by opening up his land to displaced tenants. Subsequently, the Desert Mobile Home Park was established on Torres Martinez tribal land near the Salton Sea (U.S. Department of Housing and Urban Development 2008). Home to an estimated 6,000 people, mostly farmworkers, the park has become the poster child for poverty and a well-documented exposé of Third World conditions that exist only 30 minutes from some of the most expensive resorts and real estate in the United States, such as Rancho Mirage, Indian Wells, and Palm Desert (Kelly 2008).

Nicknamed Duroville, and even more commonly known as Duros, the trailer park has been plagued by environmental problems since its inception. Cited problems include dirty tap water, sewage disposal in open ponds, seepage of sewage into the ground, and an unsafe electrical system. Duros has attracted much unwanted media coverage and is now facing a second federal lawsuit brought by the Bureau of Indian Affairs to shut down the park (Moore 2007). While federal officials are worried about displacing Duros's residents, they also claim that they cannot continue to turn a blind eye to the dangerous conditions at the trailer park.

"At least Rosa Parks had a choice, we don't even have a bus stop" is a sample of some graffiti that decorate the walls of Duros. It is an eloquent testimonial to the frustration and feeling of futility that pervades trailer parks such as Duros. Located near agricultural fields, most Duros residents are marginalized farmworkers, working long and grueling hours for minimum wage, or just above it. They fear authorities and the threat of deportation. Most do not speak English. They would like to move to another place that is safer for themselves and their families, but they see Duros as better than nothing. They fear that when the park inevitably closes, they will be out on the street with no options available to them.

The Nonprofit Sector Responds

Clearly, Riverside County's heavy-handed decision in 1999 had severe consequences. In response, Catholic Charities, the Diocese of San Bernardino, California Rural Legal Assistance, the State Department of Housing and Community Development, the U.S. Department of Housing and Urban Development, the Coachella Valley Housing Coalition, and concerned individuals moved quickly to block the immediate closing of the parks and the suit against the tenants. Park owners, with an unusually myopic perspective, formed an organization to present themselves as victims of the county's effort to close their illegal parks. At the same time, tenants lacking affordable housing were forced to drag their run-down trailers to other unsafe parks like those in Duroville, primarily on sovereign Indian land.

Fourth District county supervisor Roy Wilson, a staunch advocate for affordable housing, met with the concerned groups to discuss alternatives to the immediate eviction of hundreds of very low-income families. The tenants were dropped from the lawsuit, and plans were developed to provide financing to the park owners to bring their parks up to health and safety standards.

Through the intervention of the Catholic diocese, farmworkers, advocates, property owners, and community-based organizations (including CVHC), consensus emerged to repair rather than shut down these "Polanco" parks. The County of Riverside Economic Development Agency (EDA) agreed. The county restructured its grants and developed five new programs to help tenants, as well as property owners, improve living conditions in mobile home parks of the Coachella Valley in unincorporated Riverside County (Riverside County Economic Development Agency 2008). Two of these programs gave park owners loans at 3 percent interest to improve properties that were in danger of closing because they failed state and local codes. Owners could use funds to update existing housing, purchase new or recently manufactured housing units as replacement housing, and upgrade common areas, infrastructure, and related facilities (Kelly 1999). The loans, with 30- to 40-year repayment terms, had to be used to improve living conditions for low-income agricultural workers. A third program provided park owners with "forgivable loans," or conditional grants. These defrayed up to $10,000 in county-assessed fees per housing unit associated with rehabilitating low-income farmworker housing. The final two programs provided outright grants and "forgivable loans" to low-income, mobile-home owners living in substandard parks. The county gave grants of up to $3,000 to mobile-home owners to make repairs that added at least 10 years to the life of their substandard properties. The county also offered individual mobile-home owners $30,000 loans, at zero percent interest, that could be forgiven after 10 years if the unit was deemed beyond repair and turned over to the county to be destroyed at the time the owner accepted the loan.

Although mobile-home park tenants took advantage of the programs, few park owners did so. Most rejected them because of provisions in California law that require long-term affordability covenants (45 years for home ownership and 55 years for rental housing that receives state or local government funding). They wanted to retain options to sell land to private developers, because land prices were on the rise. Other park owners could not use the grants because of ownership title or land use problems. Some mobile home parks were built on too-small parcels, violating minimum zoning requirements. In other cases, families and friends often jointly purchased lots, building several houses on them without meeting local land use ordinances. Sometimes, multiple families purchased home sites together but could not agree on improvement loans.

Since the grant and loan programs were launched in 1999, CVHC has worked closely with Riverside County to develop additional housing opportunities for many of the farmworkers displaced from the "Polanco" parks. CVHC has moved 500 families into newly built rental and self-help home ownership housing in the rural communities of the Coachella Valley.[2] Las Palmeras Estates was an existing park with 77 lots that had never been occupied. CVHC purchased the park, then designed and placed 77 new rental homes on the vacant lots. The park includes a swimming pool, after-school homework and computer classes, and other amenities.

The CVHC also developed a new mobile home park called Paseo de los Heroes in the impoverished agricultural settlement of Mecca. Paseo de los Heroes has 106 lots, a child-care center, preventive medical screenings, after-school homework, computer classes, and a soccer field. All of the residents lived previously in "Polanco" parks. Their former unsafe trailers were destroyed, and occupants received a grant in the range of $30,000 to $40,000 from the county to purchase a new manufactured home to place in the park (Coachella Valley Housing Coalition 2001).

The CVHC also worked with Riverside County to develop 48 new contractor-built homes in the city of Coachella for families displaced from "Polanco" parks. The CVHC developed Las Mañanitas specifically for the migrant farmworkers living in Mecca; the apartment-style housing rents for $30 per week per worker. In 2003, National Public Radio (NPR) recognized the merits of Las Mañanitas and featured the development as a success story of migrant housing. NPR also profiled stories on CVHC's self-help program and senior housing for retired farmworkers the same summer (NPR 2003).

Effective Advocacy Approaches

Coachella Valley Housing Coalition's approach has proven successful in resolving many farmworker housing problems. The organization has a long history in the Coachella Valley. It was founded in 1982 by a group of community leaders, including Carole Harper, a legal services lawyer; Sylvia Montenegro, a member of the school board and a Catholic Charities community worker; and Father Ed Donovan, a missionary to migrant workers. They came together to persuade business leaders, farmworker union members, and others to make a difference by starting an organization with the single purpose of replacing the cartolandias with decent farmworker housing. They established the nonprofit with the mission "to help low-income families improve their living conditions through advocacy, research, construction, and operation of housing and community development projects" (Coachella Valley Housing Coalition 2001).

The Coachella Valley Housing Coalition, based in the city of Indio, has since evolved into a nationally recognized nonprofit developer. It has taken a leading role in developing affordable rental and homeowner-occupied housing opportunities to low-income residents and agricultural workers in Riverside, San Bernardino, and Imperial counties. Early on, CVHC recognized the need for additional resident services to fully serve the hardworking farmworker families. In the late 1980s, residents expressed a need for child-care services at CVHC's farmworker housing apartments Pie de la Cuesta and Las Casas Apartments. CVHC obtained funding directly from the California Department of Education to provide child-care centers at each site. Today, CVHC's multifamily developments offer community services such as child care, after-school programs, computer classes, art classes, music and dance programs, and ESL (English as a Second Language) and citizenship classes. At CVHC's Paseo de los Heroes Mobile Home Park, the children of migrant farmworkers are served by the Migrant Head Start Center, which provides an educational child-care program for working families. At farmworker housing apartments Pie de la Cuesta and Las Casas Apartments, CVHC built and secured funding needed to operate the two child-care centers. For many years, CVHC's Nueva Vista Clinic in the Nueva Vista Apartments was Mecca's one and only medical center. To date, CVHC has completed a total of 2,184 affordable multifamily units and approximately 1,410 mutual self-help homes owned by low-income families.[3]

Like CVHC, other nonprofit California housing developers and nonprofit organizations have addressed farmworker needs throughout colonias and other areas of the state. California has strong nonprofit housing developers in most regions of the state, with many of the more experienced groups working in rural communities. Self Help Enterprises (SHE), based in Visalia, has been developing sweat equity homes throughout Central California for more than 40 years. The organization is a leader in rural housing throughout the United States. Self Help Enterprises, Peoples' Self-Help, South County Housing, Community Housing Improvement

Program, Rural California Housing Corp, and CVHC house thousands of farmworkers across the state (Coachella Valley Housing Coalition 2001; Community Housing Improvement Program 2008; People's Self-Help 2008; Self Help Enterprises 2004; South County Housing 2005).

The California Coalition for Rural Housing, a state network that links these groups, also has been effective in making the need for rural housing known at the state capitol. The organization's efforts have been bolstered by other California-based organizations such as Housing California, Rural Community Assistance Corporation, and Southern California Association of Non Profits. On the national level, the Housing Assistance Council and the National Rural Housing Coalition have been effective in raising the awareness of the need for adequate farmworker housing. Together, their advocacy has produced results: in California in 2006, voters passed Proposition 1C, a $2.1 billion bond initiative for affordable housing to serve low-income families and individuals throughout the state, including $135 million for the Joe Serna Jr. Farmworker Housing Grant Program. Groups in California have been effective in combining state and federal tax credits; the tax credit program complements the existing state affordable housing funds administered by the California Department of Housing and Community Development (State of California 2005) and the California Housing Finance Agency, as well as locally allocated resources. California law requires cities and counties to set aside 20 percent of their redevelopment project area tax increment fund for affordable housing. In addition, federal resources have helped fill the gap. The U.S. Department of Agriculture Rural Housing Service (RHS), in particular, has been a consistent and reliable source of funding for rural home ownership and rental projects, as well as for community and water and sewer facilities. USDA's RHS California directors and staff have been strong advocates for rural housing and have worked hand in hand with nonprofit developers throughout the state for many years.

Nonprofit Challenges in Developing Affordable Housing

Over the past 40 years, concerned local residents have formed some non-profit housing corporations to develop homes for low-income farmworkers in the Coachella and Imperial Valleys. Most have not survived.

Many factors have contributed to often insurmountable challenges. First, land cost is a huge obstacle for nonprofits. Almost all developable land had been purchased by major corporate developers or by "flippers," investors who purchase land and sit on it, or develop lots and sell as the market heats up. Acreage prices of finished lots have multiplied by factors of five to ten or more in the past decade. Due to the recent drop in the overall real estate market, lot prices are starting to come down. However, they have not fallen enough to make most affordable housing projects viable.

Second, the cost of bringing basic infrastructure to a developable site is usually prohibitive unless the project is for hundreds or even thousands of units. Many of the rural communities with the greatest need for housing for farmworkers lack municipal water and sewer systems, adequate roads, and utility access. In large parts of the Coachella Valley, significant water challenges complicate the problem, such as high water tables, excessive arsenic content, or no nearby connection to the water system. Few nonprofit organizations are equipped to develop on that scale.

Third, most start-up local nonprofit housing organizations lack the capital and experience required to bring projects to fruition. Funding is increasingly difficult to access as more developers pursue fewer dollars. Private developers compete with nonprofit housing development organizations for local redevelopment agency funds, state funds, and tax credit allocations as well as for U.S. Department of Agriculture–Rural Development 502 single-family loan funds. Projects often take five or six years to bring to fruition. The nonprofit organization must have sufficient resources or a stream of income to carry itself during that period, with experienced staff to guide it in the process. These staff are hard to find, and harder to hire without resources to pay competitive salaries and an expectation that the employment will continue for a few years.

Of the nonprofit organizations that have survived, many have had to leave the affordable-home-building business due to the aforementioned challenges. They include Campesinos Unidos Incorporated (CUI), based in Imperial County. Incorporated in 1971, CUI for many years operated a successful self-help housing program that produced 100 self-help homes for very low- to low-income families. In 2006–7, CUI produced its final self-help community, 18 homes in the rural community of Holtville. CUI eliminated its self-help program due to difficulties qualifying prospective families for USDA loans; the families had either too little income or too much debt. Nevertheless, CUI continues to operate successful child-care and other social service programs in Imperial and Riverside counties. CUI now refers low-income families to CVHC's Mutual Self-Help Program.

Calexico Community Action Council is another Imperial County nonprofit that has found it difficult to remain in the affordable housing development business. Twenty-eight years ago, the Calexico Community Action Council produced 299 farmworker restricted modular homes. At the time, funding was available through the Imperial County Economic Development Agency for rural housing serving the very poor. Plagued by the difficult conditions of the market, Calexico Community Action Council now mostly concentrates its single-family housing efforts on purchasing and rehabbing existing homes. However, it has also focused efforts on larger-scale, rental housing: it is currently working on a 134-unit senior housing tax credit development.

Desert Alliance for Community Empowerment (DACE), a nonprofit organization formed in 1999 by the County of Riverside to administer its federally funded Empowerment Zone, has also faced development challenges (Desert Alliance for Community Empowerment 2008). DACE's service area, which encompasses rural eastern Riverside County to the California/Arizona border, has focused on providing basic infrastructure to parcels that are remote and improperly zoned. Much of this land is within the territory or sphere of influence of a Native American tribe that to this day has not implemented planning and development procedures that would enable developers to build housing.

DACE has successes in other areas. It has built showers for migrant farmworkers in the community of Mecca, a nonprofit resource center in the city of Coachella. It has helped form various nonprofit divisions, such as Rancho Housing Alliance and Poder Popular. DACE also provides technical assistance to unpermitted park owners working with the county to bring their communities up to county code. Housing developments planned by DACE, but not yet completed, include the San Felipe Migrant Housing and Community Center, a 48-bed facility for traveling farmworkers, and the Mecca Migrant Housing Center. DACE plans to build a three-quarter-mile water pipeline to bring clean water to the 100 Palms colonia.

Summary

Clearly, many challenges face smaller local nonprofit organizations that have attempted—often unsuccessfully—to build affordable farmworker housing in the current environment. While some larger affordable housing nonprofit developers such as CVHC and SHE have succeeded, demand for affordable housing for farm laborers far outstrips supply. Seriously substandard mobile home parks still dot California's agricultural landscape. A spectrum of housing types is needed—community-owned rental housing in rural cities and towns, homeownership opportunities for farmworker and low-income families, emergency housing and units for short stays on or near farms and orchards in remote areas. A wide-ranging continuum is essential to meet the needs of this diverse group: unaccompanied migrant workers, migrant workers who travel back and forth between the United States and their home country, migrant worker families who follow the crops but stay within the United States, and families who would like to put down roots in an agricultural community.

These permanent and temporary camps are where more federal colonias funding, and other federal, state, and private resources, are most desperately needed. A more clearly defined policy is essential to allow federal funds to assist people living outside the narrowly defined geographic regions of colonias. Currently, the federal definition excludes more-urbanized counties, like Riverside County, and those agricultural settlements beyond 150 miles of the U.S.–Mexico border. A revised definition, inclusive of the broad range of farmworker locales and service needs, would greatly assist California housing development organizations. It would enable CVHC and other nonprofits to expand assistance to the people who are often disenfranchised, work long, grueling hours in the agricultural fields, and return home to appalling and unsafe housing.

Notes

1. Riverside County is home to eight of the state's thirty-two federally recognized colonias. All have been designated as colonias by their respective county governments (Mukhija and Monkkonen 2006). However, few in the California affordable housing industry utilize the term, as it depicts dire housing conditions along the U.S.–Mexico border. In California, unsafe, substandard housing is not relegated to the border regions. These housing conditions more often are found in farm labor and migrant

worker camps that stretch north across the state and mirror the conditions found in colonias across the country.

2. One of CVHC's first projects was a farmworker housing complex called Pueblo Nuevo, a 50-unit development that had more than 500 farmworker applicants.

3. Through CVHC's mutual self-help program, families in groups of 10 to 12 provide "sweat equity" by helping to build their own homes and those of their neighbors. Families working together in this mutual self-help environment create close-knit communities, which in turn produce safe neighborhoods and community pride. They also learn construction skills that allow them to maintain the upkeep of their homes.

PART III

Colonias Health and the Environment

Living Betwixt and Between

CONDITIONS OF HEALTH IN
BORDERLAND COLONIAS

Marlynn May

THIS FINAL SECTION of the book explores public and environmental health in border colonias. As with previous sections that dealt with economic and community development, readers will find that public and environmental health conditions impose enormous hardships on colonia residents. It is difficult, perhaps impossible, to identify which aspect—economy, community, or health—is at the core of these hardships, because they are related. But it is safe to say that health is embedded in the complex maze of economic and social forces that shape everyday life. As much as anything, the data and case studies reported in this section point to these complex relationships.

In this chapter, I provide a broad-based perspective on conditions of health in colonias across the entire U.S.–Mexico border. While colonias in different states will have more of one or another of the health issues identified here, the discussion is germane to all colonias and the people who live in them. But the bases of health quality and health care are the central themes of the chapter. I present a model that integrates economic, social, and cultural forces so that colonias are positioned in the broader array of forces that shape health and health care.

The chapter consists of three sections. In the first section I summarize principal health problems and link them to economic and social conditions in the border region. The second section presents a systems-based model that anchors colonias health to the broader social, economic, and political environment. The model explains how and why colonias face such severe health problems, and shows why health care and delivery are hindered. The third section summarizes principal programs and organizations that respond to colonias health. I do not provide a comprehensive listing, because there are literally dozens of federal, state, and nonprofit agencies and organizations involved with colonias and border health. Instead, I direct attention to those agencies and organizations that deal with health broadly in the border region. The chapters that follow discuss some of the locally based nonprofits within border states.

Conditions of Health in Colonias

Studies of health in the border region have found far greater incidences of disease and illness than in other parts of the United States. In counties that lie within 62 miles (100 kilometers) of the U.S.–Mexico border, researchers found that incidences of infectious diseases such as measles, hepatitis A, rubella, shigelloses, and rabies are two to four times higher than across the country (Collins-Dogrul 2006; Weinberg et al. 2003), while others reported elevated rates of salmonella, tuberculosis, and dengue fever (Rodríguez-Saldaña 2005). Disproportionately high rates of HIV/AIDS are common in cross-border cities such as Ciudad Juárez–El Paso and Tijuana–San Diego, where drug use is rampant (Moyer et al. 2008). Alcoholism, the cause of many preventable illnesses, is widespread but varies according to location and depth of acculturation (Caetano et al. 2008; Lara et al. 2005). Diabetes is perhaps the most pressing preventable health problem in border colonias, mainly because of the large Hispanic presence. Across the country, the rate of diabetes for Hispanics is nearly twice that of whites and, among the Hispanic population, Mexican Americans have the highest rates of all (Cohen and Ingram 2005). The border region is also home to millions of farmworkers who suffer from a range of injuries and illnesses. Diseases and illnesses such as cancer, skin rashes, and eye damage result from exposure to pesticides and chemicals, allergens, dust, and intense sunlight (Arcury and Quandt 2007; Mills and Yang 2007).

These health problems arise from both environmental and social factors. In terms of environment, observers have long associated poor health in colonias with infrastructure deficiencies, especially the lack of potable water, government-regulated landfills, sanitation treatment facilities, and paved streets and roads (Evans and Kantrowitz 2002; U.S. Environmental Protection Agency 2007a). Each of these deficiencies diminishes health through the spread of pathogens, exposure to toxic materials, and airborne pollutants that cause numerous illnesses. The human-built environment affects colonia residents in other ways. Dilapidated housing, the absence of home heating and cooking facilities, and the paucity of parks and playgrounds, recreation centers, and safe open spaces compromises engagement in healthful lifestyles, especially among children (Auchincloss et al. 2008; Joshu et al. 2008; Keim 2005; Metzger, Delgado, and Herrell 1995).

Long-standing economic, social, and political inequities underlie many of the health problems witnessed in colonias. These inequities arose from decades of violence and intimidation that ripped across the border from Texas to California, as the dominant white society attempted to reduce Mexicans to second-class status (Martínez 1994, 2006). The vestiges remain today as Mexican Americans struggle for cultural identity and access to education, employment, and participation in the political arena (Alvarez 1995; Mukhija and Monkkonen 2006). Poverty and deprivation are the most visible signs of these deep-seated conflicts. As of 2006, per capita incomes in 24 counties bordering Mexico (15 in Texas, three in New Mexico, four in Arizona, and two in California) lagged well behind the country as a whole. Per capita income in Texas border counties equaled $14,200; $12,500 in New Mexico; $16,000 in Arizona; and $18,000 in California, compared to $21,587 for the country (Salant and Weeks 2007).

These, and other health issues, have been targeted by the U.S.–Mexico Border Health Commission. The commission's *Healthy Borders 2010* (2003) report discussed them both as discrete problems of disease and as a cluster of health issues. The report focused attention on 11 specific disease concerns found in colonias and presented abundant evidence of these major health issues. It also established a set of objectives aimed at improving conditions of health on the border in the years to come.

Colonias Health in Perspective: A Systems Approach

The conditions described above are perhaps best understood by placing them in the context of a larger set of social determinants of health in which colonias are nested (Irwin and Scali 2007). Specifically, colonias are understood to be community subsystems nested within larger social, economic, and cultural systems, all of which affect health and the availability of, and access to, health care and disease prevention. Understanding health and colonias from this perspective also helps explain why it is so difficult to come to grips with and improve the conditions leading to poor health.

Social, economic, and cultural systems are a complex array of institutional structures and processes organized around sets of rules and policies designed to govern, control, and protect the distribution and consumption of goods and services, both within and outside the system. A system has a "logic" by which its goals and objectives are achieved. Systems exist in "layers" such that any given social, economic, or cultural system or subsystem resides in the context of other surrounding comprehensive systems that influence the opportunities and boundaries in which a subsystem operates. In theory, any given system's optimal functional efficiency occurs when it reaches maximum synchronization with the surrounding systems, although this seldom occurs.

Through complex sets of system interactions, each subsystem strives to maintain its own autonomy and logic. As system–subsystem synchronization diminishes, mutually beneficial outcomes of the several systems involved are reduced, potentially subverted. Colonias exist as less powerful systems in a complex set of larger, more powerful, organized systems.

Figure 11.1 presents a visual image of the embeddedness of colonias in four major systems, with access to and influence of each system on colonias residents' lives arrayed from more to less (inside to outside). The two outside circles, representing economic and health-care delivery systems, are more remote and "filtered" by the two inner circles—the borderlands and the sociocultural environment of colonias. Adding to the complexity, each of the systems has a Mexican and a U.S. dimension, different in content and meaning. Colonia residents, therefore, maneuver multiple systems, many of which do not even recognize the needs and assets in the colonias subsystems. By their very nature—small, unincorporated communities with minimally developed physical and social infrastructure— colonias exist marginally and largely invisibly among surrounding systems, with which they have asynchronous and conflicted relationships at best. It becomes abundantly apparent that colonias and their residents exist "betwixt and between" a number of influencing systems.

An example illustrates the point. The vast majority of colonias residents are first- and second-generation, primarily from Mexico, many with vivid knowledge of and affinity with the social, cultural, and health-care systems of Mexico (Anderson and Gerber 2007). Colonias residents

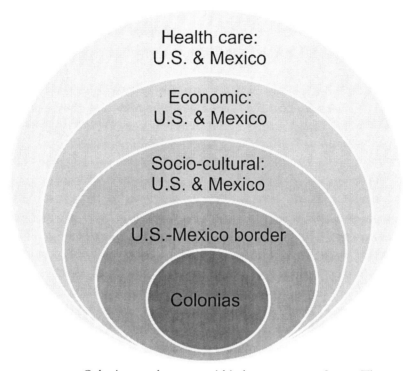

Health care:
U.S. & Mexico

Economic:
U.S. & Mexico

Socio-cultural:
U.S. & Mexico

U.S.-Mexico border

Colonias

FIGURE 11.1 Colonias as subsystems within larger systems. *Source*: The author

sustain an affinity socially and culturally with Mexico (in varying degrees, of course), yet the border itself represents a marginalizing (separation) from Mexico, increasingly so in the current climate of anti-immigration in the United States. Maneuvering this divide becomes increasingly complex and confusing.[1]

Access to Health Care in Colonias

The "betwixt and between" dilemma is boldly illustrated by issues related to access to health care. The U.S.–Mexico Border Health Commission's *Healthy Border 2010* (2003) put access at the head of the list of their conditions of health in colonias. Access trumps all other conditions because, regardless of how good the health-care delivery system might be, people will suffer if it is not accessible. Figure 11.1 provides an image of how and why this is the case. The health-care delivery system exists remotely from colonias and is "mediated" by a plethora of other system institutions.

Viewing access to health care in the context of figure 11.1 is crucial in another way: it moves perceptions of conditions of health beyond thinking primarily in terms of health as an absence of disease. It invites us to think in terms of *community health* (Pappas 2006). Community health encompasses things like access to potable water, sewer service, passable roads, substantial housing, adequate disposable income, and availability of transportation (both public and private). The fact is that colonias are buried in surrounding social, political, and economic systems that often have only minimally enabled—and in other ways disabled—access to community conditions of health (Davidhizar and Bechtel 1999; National Association of Community Health Centers 2007). Without access to positive conditions of community health, colonia residents' capacity to consume and practice curative and preventive health care is diminished.

The California Department of Health Services (Belshe and Shewy 2003) made this point unequivocally clear by noting that preventive health-care measures such as diet, nutritional counseling, and regular screening go a long way in mitigating longer-term illnesses. Preventive measures work best when a person is under the care of a health care provider who acquires familiarity through regular and sustained evaluation and counseling. Regrettably, minorities in the United States are far less likely to receive this sort of preventive health care. Twenty-eight percent of Mexican Americans, for example, do not have access to preventive health care. African Americans and Anglo-Americans fare better, with 15 percent and 13 percent respectively not receiving regularly scheduled preventive care (Belshe and Shewy 2003). The diminished conditions of access to health care result, in large part, from asynchronous relationships—sometimes intentionally created by the surrounding systems, other times occurring unintentionally—between the colonias subsystems and the larger systems identified in figure 11.1.

The Health Care Delivery System

Because regular, sustained health care for colonias residents is variously mediated and diverted through social, economic, and cultural systems (fig. 11.1), the health-care system itself is part of the problem. The result is that its providers, institutions, and services are unevenly available to, and accessible by, colonias residents.

Health Workforce Distribution. The health-care workforce has been historically remote to colonias, largely as a function of the uneven distribution of medical personnel in the U.S.–Mexico border counties and within the specific geographic context of colonias.

The ratio of primary and specialty physicians to population varies across border states, but some similarities exist (Health Resources and Services Administration 2007a, 2007b, 2007c, 2007d). In Texas and New Mexico, the ratio of physicians (primary and specialty) to populations within 62 miles of the border is consistently lower than in other parts of the respective states. Similar conditions exist for ratios of oral health professionals, allied health professionals (physician's assistants and nurse practitioners), and mental health professionals (psychiatrists and psychologists). Two factors explain a major portion of this uneven workforce distribution: the rural locations of most colonias residents and a lack of consistent and sustainable (in some cases, no) public transportation; both factors highlight the colonias residents' isolation.

Interestingly enough, the distribution of health-care workers along the Arizona and California borders differs from that of Texas and New Mexico. In many cases, the workforce ratios are generally better in California and Arizona than in New Mexico and Texas. Even more puzzling is that in Arizona the ratio of physicians per 100,000 population within 62 miles of the border *exceeds* the ratio for the state as a whole, and in California comparable ratios are nearly the same. In both Texas and New Mexico the ratios within 62 miles of the border are well under the comparable ratios for each state.

The reality is that the Texas and New Mexico ratios are closer to workforce distributions along the border. Arizona (in Tucson) and California (in San Diego) have major universities with medical facilities in areas near the border, unlike New Mexico and Texas. Nonetheless, colonia residents are, by and large, still isolated from these concentrations of health care near the border.

It remains to consider whether access to mental-health care is better due to a more even distribution of mental-health workers. Unfortunately, it is not. The pattern observed above with physicians and allied workforce professionals continues with psychiatrists and psychologists. And once again, the largest ratios of psychiatrists to population in border counties versus the state as a whole are found in California and Arizona, for the same reason mentioned above.

Health and Preventive Care Insurance. Another major factor in understanding conditions of health among colonias residents is the availability of reasonably priced health insurance. It is important to note, first, that the availability of health insurance at a cost that is affordable is becoming a greater problem generally in the United States. Gilmer and Kronick (2001) predicted that if insurance costs continued to rise faster than income, by 2009 insurance cost could rise more than 50 percent, assuring that the numbers of uninsured will continue to increase as the cost of health insurance and health care increase.

The lack of health insurance imposes hardship across a wide spectrum of the U.S. population. Fronstin (2005) indicated that in 2004, about 210 million nonelderly Americans had health-care coverage. On the other hand, nearly 46 million Americans (18 percent) were uninsured as of 2004, up from 45 million the year before. The size and growth of the uninsured population is troubling, because they are far more likely to forgo preventive health care and emergency treatment when needed. This leads to chronic (yet avoidable) health problems and advanced stages of illness when treatment is finally sought, which raises the probability of death while hospitalized. It is not surprising, therefore, that the uninsured are more likely to die at a younger age (Agency for Healthcare Research and Quality 2005).

Colonia residents are even less likely to have health insurance, because many live well below the poverty line and cannot afford health insurance, and it is often the case that those with higher-paying jobs do not receive health coverage as part of a benefits package. Instead, most are employed in construction, farm, and other forms of manual labor and service jobs that carry minimal or no fringe benefits. The majority have not finished high school, and most are Hispanic (Cunningham et al. 2006). The situation for unauthorized immigrants is even more burdensome, because they are typically denied access to public health care (Pagán and Pauly 2006; Schur and Feldman 2001). The data on the uninsured (i.e., without employment-based, individually purchased, or Medicaid insurance) in the four border states (within 62 miles of the border) confirm this conclusion. In Texas, nearly 42 percent of border residents do not have health coverage. New Mexico residents fare better, where 24 percent of the border population are without health insurance. Arizona and California have much smaller uninsured border populations, with 14 percent and 15 percent respectively (Health Resources and Services Administration 2007a, 2007b, 2007c, 2007d). These data are particularly compelling given that Texas, by far, has the largest numbers of colonias and residents, with New Mexico following.

Health Care Infrastructure. Another consideration in understanding conditions of access to health care in colonias is the paucity and uneven distribution of physical health-care delivery infrastructures. A report by the National Latino Research Center (2004), for instance, found an enormous need for investment in local health infrastructure in California's agriculturally rich Imperial County, where farmworker families struggle with a range of health problems. This finding is distressing in itself, but particularly troublesome because the lack of health infrastructure was recognized long ago yet little effort has been made to address it.

One early method for confronting gaps in access to health care was to improve financing and increase the number of health clinic and hospital resources in hard-to-reach places with major proportions of under- and unserved populations. For example, in 1977 the Rural Health Clinic (RHC) Program set out to address the inadequate supply of physicians in rural areas (National Association of Community Health Centers 2007). This program provides qualifying clinics and other providers payment on a cost-related basis for outpatient and certain non-physician services. To achieve its mission, the RHC Program serves areas designated and certified by the U.S. Department of Health and Human Services as health professional shortage areas.[2]

Complementing the RHCs are the Federally Qualified Health Care Centers (FQHCs). All organizations receiving grants under Section 330 of the Public Health Service Act are FQHCs. They are mandated to provide a range of services for all ages in addition to primary care and preventive health, such as dental and mental health services, transportation necessary for adequate patient care, and hospital and specialty care. Sometimes called "safety net providers," FQHCs have been a major positive development in making health care more widely available. They make reasonably priced and accessible health care available geographically, financially, and culturally (Hadley and Cunningham 2004). Even so, federal programs do not come close to eliminating the health care gap between those covered by private insurance and government-sponsored programs. This applies especially to the border region (Hunter et al. 2003).

Colonia Health: Programs and Binational Initiatives

The problems of border health and health delivery have drawn the attention of numerous binational, federal, and state agencies, as well as nongovernmental organizations (NGOs). This concluding section summarizes well-known binational and federal agencies that work along the entire length of the border, but it is noteworthy that the states of Texas, New Mexico, Arizona, and Califonia sponsor other programs that are geared to local needs. Various NGOs, both faith-based and secular, also provide much-needed health care as they work tirelessly to meet the needs of border dwellers, many of whom reside in colonias. Others reach out to farmworkers and the immigrant population who, because of their unauthorized status, are often underserved by government agencies. Some state-sponsored programs and some initiatives launched by NGOs are showcased in subsequent chapters.

The U.S.–Mexico Border Health Commission provides the most extensive coverage of health issues in the border region. As a binational organization, formed in 2000, it unites federal and state health officials and professionals in ten border states: six in Mexico and four in the United States. It serves the health needs of all U.S. communities located within 62 miles (100 kilometers) of the borderline. As a binational organization, its mission is to provide leadership in identifying and highlighting the most prevalent health problems along the border and advocating for and monitoring the improvement of those health conditions. In its *Healthy Border 2010* report (U.S.–Mexico Border Health Commission 2003), the commission identified 11 target areas of health promotion and disease prevention. For each of the target disease conditions, the commission presents goals (some very specific) to be achieved in both Mexico and the United States in reducing disease prevalence. The 10 disease target areas can be organized into three general headings: chronic diseases, preventive health, and environmental health. Subsumed under chronic diseases are cancer, diabetes mellitus, asthma, HIV/AIDS, and respiratory disease. The preventive health target category includes maternal, infant, and child health; mental health; oral health; immunization and infectious diseases; and injury prevention. Environmental health targets include exposure to a wide variety of hazards affecting border residents—air, water, soil, no or substandard drainage and sewer facilities resulting in contaminated water and lack of potable water—and pesticide poisoning hospitalization.

The U.S. Environmental Protection Agency is another binational program that applies to the entire length of the border. The EPA's goals and objectives are reported in its *U.S.–Mexico Environmental Program: Border 2012* (2007a). This is a collaboration between the United States and Mexico to improve the environment and protect the health of the entire border population. The EPA targets twin (cross-border) cities in the border region, because they house about 90 percent of the population. The EPA is especially concerned with physically based causes of health problems such as insufficient infrastructure (potable water, sanitation, paved streets and roads), because they are the source of many illnesses. The EPA also addresses issues of air pollution and air quality monitoring in the region's largest cross-border cities. To meet this challenge, the Border 2012 program has established six goals: reduce water contamination, reduce air pollution, reduce land contamination, improve environmental health, reduce exposure to chemicals as a result of accidental chemical release, and improve environmental health.

The U.S. Geological Survey (USGS) developed the U.S.–Mexico Environmental Health Initiative to provide Web-based mapping and research tools that enable exploration of a range of environmental health issues that span the U.S.–Mexico border (U.S. Geological Survey 2008). The USGS provides detailed mapping and analysis facilities that enable investigation of a range of environmental health issues that stem from rapid population growth and urbanization in the border region. These include infrastructure, water quality and depletion, airborne pollutants (especially in and near major cross-border urban centers), and groundwater contamination resulting from agriculture and mining.

The U.S.–Mexico Border Health Association is the longest-standing binational health program in the border region. Founded in 1943, the assocation continues its long tradition of providing health care to communities on both sides of the border (U.S.–Mexico Border Health Association n.d.). The binational mission is accomplished by bringing together health professionals from Mexico and the United States in all four border states. The association handles a broad range of health issues but focuses on the prevention of infectious diseases such as HIV/AIDS and tuberculosis, substance abuse, environmental health, and education. Some of the programs are sponsored by the Centers for Disease Control and Prevention, but the association relies on private donations for many of the programs offered.

The U.S.–Mexico Border Centers of Excellence Consortium, based at the University of New Mexico, aims to fill the shortage of health-care professionals in the border region, especially for Hispanics (Hispanic and Native American Center of Excellence n.d.). This is accomplished by providing training for Hispanic health-care professionals and investigating the needs of predominantly Hispanic communities. The consortium also monitors funded research projects that target border health issues, including cancer, HIV/AIDS, diabetes, and cardiovascular disease. It brings together university-based health science centers in Texas, New Mexico, Arizona, and California, as well as the U.S–Mexico Border Health Commission.

There are other, less-recognized organizations and agencies that warrant mention. First, USA–Mexico Border Health is a Web-based project funded by the U.S. Department of Health and Human Services through its Office of Rural Health Policy (USA–Mexico Border Health 2008). The Web portal provides assistance in identifying funding agencies, grant writing, and information on numerous border health issues. It caters to the needs of communities located within 62 miles of either side of the border, from Texas to California. Second, the Centers for Disease Control and Prevention are engaged in many collaborative projects, some of which are binational, that deal exclusively with the border region (Centers for Disease Control and Prevention n.d.). These include public and environmental health issues such as diabetes, respiratory ailments, and environmental health hazards. Finally, the U.S./Mexico Border Counties Coalition conducts research on a range of issues that affect the border, including the rising cost of health care (U.S./Mexico Border Counties Coalition 2002). They find a substantial shortfall in funding for hospitals and clinics located in the 24 border counties and attribute some of the cost to unauthorized immigration.

Summary

In the U.S.–Mexico border region, poverty and deprivation are the rule rather than the exception. These conditions arose from age-old forces that led to the deep-seated inequality and social injustice that we see today. From Texas to California, colonia residents struggle in the mire of history as they confront a host of problems.

It is impossible, perhaps inappropriate, to speak of health as a separate issue, because it is connected to the mix of economic, social, and political forces that weave the very fabric of society. This chapter responded to this interdependency by focusing on the interplay of economy, society, and health, summarizing the principal public and environmental health issues, placing them into a sytems-based model, and describing several organizations that provide valuable health services in the border region. My efforts here aim to bring these issues forward, rather than delving deeper into any particular theme. Readers will find much more depth as subsequent chapters explore specific health issues in greater detail, especially the role that NGOs play in health-care delivery.

Notes

1. There are multiple ways of designating what represents the U.S.–Mexico "border." I use this one because it is the most focused way to think geographically and politically about the U.S. side of the border, but I also recognize that there are good reasons to designate the border more broadly. One reason is that it is an empirical question as to how far the border's influence extends beyond the border.

2. See Taylor (2004) for an excellent review of community health centers, the umbrella concept under which rural health clinics exist.

12

Colonias Health Issues in Texas

Sergio Peña and E. Lee Rosenthal

NUMEROUS HEALTH ISSUES in Texas colonias have drawn the attention of federal and state agencies as well as nongovernmental organizations (NGOs). Federal and state agencies have favored place-based solutions, especially infrastructure upgrades (potable water, sanitation, and paved streets and roads), while NGOs have pursued people-based strategies. These efforts are certainly needed, but, at a deeper level, there is little conceptual understanding of how, and why, colonias emerged as unhealthy places.

This chapter fills the gap by examining both space/place and human dimensions of colonias health. In the first instance, we explore the relationship between space and colonias health by responding to the following question: how does space or place shape health among colonia residents? Our premise is that the way space is organized goes a long way in explaining varying levels of health and health care. In the second instance, we look at how people's background and behavior affect health. The following question guides our analysis: how do biology, personal behavior, and environment shape health outcomes? While space/place and human dimensions are interrelated, policies and programs emphasize one or the other. We argue that an integrated approach to colonias health and health care will meet with greater success.

The chapter is organized into three sections. The first identifies the types of illnesses and disease prevalent in Texas colonias and shows how they have been linked to the lack of infrastructure. The second section deals with the physical (space/place) and human dimensions of colonias health. We present a conceptual model that links space/place to the health disparities that colonias face. Finally, we describe policies and programs that target both people and place by focusing on the community health worker approach, also known as the *promotores(as) approach.*

Colonias and Health Issues in Texas

About two decades have passed since colonias emerged on the public policy agenda in the state of Texas. From the outset, colonias were treated as unregulated subdivisions that lacked the basic infrastructure found in conventional subdivisions (Mukhija and Monkkonen 2007). For this reason, in 1989 the 71st Texas legislature passed Senate Bill 2, creating the Economically Distressed Area Program (EDAP) to provide basic infrastructure. Since then, the Texas Water Development Board (TWDB) has conducted comprehensive studies and assessments of Texas colonias.

The Texas legislature was moved to action because of the size of the colonias population and the severity of conditions they have faced. Using TWDB data, Carter and Ortolano (2004) estimated that there were approximately 1,500 colonias in Texas and about 400,000 residents. A more recent report set the number of colonias at 1,786, with an estimated population of 359,825 (Institute for Policy and Economic Development 2006). Five counties house about 94 percent of the colonias population: Hidalgo (156,132), El Paso (77,864), Cameron (47,606), Starr (34,742), and Webb (21,022). The institute's report emphasized the connection between physical infrastructure and public health, which remains a critical problem in Texas colonias. The report developed a threefold typology that classified colonias according to the level of infrastructure available and associated health risks. The first category of colonias was assigned the lowest health risk and greatest access to infrastructure such as potable water, wastewater, paved roads, drainage, and solid waste disposal. This set accounts for 36 percent of all colonias and 40 percent of the total population. Colonias in the second category are exposed to "intermediate" health risks because some infrastructure is available, such as paved roads and solid waste disposal. Twenty-two percent of colonias and 29 percent of the total colonia population fall within this category. Finally, colonias in the third group have the highest health risk because they lack access to basic infrastructure such as potable water and wastewater treatment. This category claims 25 percent of colonias and 17 percent of the population. In sum, about half of the residents (46 percent) live in intermediate or high health-risk colonias.

Monitoring health risks in colonias is challenging, because most data are reported at the county level. Thus, colonia health-related data, for the most part, are generated through case studies (Haass et al. 1996; LaWare and Rifai 2006; Leach et al. 2000; Ortiz, Arizmendi, and Llewellyn 2004; Ramos, May, and Ramos 2001). The theme common to these studies is that health risks or illnesses prevalent among colonia residents are often infectious and communicable diseases linked to unsafe drinking water and substandard sanitation. Hepatitis A, shigellosis, typhoid, salmonellosis, and giardiasis are among the most common diseases mentioned.

While not optimal, county-level data provide a general picture of the health problems confronting colonia residents. More so, these data illustrate the importance of space, or place, in understanding colonia health issues. We expect, for example, that counties housing the majority of the colonias population will exhibit higher incidence rates for illnesses related to unsafe water and poor sanitation. Doyle and Bryan's study (2000) of border health supported this claim. Their study investigated border health for the years 1990–98 by comparing illness incidence rates for three regions: (1) the border region, which includes 48 counties located within 100 kilometers of the border; (2) border states excluding the 48 counties; and (3) the entire United States. They found that incidence rates in the 48 border counties (region 1) were greater than in the border states (region 2) for food-borne botulism, human rabies, brucellosis, diphtheria, rubella, hepatitis A, legionellosis, mumps, shigellosis, pertussis, measles, and salmonellosis. Compared to the nation as a whole, the border region scored comparatively high on the incidence of brucellosis, food-borne botulism, Hansen's diseases, measles, rabies, hepatitis A, plague, diphtheria, cholera, shigellosis, rubella, hepatitis B, tetanus, mumps, typhoid fever, and salmonellosis. These results are consistent with those reported by Haass et al. (1996), who found higher incidence rates in El Paso's colonias for Campylobacter enteritis, hepatitis A, and salmonellosis.

Space, Class, and Health in Colonias

The data reported above clarify the relationship between location and health by linking geography, or space, to the incidence of illnesses. Our conceptualization of space and health builds on three interrelated factors: space/place, social class, and differential levels of health. As noted above, space is important because it captures the relationship between location and illnesses that are related to poor sanitary conditions (infrastructure).

Thus, understanding how urban space is produced and organized is critical. Social class is also important, because the socioeconomic profile of colonias reveals an obvious class/ethnic bias (e.g., low levels of educational attainment, Hispanics, low-skilled blue-collar workers).

Two theoretical traditions are often used to explain how urban space is produced and organized: neoclassical economics and critical theory based on Marxist analysis.[1] The neoclassical approach argues that market forces govern the production and organization of urban space (the built environment). From this perspective, the market is a neutral institution that allocates resources (land and location) to the highest and best use. Thus, access to housing, land, and other goods and services such as health are determined by the ability and willingness to "outbid" competitors by paying the most. Furthermore, the lack of health services or access to decent and affordable housing is seen as a market failure. Government intervention is often used as a mechanism to "fix" these market failures, which are labeled externalities, monopolies, asymmetric information, and public goods (Levy 1995). Public choice, a variant of neoclassical theory, views political decisions and policies similarly. In this case, politicians, consumers, and bureaucrats are considered rational actors that seek to maximize their benefits. Thus, instead of focusing on market failures, public choice points to "government failures." As such, colonias arise from the government's failure to uphold its primary function of police power: to protect the public's health, safety, and welfare.[2]

In contrast, critical or Marxist theory emphasizes social relations across space. The argument central to the neo-Marxist perspective is that we must delve deeper into the "fetishism" of space, because the physical object we call "city" is linked to societal relations (class, gender, race) found in cities (Castells 2000; Harvey 2002; Soja 1980). Cities affect the spatial arrangement of urban space as they facilitate capital accumulation, the essential condition of capitalism (Harvey cited by Allmendinger 2002). Thus, urban space is the tangible outcome of class relations and struggle, rather than the neutral or class-blind product of market forces.

Neoclassical economists (and most urban planners) and Marxists hold far different perspectives on how society clusters across urban space. In the first case, economists and planners see the clustering (spatial segregation) of social groups as a "sorting" process that is guided by market forces, in this case the urban housing market. The wealthy live among the wealthy because they have the wherewithal to do so, while the poor are excluded. This sorting leads to the formation of upscale neighborhoods and middle-class housing districts, while colonias, where the poor live, are isolated well beyond the urban fringe because land (housing) prices are lower. In the second instance, Marxists pin the formation and isolation of colonias to complex social and class relations rather than neutral market forces. They argue that, historically, the poor, and minorities in particular, were denied access to institutions such as education and health care, thereby precluding social mobility. These social relations, which embody class-based and racial discrimination, perpetuate poverty and social isolation over time. The urban landscape, therefore, is itself an expression of social relations and class struggle. Regardless of the paradigm used to explain colonia formation, the outcome is the same: spatially isolated communities (colonias) that often lack basic infrastructure and reveal higher rates of illness.

The field of public health is rich in the study of social inequality, geography, and health (Curtis 2004; Kreiger and Zierler 1996; Marmot and Wilkinson 1999). Marmot and Wilkinson argued that there is a strong relationship between poverty and health; those traditionally excluded from mainstream society—minorities, refugees, the unemployed and the homeless—experience poor health. Curtis (2004) examined the relationship between inequality and health by drawing on critical theory and the geography of urban landscapes. She argued that "the geography of health is focused on the ways that health of populations is differentiated between places and the range of factors that explain these differences. The concept of landscape has often been used to convey the idea of system factors and processes that interact in particular settings to produce geographical variations" (Curtis 2004, 22–23).

An Explanatory Model of Health Disparities in Texas Colonias

The above discussion demonstrates how and why colonias emerged as spatially isolated communities that expose residents to higher health risks because of infrastructure deficiencies. We now develop an explanatory model that summarizes how social, economic, and political forces lead to differential health outcomes. The model draws on the critical theory perspective by highlighting structural causes.

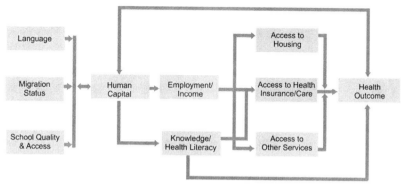

FIGURE 12.1 An explanatory model of colonias health. *Source:* The authors

The explanatory model presented in figure 12.1 demonstrates how health outcomes arise from a series of direct and indirect social and structural relationships. As described above, structural and class/ethnic relations often exclude colonia residents from acquiring human capital. Of the factors that preclude gains in human capital, education is perhaps the most important, because it is correlated strongly with income or earnings potential. Education is an investment people make in themselves with the expectation of improving social mobility. But colonia residents typically have lower levels of educational attainment than the population at large. In Texas, approximately 83 percent of the population has at least a high school diploma, compared to 31 percent in Starr and Hidalgo counties, where the majority of colonias are found (Ortiz, Arizmendi, and Llewellyn 2004). This is expected, because structural inequities favor funding for education in more wealthy suburbs at the expense of colonias. This demonstrates the importance of space/place in reproducing poverty versus privilege. Other factors, such as language and migration status, affect the ability to build human capital (Davidhizar and Bechtel 1999). Language skills (reading, writing, speech) are closely associated with income, because they open the door to education and employment. Migration status has become a far more critical issue in recent years, as the public and Congress seek to deny education to unauthorized immigrants. While Texas provides bilingual education, immigrant status often precludes access. This once again demonstrates how institutional and structural biases perpetuate inequality across the urban landscape.

Figure 12.1 shows that human capital is the gateway to differential health outcomes, because it shapes earning capacity and health literacy. Employment and higher incomes facilitate access to safe housing or shelter (which is serviced by adequate infrastructure), health insurance, and other services. Access to insurance affects the quality of health by opening the door to preventive and curative health care. It is estimated, for example, that 25 percent of Texas residents lack insurance; the percentage in Texas border counties ranges from 23 percent in Jefferson Davis County to 38 percent in Hudspeth County (Institute for Policy and Economic Development 2006). Two case studies of colonias in Starr and Hidalgo counties estimated the uninsured population at 42 percent (Ortiz, Arizmendi, and Llewellyn 2004). It is noteworthy that about two-thirds of colonia residents are U.S. citizens, and many are eligible for government-sponsored health insurance such as Medicare, Medicaid, or the State Children's Health Insurance Program (SCHIP). Colonia residents, however, are often unaware of these programs despite their eligibility (Eldridge 2002).

Access to health insurance cannot be explained without accounting for structural and institutional biases in the U.S. health-care system, in Texas in particular. The reliance on the market to provide health care is deeply embedded in the United States. But this market system precludes certain populations from accessing health care, because they are unwilling or unable to pay for health insurance and/or medical care. Because health care organizations (HCOs) operate under economies of scale, the larger the pool of participants, the lower the costs of premiums (Curtis 2004). It is more common for larger firms or employers to offer insurance as a fringe benefit, but this means that employee productivity must exceed the cost of insurance premiums. Therefore, employees working for larger corporations are more likely to be insured. But colonia residents face a far different health insurance environment. Some studies (Eldridge 2002; Ortiz, Arizmendi, and Llewellyn 2004) emphasized that colonia residents are a classic example of a "reserve labor force" that holds menial jobs and faces a higher-than-average rate of unemployment. As a consequence, they are less likely to be insured.[3] A recent study found that unemployment in five Lower Rio Grande Valley colonias ranged from 20 percent to 60 percent, while the rate for the State of Texas equaled 7 percent. Residents in these colonias were usually employed in agricultural work (30 percent), construction (24 percent), and factory work (15 percent) (Federal Reserve Bank of Dallas 2007). Class and ethnic differences, therefore, filter through the marketplace and deepen the social divide between the haves and have-nots.

The lack of access to other services, such as transportation and child care, contributes to differential health outcomes. Transportation is especially important for minorities and low-wage earners, because jobs are most often found well beyond places of residence (Diaz 2005; Esparza and Donelson 2008; Levy 2006). The lack of access to these jobs and services, therefore, lowers earning capacity.

As figure 12.1 indicates, health literacy is also instrumental in shaping the quality of health and health care. It is widely understood that educated people are more likely to adopt forward-looking health habits. These include regular exercise, healthful diets, familiarity with health risks, and better knowledge of how to access health-care services.

The Human Dimension of Health in Texas Colonias

To this point we have summarized space/place-based health problems in colonias and linked them to broader social and economic forces. This section considers how the human dimension of health leads to differential health outcomes. Our approach classifies health-related problems and the causes of illness into three dimensions. These include biological, behavioral/lifestyle, and environmental/place-based factors.

From the perspective of biology, colonia residents have the same probability of developing certain illnesses as the broader group they are part of—Hispanics, in this case. Hispanics and African Americans, for example, are more likely to develop diabetes than are white non-Hispanics. Even though colonias residents have an equal chance of developing certain illnesses, a principal difference is whether they have access to primary, secondary, and tertiary medical care services. Differential levels of health, therefore, are related to several factors, including biology and economic means.

The second dimension of health deals with personal behavior. In this case, poor health is related to the choices people make and the health-care services that are available. Cardiovascular disease (hypertension, heart problems, unhealthy levels of cholesterol), for example, is associated with personal choice (diet and exercise) and biological factors (genetics) as well as access to care. This, once again, brings socioeconomic status forward, because it is related to risk taking and health. Persons of higher socioeconomic status consume healthier food and spend more hours exercising (Ehrenberg and Smith 2000).

The third dimension, environment, is particularly important, because it emphasizes space/location. There are several scales of space, ranging from the most intimate and personal to public spaces (public plaza, street), that relate to people's well-being (Madanipour 2003). In other words, the physical and social environment people experience affects health. For instance, crowded living conditions within a house shape personal space, while the lack of usable public spaces (e.g., parks) may limit physical activity and may provoke risky behaviors that have health implications (Dannenberg et al. 2003; Frumkin 2003). Wallisch and Spence (2006), for example, found higher rates of binge drinking and alcohol dependence among colonia residents than in urban areas in El Paso.

In summarizing this section, it is important to emphasize that the space/place and human dimensions of colonias are interdependent. Colonias emerged from deep-rooted socioeconomic, structural, and political forces that led to communities rife with unhealthful environments. These environments, in turn, shape personal health through the loss of private and social space and the adoption of unhealthful (risky) behavior that lessens quality of life and longevity. While the influences of place versus people are difficult to untangle, policies and programs treat them as separate issues.

Policies, Health, and Health Care in Colonias

There is no doubt that colonias and their residents require assistance to meet immediate and longer-term health needs. It has long been the case, however, that policy and programs focus on either the physical or the human dimension of colonias health. This section looks more closely at policies and programs by describing the community health worker approach, one of the most successful people-based initiatives in the Texas–Mexico border region.

Community Health Workers/
Promotores(as) in Texas Colonias

People-based programs have proven successful in meeting the health and health-care needs of colonias. They emerged in part because colonia residents do not have health insurance, health care, or even health promotion services. Few colonia residents have jobs that provide health coverage, and recent changes in Texas law concerning Medicaid have left a growing number of people without government-supported health insurance (Eldridge 2002). This applies to persons residing legally in the United States as well as to undocumented immigrants who entered the country after August 1996. The lack of public and private insurance shifted the burden for health care to the nonprofit sector (Eldridge 2002).

Community health centers (CHCs) throughout Texas have been filling the vacuum left by private and public sectors (Perez and Martinez 2008). According to the Texas Association of Community Health Centers (n.d.) there are thirty-seven centers scattered across the state, with ten located near the border: two in El Paso and the remainder in the Lower Rio Grande Valley of south Texas. There are four types of CHCs: (1) community health centers; (2) migrant health centers; (3) rural health clinics, and; (4) federally qualified health center look-alikes (Eldridge 2002). Community health centers target populations that are least likely to receive primary and preventive care.

Community health workers, also known as *promotores(as)* (CHW/Ps) are among the most successful outreach health programs adopted by CHCs (Bowden et al. 2006; Olney et al. 2007; Ramos, May, and Ramos 2001). CHW/P programs are often based in CHCs, both federally recognized and free-standing, but are also housed in community and faith-based organizations. The CHW/P approach plays an increasingly important role in accessing health care in the U.S.–Mexico border region, across the United States, and abroad (Bowden et al. 2006; Davidhizar and Bechtel 1999; Mier et al. 2007; Olney et al. 2007; Ortiz, Arizmendi, and Llewellyn 2004; Ramos, May, and Ramos 2001; U.S. Department of Health and Human Services 2007; Witmer et al. 1995). Strong roots in less-developed countries, including many programs in Latin America, influenced their popularity in the Texas–Mexico region.

Promotores(as) are either volunteers or paid staff. The National Community Health Advisor Study (Rosenthal et al. 1998) and the more recent CHW National Workforce Study (U.S. Department of Health and Human Services 2007) found that approximately 75 percent of the CHW/P workforce is paid for full- or part-time work, while the remainder consists of volunteers. CHW/Ps are often recruited from communities because of their leadership skills, while at other times they simply respond to job notices. Once in the program, their education varies, but, in general, CHW/Ps' training builds on their knowledge of the community. For some promotores(as), training may last a single day, while other situations may require a year-long college program. As of 2001, Texas CHW/Ps can be certified by the state. Only two states have certification programs; Texas was the first to move in this direction (Texas Department of State Health Services 2007; U.S. Department of Health and Human Services 2007).

Promotores serve a range of roles in colonias depending on local assets, needs, and funding availability (McKnight 1995). In simple terms, CHW/Ps open doors by bridging the divide between the haves and have-nots. This is accomplished by bringing health services and colonia residents together. In some cases, this requires that CHW/P workers reach out to organizations so that resources are channeled to colonias. In other cases, promotores(as) point colonia residents to resources outside the community (Power and Byrd 1998; Swider 2002). Promotores(as) also provide information on chronic diseases, such as diabetes management, potable water, safe sanitation practices, and infectious disease control, and teach advocacy skills so that residents can access health-care resources on their own.

Two examples illustrate how programs and promotores(as) promote, or instigate, health promotion and outreach. The first example involves Clinica Guadalupana, founded in 1994 by the Sisters of Charity. The clinic is an independently operated NGO without a federal health centers system designation. Clinica Guadalupana serves residents in nine colonias near Horizon City, which is located on the outskirts of El Paso. The clinic offers primary medical care services to area residents and is currently supported by the work of one promotora who offers health education to clinic patients as a follow-up to visits with primary care providers.

The promotor(a) program has several components that have changed over time to meet the needs of the community and clinic. One unique community-building activity is a small thrift store that recycles area goods at affordable prices. The store is housed within the clinic's facility and provides a gathering place for colonia residents. Currently, one emphasis of the clinic's promotor(a) program is diabetes education. The program features a homemade "flip chart" that facilitates one-on-one and small-group *pláticas* (talks).

The second program, Migrant Health Promotion (MHP), was formerly known as the Midwest Migrant Health Information Office. It was established in 1983 through a faith-based initiative. Like Clinica Guadalupana, MHP is a free-standing community-based NGO receiving some federal programmatic support. It serves migrant and seasonal farmworkers, particularly in Texas, Michigan, and the midwestern United States. A number of Texas colonias benefit from the MHP.

A primary activity of the MHP is a training program for adult and teen migrant farmworkers so that they can become camp health aides and teen health aides. The aides, or CHW/Ps, come from the communities they serve and address individual and community development through health education and community advocacy. Like Clinica Guadalupana, CHW/Ps provide information on diabetes management; they also stress access to healthful environments and issues like avoiding pesticide exposure. They also support advocacy training programs for area residents. One program, known as Voz Latina, provided instruction on how to engage the media and local policy makers so that residents have a stronger voice in decision making.

These examples demonstrate the importance of CHW/P programs in providing health-care services to colonia residents. But these, and other programs, struggle for resources, an issue that challenges their longer-term sustainability. More so, their financial hardship highlights the nearly singular focus on programs that target physical improvements at the expense of people-based assistance.

Summary

Colonias across the entire border region confront a range of health problems, but those in Texas have received the bulk of attention. This is understandable, because Texas houses the lion's share of colonias and the largest colonias population. Poor health drew the attention of federal and state government agencies years ago, and they pursued a strategy of improving health by building and expanding infrastructure in colonias. There is no question that investments in infrastructure have produced positive results, as many illnesses are linked to poor sanitation, poor water quality, and unpaved streets and roads. But the Texas legislature continues to channel most of its resources into physical improvements despite the growing need for people-based programs and initiatives. This has placed much of the health care burden on the shoulders of NGOs that struggle to provide basic services to colonia residents, most of whom are uninsured. This means that NGOs, and promotores(as) in particular, carry a greater share of the health care load, even though their budgets are stretched thin.

This chapter sought to demonstrate the need for a more balanced approach to health care in Texas colonias. Such an approach should confront the deeper causes of inequity and disadvantage that led to the emergence of colonias in the first place. Instead of tackling these issues head-on, civic leaders and legislators have chosen to reduce the problem of poor health to physical solutions (infrastructure) while neglecting the human dimension—the care of people. We illustrated how investing in people and the provision of public spaces (e.g., parks and fitness centers), will go a long way in improving health as colonia residents reshape their vision of the future.

Acknowledgments

The authors wish to acknowledge contributions to this chapter made by Gloria Morales and Deb Benedict at Clinica Guadalupana, and Lucy Felix and Genoveva Martinez at Migrant Health Promotion, as well as other staff of these two organizations.

Notes

1. "The production of urban space" refers to how different functions or activities (residential, commercial, industrial, infrastructure, roads) are organized and distributed in space. Harvey (1985) refers to urban space as "the built environment."

2. From a perspective of planning law, local governments are granted two powers that directly impact the production of urban space. The Fifth Amendment of the Constitution grants the power of eminent domain, which authorizes government to

take land for a valid public purpose with just compensation to the owner. The police power conferred to government by the Tenth Amendment grants the authority to pass laws to protect safety and health, and to ensure comfort and prosperity to its citizens (Blaesser and Weinstein 1989).

3. Sassen (2001), using Marxist categories, distinguishes between "core" and "reserve labor" (cited in Curtis 2004). Reserve labor is normally those employees that are disposable or the first ones to be let go when the corporation needs to make adjustments. Farmworkers and blue-collar workers are facing job insecurity in the new service economy of advanced countries.

13

Social Justice and Health in Arizona Border Communities

THE COMMUNITY HEALTH WORKER MODEL

Samantha Sabo, Maia Ingram, and Ashley Wennerstrom

THE UNITED NATIONS WORLD HEALTH ORGANIZATION defines health as "a state of complete physical, mental and social well-being and not merely the absence of disease or infirmity" (World Health Organization 1986). Public health is the means through which society creates conditions that favor the achievement of optimal health within populations, and accordingly it focuses on prevention rather than treatment of disease. Public health is a collective response to groups and communities—the public as a whole—rather than to individuals. Thus, public health must be concerned with social and economic conditions that are at the core of health outcomes. Public health becomes an instrument of social justice, because it advocates for equitable distribution of the resources and circumstances that influence health, such as access to health care, adequate housing, availability of recreational areas and healthful food, and environmentally safe neighborhoods.

The magnitude of health disparities among subgroups of the U.S. population is a major public health concern and indicative of injustices that exist in our society. Latinos, African Americans, and Native Americans suffer higher rates of morbidity and mortality due to diabetes, asthma, cancer, heart disease, and a variety of other diseases than do whites.

Unfortunately, public health efforts to address health inequities tend to focus on symptoms: promoting personal behavior change through culturally appropriate educational interventions, increasing access to care through outreach and referral, improving health literacy, and improving patient provider communication. While perhaps effective in addressing individual health outcomes among target populations, these strategies have had virtually no impact on closing the gap in health status between people of color and their white counterparts. Limited success is not surprising, given that traditional public health strategies are not necessarily grounded in a social justice perspective that seeks to transform the institutions that are at the root of health inequities. Hoffrichter (2003) makes the point that it is necessary to address the systematic treatment of people as members of a definable group and ensure an equal distribution of life opportunities.

People living in colonias along the U.S.–Mexico border suffer disproportionately from the root causes of health disparities and their health outcomes. If the U.S. border region were made into a state, it would rank last in access to health care, last in per capita income, first in number of children living in poverty, first in number of children who do not have health insurance, second in rates of hepatitis deaths, and third in death related to diabetes (U.S.–Mexico Border Health Commission 2003).

With a focus on Arizona, this chapter describes health issues in border communities from a broad perspective that includes the social determinants of health. The community health worker (CHW) model is explored as a means to address health disparities through case studies in two communities along the Arizona–Sonora border. Finally, recommendations to enhance the potential for the CHW model to address the root causes rather than symptoms of health inequities by advocating for community organization and empowerment are provided.

Social Disparities and Access to Health Care in the U.S.–Mexico Border Region

The U.S. border population has more than doubled since 1970, from 3.1 million people to 6.6 million people in 2000, and is projected to have 9.4 million people by 2020 (U.S.–Mexico Border Health Commission 2003). The border state of Arizona experienced the greatest increase in population, growing by more than four million people over the last 30 years. A growing percentage of the border population is of Latino origin. U.S. Census Bureau estimates for 2006 indicate that nearly 15 percent of the U.S. population identify themselves as Hispanic, while over

29 percent of Arizona's population is Hispanic. In border counties percentages fluctuate between 25 percent and 99 percent. These populations reflect a relatively young population and a high birthrate, as well as increased migratory flow northward from Mexico. Educational attainment among the U.S. border population, a fundamental indicator of social equity, is among the lowest in the nation and is even more striking based on proximity to the border. In Arizona, 50 percent of Nogales City residents in Santa Cruz County do not have a high school diploma or GED equivalent, compared to 25 percent of all residents in that county, a trend that is observed in all Arizona border cities (Arizona Department of Health Services 2003). Poverty rates are among the highest in the nation (U.S.–Mexico Border Health Commission 2003).

Access to Health Care

From a public health perspective, access to health care is the major indicator of social equity and a barometer of social justice. Access to care, including preventive care and general health information as well as the diagnosis and treatment of health problems, is critical to creating and maintaining healthy communities. For the purpose of this chapter, access to health care provides the lens through which to analyze problems and solutions.

Health insurance is the single most significant contributor to accessing care (Centers for Disease Control and Prevention 2004; Cohen, Meister, and de Zapien 2004; Parchman and Byrd 2001). On average, one-third of border residents do not have health insurance, and in some communities the percentage of uninsured is as high as 60 percent (Bastidea, Brown, and Pagán 2008). Among border residents in Arizona, those least likely to have health insurance include the unemployed (47 percent), those with less than a high school education (43 percent), and Hispanics (43 percent), further evidence of the association between access to care and other social inequities (Arizona Department of Health Services 2007). Uninsured residents in border comminutes are also more likely to deprive themselves of health care because of cost (U.S. National Center for Health Statistics 2006). The uninsured, and many times the insured, seek low-cost health care and the accessibility of Spanish-speaking providers across the border into Mexico (Hunter et al. 2003, 2004;

Landeck and Garza 2002; Macias and Morales 2001; Seid, Stevens, and Varni 2003).

However, insurance is only one aspect of health access. Even those who are eligible for federally funded insurance do not necessarily avail themselves of the resource. In Arizona in 2007, only 50 percent of children eligible for SCHIP (State Children's Health Insurance Program) or Medicaid insurance programs were currently enrolled in those programs, a percentage likely to be lower in border communities.

Other factors related to health-care access include having an adequate number of primary health-care providers, and in particular Spanish-speaking providers, culturally competent health-care organizations, health-care specialists, and specialty care requiring advanced technology, all located within reasonable proximity to the population in need. In border counties there are scarce health-care resources, insufficient hospital beds, few doctors, and fewer nurses and dentists. The majority of border communities are recognized and designated as health professions shortage areas (HPSAs).

Disempowerment of Border Communities

There is growing concern that the militarization of the border in response to immigration increases the stress of residents both documented and undocumented and negatively impacts their ability to access health and other services. Over the past few years, scholars, human rights groups, and journalists have found that U.S. Border Patrol enforcement practices and increasing political hostility (e.g., so-called "civil patrols" of anti-immigrant Americans along the border) toward Hispanics have created a climate of profound fear within the Hispanic community (Romero and Marwah 2005; U.S. Commission on Civil Rights 2002), resulting in underutilization of health and human services by the border population. Furthermore, recent legislation in Arizona denying undocumented immigrants access to public housing, public health care, a college education, publicly funded child care, and utility assistance has intensified the problem. Human services not even yet affected by such legislation have seen a drop-off in the level of participation by Hispanics due to fear that they will be harassed, lose their immigration documents, or be apprehended by U.S. Border Patrol agents.

The Community Health Worker Model

From a social justice perspective, solutions to the glaring health disparities in border communities lie in the potential for border residents to increase their participation in the civic process, to generate collective action, and to pressure private and public institutions to create a more egalitarian system that protects health (Wallack 2003). The current climate of fear and disempowerment, to even utilize available services, speaks of the challenges facing attempts at community organizing. For example, only 38 percent of registered voters in Santa Cruz County participated in the 2002 elections, compared to 56 percent for the state (Arizona Secretary of State 2002).

Community health workers (CHWs), also known as promotores(as), community health advisors, lay health advisors, outreach workers, and community health advocates, have been working with Latino populations along the U.S.–Mexico border for several decades. CHWs are well-respected, indigenous community members who seek to eliminate prominent health problems by increasing health-care utilization, providing health education, and advocating for patient needs. CHWs have successfully increased health knowledge and/or health service utilization in many areas, including nutrition (Elder et al. 2005), diabetes (Corkery et al. 1997), chronic disease screening (Hunter et al. 2004), and cancer screening (Hansen et al. 2005; Navarro et al. 1998).

CHWs also have the capacity to address the root causes of health disparities. CHWs have an intimate knowledge of community needs and extensive awareness of community resources, and are considered leaders among their peers. These qualities place CHWs in a unique position to represent their communities and advocate on a community level by pressuring lawmakers to pursue structural changes that will address health inequities.

Use of the Promotor(a) Model in Arizona Colonias

Since the launch of Comienzo Sano in 1987, a prenatal outreach and education intervention in Yuma County along the U.S.–Mexico border, researchers in southern Arizona have collaborated with border communities in Yuma, Santa Cruz, and Cochise counties to develop, implement, and evaluate programs utilizing the CHW model. Comienzo Sano was eventually sustained as a line item of the Arizona Department of Health Services budget and is now implemented in rural and underserved communities throughout Arizona (Meister and de Zapien 1989; Meister et al. 1992). Since that time, several CHW organizations have been initiated in border counties, with projects addressing chronic disease, environmental health, infectious disease, violence, and substance use. A common attribute of all programs is that CHWs advocate for members of their community to gain access to health-related resources.

There is limited academic research on the role of CHWs as community organizers. But one Arizona border project, the Border Health Strategic Initiative (Border Health ¡SI!), built on an academic–community partnership and funded by the Centers for Disease Control and Prevention from 2000 to 2003, was a comprehensive diabetes prevention and control program that centered around the use of CHWs to work across multiple domains of the community (Cohen and Ingram 2005). CHWs were crucial in engaging the community to address environmental changes conducive to health, and in successfully mobilizing program participants to lobby local politicians for increased funding for recreational areas (Meister and de Zapien 2005).

The remainder of this chapter uses case studies of diabetes and childhood obesity to explore the potential of CHWs as instruments of social change. We also discuss the CHW model's potential for addressing the core determinants of health disparities through community advocacy.

The Campesino Diabetes Management Program. Yuma County, Arizona, located along the border adjacent to Sonora, Mexico, is known as the lettuce capital of the nation. Yuma County has the largest number of farmworkers in the state: an estimated 35,000 to 60,000 farmworkers during the peak growing season. Strenuous labor, poverty, and social isolation place farmworkers at high risk for health problems and severely limited access to health care (California Institute for Rural Studies 2000). A 2002 survey found that only 10 percent of Yuma farmworkers completed the equivalent of a high school education (Yuma Private Industry Council 2002). The Arizona Department of Economic Services estimates that the average annual family income for farmworkers equals $13,440. Lettuce workers may earn up to $7 per hour, but the average is $5.50 to

$6 per hour. During growing season, their day spans 12 to 14 hours in the fields and often includes commuting long distances to and from work. The long day combined with odd work schedules, language barriers, lack of insurance, and constant migration hinders the ability of farmworkers to access services. This causes a considerable gap in health-care access; the California Agricultural Workers Survey documents that 68 percent of male participants have never seen a doctor. More than two-thirds of the men and women have never had an eye exam, and there is extremely low access to dental care, as reflected by the high proportion of dental problems in the study sample. A household survey of farmworkers conducted in Yuma in 2007 finds that nearly half (46 percent) have no medical insurance, and 28 percent do not access needed medical care because of cost.

The Campesino Diabetes Management Program (CDMP) was created by Campesinos Sin Fronteras (Farmworkers without Borders), a promotor(a) program in South Yuma County serving farmworkers. The CDMP was one of eight demonstration projects funded by the Robert Wood Johnson Foundation Diabetes Initiative. The CDMP sought to build community support for diabetes self-management, because it is a growing health threat among farmworkers. The prevalence of diabetes in the Mexican American population is at least two to three times greater than among non-Hispanic whites (Bastidea, Cuéllar and Villas 2001; Health Resources and Services Administration 2000), and they are two to three times more likely to suffer from serious secondary complications (Garcia et al. 2001; Haffner et al. 1988; Haffner et al. 1990; Hanis et al. 1983). These challenges do not escape the farmworker population in Yuma County; in a Yuma household survey of farmworkers, 16 percent reported having been diagnosed with diabetes. The CDMP embraced the rationale that promotores(as) can build effective social support among diabetics in farmworker communities and, in so doing, improve self-management behaviors and clinical outcomes (Ingram et al. 2007).

Promotores(as) developed project activities and provided services that respond to the working hours and seasonal nature of farmworker communities. Participants determined both the duration and intensity of their involvement, rather than being forced into a controlled intervention. Promotores(as) supported participants through telephone calls and home visits, by encouraging more participation from those who did not attend meetings regularly, and by continuing to (re)invite nonparticipants. In crisis situations, promotores(as) increased their contact and at times made hospital visits. Weekly or biweekly support groups, facilitated by the promotores(as), became the principal CDMP activity. The gatherings were designed to provide information, build shared empathy, and create a support network. Emotional health was a common theme in group meetings, and, based on participant input, stress and depression became major topics. Patient advocacy was also a core component of the program.

The collaboration and commitment of the Sunset Community Health Center (SCHC) was essential to the CDMP. A promotor(a) at the clinic handled cross-referrals, provided basic diabetes education, set appointments for CDMP participants, and interacted with providers on patient issues. Over a two-year period, 260 people were recruited into the program. The CDMP participants were older, with an average of 59 years of age. Females comprised three-quarters of the participant population. Thirty-four percent of the 260 participants reported having no insurance, and 34 percent reported not having a regular doctor.

The CDMP had the luxury of resources for project evaluation that are found rarely in promotor(a) programs. In addition to collecting clinical data and conducting periodic questionnaires, promotores(as) carefully tracked their interactions with program participants and recorded comments for each contact. Over the course of approximately three years, the promotores(as) documented roughly 14,000 contacts with 260 CDMP participants. Among the 260 participants, promotores(as) provided a total of 120 advocacy services to 68, or one-fourth, of CDMP participants. The majority of these received more than one advocacy service.

The CDMP focused on self-management of a specific disease to minimize health complications. Advocacy activities, therefore, tended to focus on individual rather than community advocacy. A qualitative analysis of advocacy comments reveals that the majority of contacts were related to medical care (76 percent). Specific types of advocacy included helping participants find a medical home, completing and submitting insurance applications, providing medical advocacy in appointments, assisting participants in making timely or urgent medical appointments, and accessing free diabetes education. Medication is a cornerstone of diabetes care, and promotores(as) spent a substantial part of their contacts ensuring that participants were able to access medical supplies from insurance providers, including glucometers, strips, lancets, shoes, and medical transportation.

Promotores(as) often found that their advocacy required social support for retired farmworkers who are chronically ill and live in isolation. Promotores(as) also accessed free glaucoma exams for participants without insurance and provided health screenings and referrals to connect participants to the health care system. In a couple of cases, promotores(as) helped participants work through the process of obtaining medication.

In addition to medical care, advocates helped participants access community services. This can empower community members who are often unaware of their right to access a variety of resources and services. One example involved signing up participants for library cards. The promotor(a) indicated, "We took the group to the library to teach them how to look up information about diabetes and we helped them sign up for a library card." In several cases, the promotores(as) helped participants with paperwork related to Social Security or disability compensation. Promotores(as) also found themselves helping with basic needs such as food boxes and house repairs.

These activities demonstrate how promotores(as) advocate successfully by helping individuals overcome barriers to diabetes self-management, access resources, and participate in the public arena. This type of support empowers the community as knowledge and learning spillover over from family members to friends. This case study demonstrates the intimate relationship that promotores(as) have with the community, and their feeling of responsibility for confronting problems. Community advocacy seems a natural step in the progression of CHW efforts.

Steps to a Healthy Family (Pasos a una Familia Saludable). This program responds to the problems of overweight and obesity among Arizona border youth. These are serious problems across the nation, and in the border region in particular. Seventeen percent of children and adolescents in the United States are overweight, three times the percentage 30 years ago (Ogden et al. 2006). Childhood overweight and obesity raise the risks for the leading causes of death, including diabetes, cardiovascular disease, and cancer. Childhood overweight imposes even greater threats to ethnic and economically marginalized groups that already reveal major disparities in health and wellness. According to Ogden et al. (2006),

Mexican American children and adolescents are significantly more likely to be overweight than their non-Hispanic white counterparts. In Arizona border counties in 2006, the percentage of high school students reporting a body mass index (BMI) at or above the 95th percentile was higher (14 percent) than Arizona's youth (12 percent). In Santa Cruz County, where Steps to a Healthy Family is targeted, upward of 18 percent of girls and 17 percent of boys were at risk of becoming overweight. Seven percent of girls and 17 percent of boys were currently overweight (Youth Risk Behavior Surveillance System 2007).

Like so many youth in the United States, few adolescents in the Arizona border region heed recommended levels of nutritional and physical activity. Survey data (Youth Risk Behavior Surveillance System 2007) indicate that as of 2007, only 17 percent of Arizona border youth reported eating the daily recommended five or more fruits and vegetables required for maintaining good health. Twenty-nine percent were physically active for the recommended 60 minutes for five days of the week. Survey results also indicate that half of all border youth tried to lose weight or to keep from gaining weight (68 percent) through exercise and consuming less food, fewer calories, or less fat. These are positive prevention efforts, even proactive. But they are often coupled with negative weight loss behavior such as fasting for 24-hour periods (13 percent) and using diet aids in the form of pills, powders, or liquids without a doctor's advice (8 percent). Such self-harming behaviors are detrimental to youth's ability to maintain long-term health, academic achievement, and positive self-image and self-esteem. Finally, in 2007, one-third of border youth reported signs of depression, 15 percent considered suicide, and 10 percent had attempted suicide during the last year.

It is important to reflect on the basis of obesity among America's youth, especially those living in the border region. In simple terms, obesity is socially produced and evolves from interactions between the individual child and her or his environment. By this we mean that children respond to a multitude of socio-environmental factors that impact their decisions to "be healthy." In this regard, the built environment is particularly important, because it offers opportunities for healthful behavior. Publicly provided infrastructure such as parks, playgrounds, and sidewalks encourage children to engage in activities that promote health. At other times, however, the environment can thwart efforts to engage in healthful activities. These include real or perceived threats and dangers such as the absence of lighting and sidewalks, neighborhood decline, crime, "stranger danger," and roaming dogs, to name a few (Krahnstoever-Davison and Lawson 2006). These obstacles to building children's health are especially important in border colonias, because they often lack the infrastructure needed for safe and healthful environments.

These deficiencies, coupled with limited household budgets, prevent many parents from providing safe environments and encouraging healthful diets. Parents with limited financial resources and time cannot prepare meals at home or offer quality "family time" at the dinner table. Both these behaviors are associated with healthy weight in children (Krahnstoever-Davison and Lawson 2006).

Steps to a Healthy Family was developed within the context of the Mariposa Community Health Center (MCHC) Platicamos Salud Health Promotion Division. Project funding was provided by the Steps to a Healthier Arizona Initiative, funded by the Centers for Disease Control and Prevention and the Arizona Department of Health Services. Healthy Families is based on the CHW model and seeks to transform families experiencing childhood overweight by fostering communication and active relationships within families. The program also seeks to equip children and parents as advocates that promote change in the broader community.

Steps to a Healthy Family targets third- through fifth-grade children with body mass indices at or above the 95th percentile and includes the participation of at least one parent or guardian. The program spans a six-month period and consists of two 12-week phases. The program features weekly two-hour sessions that are facilitated by a nutritionist, a behavioral specialist, a physical educator, and a promotor(a). The first 12-week phase focuses on family awareness of healthful habits and communication. Participants discuss current approaches to healthful nutrition for families. They also explore physical activity through interactive family-oriented games. Family education stresses learning about positive reinforcement, emotions and eating, identifying overeating triggers, strategies for communication, self-talk, self-image, and self-esteem exploration.

The second 12-week phase emphasizes family readiness to change and individual goal setting. Families are encouraged to put in motion information acquired about healthful nutrition, family-based physical activity, and game time learned in the first session. At the end of each weekly session, children and parents set a weekly goal for discussion at the next session. During weekly sessions families learn strategies to increase fruit and vegetable intake and replace soda and sweet drinks with milk and water products. Family meal time and meal planning are introduced, as well as media literacy and television viewing and screen time. Physical activity is reinforced with a structured martial arts programs that claim 30 minutes of each two-hour session. Families are encouraged to supplement physical activity with participation in weekly structured school or community-based sports activities. Program organizers provide community resources to families concerning free and reduced-cost activities that promote physical activity and group play.

Since 2005, twenty families have participated in the Steps to a Healthy Family program, with children ranging from six to twelve years of age. Approximately two-thirds were girls. The 23 parent and guardian participants were predominantly female (86 percent). Families are Latino (95 percent) and predominantly of Mexican heritage. One-third of parents (34 percent) have less than a high school education, and 17 percent completed elementary school only. Almost half (48 percent) of families rely on publicly funded health-care mechanisms like Medicaid, Medicare, and the MCHC plan, which covers those who do not qualify for other federal programs. Seventeen percent of families reported no source of health care, while 21 percent had private U.S. insurance, and 13 percent accessed health care through the Mexican private sector. A little less than half (43 percent) of parent participants had someone they thought of as their primary care physician, and 17 percent of families went without medical attention in the prior year due to cost.

As the CHW model prescribes, Steps to a Healthy Family ensures that participant families have access to health care, and supports families in developing long-term relationships with primary care providers. Steps to a Healthy Family took the lead in connecting the dots between patients and providers by emphasizing dialogue and strong patient–provider relationships as the centerpiece of empowerment. CHWs and other program staff worked with clinic insurance liaisons to help families apply for publicly funded health access mechanisms.

The program also worked with families to advocate for policies that address school and community environments. Steps to a Healthy Family brought parents and school health personnel together to learn how to advocate for more nutritious school lunches and better physical education through a Family Health Advocacy Forum. The Advocacy Forum stressed the role of the built environment in enabling family activities outside the home. More than half of the Steps to a Healthy Family parents (56 percent) described living in neighborhoods beyond walking distances to a park, playground, or open space. Sixty-four percent believed the park or playground nearest their home was not safe during the day. Parents participating in the program believed that there are mechanisms to voice concerns about inadequate school services or resources (85 percent). They also expressed comfort in voicing their concerns (63 percent), and more than half (63 percent) actually do so more than half the time.

To better engage these already active families, community partners of the larger Steps to a Healthier Santa Cruz County Initiative developed a collaborative of 11 local youth-focused health and social service agencies, which included community health workers, to plan and organize a family health advocacy forum. The objective of the forum was threefold: (1) develop a collaborative of Santa Cruz County health and social service agencies and university partners to increase leadership and advocacy skills among all agencies and the families they serve; (2) inform parents and teens about the health status of their community through the most recently available Youth Risk Behavior Survey (YRBS) and Behavioral Risk Factor Survey (BRFS) data; and (3) develop an advocacy plan for neighborhood and community change.

Program organizers selected components of the University of Arizona Cooperative Extension's Arizona Community Training (ACT) curriculum and developed a bilingual workshop for parents and teens. A parent-versus-teen "jeopardy" game was developed to present the Santa Cruz County YRBS and BRFS data. This game engaged parents and teens in learning about the differences and similarities in youth and adult health behaviors, such as tobacco use, physical activity, and nutrition. Some families had reported prior experience in advocating for change with school boards and school administration. After the forum, parents and teens reported increased knowledge and confidence in their ability to advocate for or make changes in their home and family (70%), school (73%), neighborhood (81%), and county or state (85%).

The collaborating partners of the forum were activated by the process of planning and implementing the forum. Members continue to meet and focus on a county-wide initiative to increase enrollment of eligible children into the Arizona Health Care Cost Containment System (AHCCCS) KidsCare program, with the long-term goal of establishing school-based health centers.

Summary

Closing the gap in health disparities among communities on the U.S.–Mexico border will require drastic changes in the political sphere. Foremost is acceptance of health as a human right and the need to engage the most vulnerable populations and create a collective voice that resonates with agency and power. There is evidence that CHWs in Arizona are communicating with elected officials and political bodies, as well as with health and social service agencies, about making changes in their communities (Ingram et al. 2008); however, it is rarely the program focus. Community health worker training and job roles/responsibilities fail to stress the role of community advocacy and leadership, partly because CHW employment opportunities tend to stem from grant-funded programs that focus on short-term individual health outcomes. A collective shift in the field is needed to increase CHW community advocacy and address the root causes of health disparities. Collaboration between CHWs across agencies should be supported, and CHWS should be "expected to function as an advocacy group, meeting together to initiate interaction among their respective networks on a regular basis to carry out community wide activities" (Eng and Young 1992). Funding organizations and community members must understand that CHWs not only work to improve the health of individuals; they also elevate community health. Ultimately, this is the domain of public health.

Acknowledgments

Campesinos Sin Fronteras in Yuma County and the Mariposa Community Health Center Platicamos Salud in Santa Cruz County are two community health worker programs on the Arizona–Sonora border that have worked tirelessly to improve community health. The authors wish to thank the promotores(as) and other staff for sharing their programs, stories, and evaluation data.

14

Urbanization and Environmental Health in Arizona Colonias

Laura Norman

ENVIRONMENTAL HEALTH PROMOTES human health by preventing or mitigating exposure to factors that diminish health. These include, for example, exposure to pathogens caused by deficient infrastructure (potable water, sanitation) and anthropogenic impacts that exceed threshold levels (air pollution). Health disparities often appear when segments of the population are disproportionately exposed to compromised environments, both human-built and natural. These disparities are most likely found in low-income minority neighborhoods in which infrastructure is substandard or lacking altogether, and where anthropogenic impacts are severe (Evans and Kantrowitz 2002; Resnik and Roman 2007). The environmental (in)justice movement has responded by linking health disparities to social and economic inequities and environmental health. It also calls for a renewed public health agenda that targets people and place equally (Brulle and Pellow 2006).

The U.S–Mexico border region brings these inequities to life, because poverty and deprivation have led to numerous public health problems that are linked to environmental sources, especially in the region's colonias (Davidhizar and Bechtel 1999; Collins-Dogrul 2006). Environmental health in Arizona's colonias takes on an added dimension, because rapid population growth, economic change, and climatic conditions have placed enormous stress on the fragile Sonoran desert environment. The hot and arid climate, scarce water resources, and varied desert land cover make the Arizona–Sonora border region particularly sensitive to the impacts of urbanization. To make matters worse, the unplanned development found in many colonias imposes negative impacts on water quality and quantity, as well as air quality—all of which culminates in increased environmental health problems for border residents. As such, colonia populations suffer disproportionately from risks resulting from substandard environmental factors.

This chapter explores environmental health in the Arizona–Sonora border region. The chapter consists of three sections. The first section builds context by discussing urbanization, population growth, and economic change in the border region historically. The second section details prevalent environmental health issues in the Arizona–Sonora border. The final section describes federal programs and projects that attempt to mitigate these problems.

Urbanization in the Border Region

Urbanization in the Arizona–Mexico border region is advancing at an alarming pace. In 2000, the combined population of southern Arizona and Sonora, Mexico, which abuts Arizona to the south, neared 1.7 million. Estimates place the combined population at two to three million by 2030 (Peach and Williams 2003). This trend follows from a long history of urban settlement, population growth, and economic transition in the U.S.–Mexico border region.

The U.S.–Mexico border was carved out the vast territories of northern Mexico and the southwestern United States. Urban settlement in the region came from Spaniards who, in the sixteenth and seventeenth centuries, ventured from the interior of Mexico northward through present-day Texas, New Mexico, Arizona, and California (Esparza and Donelson 2008; Martínez 1994, 2006). Settlement was slow during the years that followed, but the 1853 Gadsden Purchase changed the border forever. The Gadsden Purchase involved the acquisition of vast stretches of Mexican land for the sum of $10 million. It included lands south of the Gila River, east of the Colorado River, and west of the Rio Grande. Most important, the Gadsden Purchase set in place the present-day U.S.–Mexico boundary.

In the years that followed, Mexicans crossed the border at will, where they worked for the mines, railroads, and agriculture industries (Elac 1972). A network of cross-border towns emerged over time as the railroads linked them to the country's interior (Arreola and Curtis 1993; Esparza and Donelson 2008). It is noteworthy that prior to the Gadsden Purchase, many cross-border communities were undivided and shared cultural familial heritages unique to their localities. Many of these towns on the U.S. side of the border are now officially designated colonias.

World War I and World War II fueled the growth of border towns, as military installations brought waves of soldiers and their families, new industries, and economic development to the region (Esparza and Donelson 2008). Transportation improvements followed close behind, which further opened the region to urbanization. While racial and ethnic conflict had colored the border for decades, the influx of new arrivals during the war years fanned the flames, as discriminatory practices denied Mexican Americans access to education, well-paying jobs, and social mobility (Heyman 1993; Martínez 2006). This conflict deepened the poverty and deprivation that is found in many colonias today.

The Bracero Program, put in place in the 1940s, was the next impetus for border urbanization. The program, established by binational agreement, granted Mexican farmworkers entry to the United States, where they worked on farms and ranches throughout the Southwest. From the 1940s through the 1960s, over four million Mexican farmworkers entered the country. However, termination of the Bracero Program in 1964 sent millions of farmworkers back to Mexico, and many remained in border towns (Esparza, Chavez, and Waldorf 2001).

Mexico's Border Industrialization Program (BIP) followed on the heels of the Bracero Program and led eventually to the formation of Mexico's maquiladoras, the hallmark of the present-day border economy (Esparza and Donelson 2008; Esparza, Waldorf, and Chavez 2004; Martínez 2006). The BIP, enacted in 1965, sought to employ the vast reserve of labor left idle by termination of the Bracero Program. While it quelled the social unrest resulting from high levels of unemployment, it also encouraged growth in U.S.–Mexico border towns, much of which was substandard compared to current development codes.

The maquiladora economy grew over the years and has been the most transformative force in the U.S.–Mexico border region. Maquiladoras employ millions of Mexican laborers at a fraction of the minimum wage paid in the United States. Older maquiladoras were built and operated with little regulation, but newer facilities adhere to more strict building and processing codes modeled after international standards. While maquiladoras predate the 1994 North American Free Trade Agreement (NAFTA) by nearly two decades, NAFTA set the stage for the explosion of cross-border manufacturing and trade that fueled economic development in many U.S. border towns, including those along the Arizona–Sonora border (Pavlakovich-Kochi 2006). Enacted in 1994, NAFTA was designed to foster greater trade among Canada, the United States, and Mexico through the elimination of taxes on goods shipped across the continent.

The political and economic ramifications of NAFTA and the maquiladora economy are debated widely, but the environmental consequences are undeniable (Schatan and Castilleja 2005). Environmental issues include contamination of rivers and watersheds of southern Arizona and the Rio Grande Valley in Texas, where a range of toxins and chemicals threaten human populations and strain ecosystems (Buelna and Riffat 2007; Norman 2007). Air pollution is also widespread in the border region, especially in and around major cross-border urban centers such as Ciudad Juárez–El Paso, Ambos Nogales, and Tijuana–San Diego. Air pollution stems from rapid urbanization and transborder trucking: the lifeblood of the maquiladora economy (Mukerjee 2001). The environmental consequences of urbanization in the Arizona–Sonora region are detailed in the next section.

The living conditions of the maquiladora labor force have also caused severe environmental problems. The maquiladora workforce includes migrants who travel from all over Mexico, and often beyond, in search of work. Some maquiladoras provide worker housing—the modern-day equivalent of the classic "company town"—but individual dwellings are often overcrowded as family and friends join workers. This overburdens sewer and wastewater infrastructure, which contributes to the spread of waterborne pathogens. When housing is not provided or workers are unemployed, migrants often "squat," or occupy property that is not otherwise developed. This has led to the emergence of shantytowns in and around Mexican border cities.

Much of the recent population growth on the U.S. side of the border is housed in the region's colonias. In Arizona, colonias represent a wide range of community types, including some tribal communities, long-established mining towns, retirement communities, rural utility districts, and illegal subdivisions. Many colonias in southern Arizona arose from "wildcat" subdivisions that first appeared in the 1950s and became far more common in recent years (Esparza and Donelson 2008). These are developments that circumvent subdivision regulations: the codes and standards that regulate infrastructure in residential subdivisions. It is easy to bypass these regulations because the state of Arizona allows up to five lot splits before subdivision regulations kick in. This means, in effect, that landowners divide their land into five parcels without having to provide infrastructure or other on-site improvements. Each of these parcels, in turn, can be divided up to five more times so that full-blown subdivisions appear on the landscape without any infrastructure improvements, including water delivery, centralized waste treatment, paved street and roads, curbs and sidewalks, street lighting, or even street numbering systems. The soaring cost of urban living, especially in nearby Tucson, is largely responsible for wildcat subdivisions, because they offer comparatively cheap land and housing (often manufactured homes) to low-income segments of the population. At other times, however, these unregulated subdivisions are home to unauthorized immigrants and farmworkers (Esparza and Donelson 2008).

The Impacts of Urban Growth

Decades ago, a handful of small, remote towns in southern Arizona served as gateways to Mexico: far-flung outposts on the country's southwestern-most fringe. These towns were occupied by Mexican Americans who struck a balance with the fragile Sonoran desert so that environmental impacts were negligible. But over time, urbanization, population growth, and economic change transformed the border and ignited environmental impacts that increasingly affect public health. Economic and social disparities are largely responsible for these impacts, because few towns and colonias have the wherewithal to fund the infrastructure improvements needed to minimize environmental degradation. The modes and quality of development, therefore, underlie much of the environmental health risk in the region.

Land Modification

The way that land is developed contributes to many of the environmental health risks in southern Arizona and northern Sonora. First, border-lands population growth has transformed landscapes from natural cover to impervious urban land. Impervious surfaces inhibit the infiltration of water into the soil and thus act as conductors of runoff. Impervious surfaces found in urban settings include transportation (e.g., parking lots) and rooftops (Sleavin et al. 2000), which vary depending on land use and stage of development. An increase in the overall impervious surface area changes surface-water quality and runoff quantity, leading to degraded stream and watershed systems by increasing flood peaks, erosion potential, and chemical pollution (Huth and Tinney 2008). The runoff caused by impervious surfaces is a key issue in growth management and planning across the country (Arnold and Gibbons 1996), but it is especially critical in the borderlands because there are few resources to mitigate impacts.

Urban runoff contributes significantly to nonpoint source (NPS) pollutants that infiltrate water resources (Beach 2002; Boyer et al. 2002; U.S. Environmental Protection Agency 2002). Major sources of NPS pollutants found in urban runoff include sediment, nutrients, oxygen-demanding substances, road salts, heavy metals, petroleum hydrocarbons, pathogenic bacteria, and viruses. Suspended sediments are the single largest source of pollutants carried from urban areas to surrounding watersheds, where they affect wetlands, lakes, streams, rivers, and aquatic life (U.S. Environmental Protection Agency 2006).

Second, the use of unpaved roads is characteristic of borderlands and adjacent areas south of the border. As land in colonias is subdivided, communities grow and new roads are created. The placement of these roads is determined by the shortest route to larger towns and cities and the ease of their development. Residents select dry riverbeds or washes as roads, rather than allowing official planners and civil engineers to make roadway improvements. This causes a series of ecosystem impacts as habitat is disrupted, and it leads to flooding in low-lying areas, because many roads follow natural arroyos.

Third, the development of residential settlements follows a similar course of unplanned development. Colonias sprout up on unoccupied land that, at times, is located in floodplains or in areas susceptible to erosion. Erosion susceptibility increases with soil compaction, vegetation removal, and land use changes associated with development. Bare hillslopes have higher rates of surface runoff and lower rates of water infiltration than those covered with natural grasses (Brooks et al. 1997).

Air Pollution

Most of the pollution in border airsheds can be attributed to anthropogenic activities common to congested urban areas and their environs

(Mukerjee 2001). The Clean Air Act and Amendments of 1990 define a "nonattainment area" as a locality where air pollution levels persistently exceed National Ambient Air Quality Standards. The EPA Office of Air Quality Planning and Standards (OAQPS) has set National Ambient Air Quality Standards for six principal "criteria" pollutants. In the United States, many cities along the Arizona–Sonora border have been designated as nonattainment areas, including Yuma, Nogales, and Douglas, because the criteria pollutant standards have been exceeded for several years.

Particulate matter less than 10 microns in diameter (PM10) consists of small, discrete solid or aerosol particles. Sources of PM10 include windblown dust from the desert or agricultural fields, dust produced by vehicular travel over unpaved roads, and areas of high-erosion potential. The highest concentrations of atmospheric PM10 are observed in these erosion and sediment deposition areas (Heisler et al. 1999). In the border region, dominant PM10 sources include very fine sediments dispersed from poorly paved streets, unpaved roads, and unpaved parking areas.

Particulate matter in the respiratory tract is known to cause injury by itself, but the impact is heightened when combined with noxious gases. The elderly, those suffering from respiratory illness, and young children are especially prone to the harmful effects of airborne particulates. A long list of health problems arises from inhaling particulate matter, including the aggravation of existing respiratory and cardiovascular disease, shortness of breath, eye irritation, alterations in the body's defenses against foreign materials, damage to lung tissue, carcinogenesis, and premature death (U.S. Environmental Protection Agency 2007b). The Arizona Department of Environmental Quality (ADEQ) completed binational studies on air quality at three major border communities—Yuma/San Luis, Ambos Nogales, and Douglas/Agua Prieta—and identified high PM10 concentrations (Arizona Department of Environmental Quality 2006).

Water

Water is the most limited resource in the arid borderlands region. This means that population growth, urbanization, aquifer depletion, surface water usage, pollution, and climate change all threaten the availability of water resources (Nitze 2003). Water quality has been affected in two principal ways. First, as mentioned above, urbanization and development have led to increased rates of sedimentation in local watercourses. This occurs as water channels absorb runoff from rooftops and paved surfaces, which, in turn, speeds the flow of water and deposits excess sediments that disrupt the balanced ecology of streams. Disruption occurs because suspended sediments alter turbidity, the optical property of water that causes the scattering of light rather than direct penetration to the stream bottom. This diffraction prevents photosynthesis and smothers bottom-dwelling organisms. Sediments also act as carriers of nutrients and toxins, inhibit fish reproduction, and alter natural stream flow (Stringer and Perkins 1997).

Second, pollution threatens groundwater resources—the principal source of domestic water in the border region. The intentional or accidental spill of synthetic compounds on alluvial sediments can have a detrimental effect on the drinking water resources of a community. In Nogales, Sonora, a 1997–98 study conducted under the auspices of the International Boundary and Water Commission (IBWC) detected tetrachloroethylene (PCE) in groundwater monitor wells located on both sides of the border (International Boundary Water Commission 2001). Tetrachloroethylene is a colorless organic liquid used mainly in the textile industry and as a component of aerosol dry-cleaning products. In the United States, PCE carries a maximum contaminant limit (MCL) of five parts per billion (ppb) for drinking water. Individuals who drink water containing PCE in excess of the MCL over many years can develop liver problems and experience increased cancer risk. Tetrachloroethylene concentrations were found to be marginally above MCL in samples collected from Nogales Wash monitor wells in Arizona, and significantly above water quality standards set by Mexico for monitor wells in Sonora. Subsequent monitoring by ADEQ through 2007 has detected PCE in Arizona Nogales Wash monitor wells, but at levels beneath MCL. ADEQ continues to monitor groundwater wells on the U.S. side of the border (Hans Huth, pers. comm. 2008).

Mitigation

The onslaught of urbanization has produced numerous environmental impacts that diminish public health and threaten the longer-term sustainability of communities in the Arizona–Sonora region. These impacts caught the eye of various federal agencies years ago and prompted the implementation of programs and initiatives aimed at mitigation. In this concluding section, I summarize three of these programs that target monitoring and surveillance of urban development, large-scale infrastructure projects, and urban planning. Other environmental problems, such as air quality, are not specifically addressed, because their resolution involves binational agreements that affect cross-border trade. Much of this debate revolves around transborder trucking, the centerpiece of NAFTA, because Mexico and the United States have different vehicular emission standards and requirements.

Monitoring Urban Development

Nearly all communities in the United States benefit from computer-based resources that provide a wealth of information on urban growth, infrastructure, transportation, topography, and land cover. But an hour south of Tucson, Arizona, near the U.S.–Mexico border, there are far fewer analytical resources, mainly because border communities do not have funding and technical support: a sure sign of the disparities between border communities and other U.S. cities.

Responding to the deficiency in border towns, the U.S. Department of Housing and Urban Development (HUD) funded a project in 2000 that enabled the mapping and monitoring of colonias along the U.S.–Mexico Border (Norman et al. 2006; Norman, Parcher, and Lam 2004). The project was implemented by the U.S. Geological Survey (USGS) working in cooperation with the Mexican Instituto Nacional de Estadística Geografía e Informática (INEGI). The mapping and monitoring project sought to provide geographic-analysis tools to enhance the decision-making processes of local city and county planning departments. In addition to enhancing planning functions, the project sought to assist local government agencies and nonprofit organizations by providing them with tools needed to inventory larger-scale problems and propose development solutions.

The project adhered to HUD's definition of colonias. The agency defines them as rural neighborhoods located within 150 miles of the border that lack adequate infrastructure, housing, or other basic services. While HUD's definition identifies communities eligible for federal support, it does little to define their boundaries. The federal government does not define spatial units called colonias in the same way that it defines census tracts or counties. Moreover, colonias rarely fall within well-defined census divisions, so developing computer-based tools that apply to specific colonias is challenging.

For this reason, the project required the identification of colonia boundaries and the placement of all existing data into a geospatial information system (GIS) format (Norman, Parcher, and Lam 2004). This stage of the project incorporated work in sister cities along the Arizona–Sonora border, including Douglas–Agua Prieta, Sonora; Bisbee and Naco, Sonora; and Ambos Nogales. These locations were chosen for the project partly because of long-standing efforts to coordinate cross-border economic development, and partly because of their remote location and comparatively small size. These characteristics have historically made access to technology and urban services a challenge for border communities.

Digital data and local communities enabled the construction of boundaries and the GIS platform. Landsat satellite imagery was used to depict and quantify changes in urbanization so that boundaries were defined by the spatial extent of development over time. Colonia boundaries were traced onto hard-copy maps and then automated into digital format. At the same time, community members identified the locations of waterlines, sewer lines, and inadequate housing, which were placed into the data set as separate data layers. An ArcIMS Viewer was created and is available online to allow public access to the GIS project free of charge. This information can be layered to generate maps that combine geospatial, tabular, and remotely sensed data that enable visual analysis of existing deficiencies and areas in most need of development.

Large-Scale Infrastructure Projects

The rapid growth of industry and population in Mexico's northern border region has placed increased pressure on state and municipal governments to provide effective and efficient public services, particularly potable water and wastewater infrastructure. Many locations along the Arizona–Sonora border lack sewer and water lines. This led to makeshift treatment facilities, which result in even more serious water pollution and increased risks to public health.

Federal and binational agencies have funded several large-scale wastewater treatment facilities in the border region, but the problems encountered in Nogales, Sonora, highlight the challenges faced by many colonias. The main wastewater interceptor serving this city was constructed in the Nogales Wash streambed without anchoring structures. As a consequence, large runoff events caused by monsoonal precipitation dislodge pipe joints, and the pipes fill with sand. Breaks in the pipes, as well as sediment obstructions in the interceptor, cause sanitary sewer overflows (SSOs), which impact the wash adversely. Finer sediments impact the operation and maintenance of the Nogales International Wastewater Treatment Plant located in Rio Rico, Arizona (a few miles north of the border) (Huth and Tinney 2008). During periods of heavy precipitation, sand and other obstructions are washed into wastewater subcollectors, which run along streets and lateral washes. Heavier sediments settle out in the conveyance where slopes flatten, usually near or within the main interceptor. Obstructions continually and rapidly arise, and SSOs force raw sewage into washes and streets. The Nogales, Sonora Wastewater Utility (OOMAPAS-NS) repairs impacted infrastructure as needed and also chlorinates SSOs as they appear throughout the city (Huth and Tinney 2008).

The United States and Mexico have developed a cooperative plan along the international boundary to address binational water pollution challenges. The plan is based on the 1983 La Paz Agreement between the two countries and aims to protect, conserve, and improve the border region environment. The program is led by a binational team: the EPA appointed its Office of Water, while Mexico's Secretariat of the Environment, Natural Resources, and Fisheries appointed its National Water Commission (CNA). The International Boundary and Water Commission (IBWC) supported the program by expanding its role in protecting the border environment.

As prescribed by NAFTA, the Border Environment Cooperation Commission (BECC) and the North American Development Bank (NADBank) were established to assist the binational team. The BECC assists border communities by providing technical assistance and certifying infrastructure projects so that they are eligible for funding. The NADBank, in turn, facilitates financing through loans so that projects certified by the BECC can be implemented. The NADBank also manages

EPA's Border Environmental Infrastructure Fund (BEIF), supplements the EPA's loans, and leverages other funding sources (U.S. Environmental Protection Agency 2007c).

Several large-scale infrastructure projects have benefited from the binational program. Current border infrastructure projects in the Arizona and Sonora region include expansion of the wastewater collection system in Agua Prieta, Sonora; wastewater system improvements in Bisbee and Douglas, Arizona; wastewater collection and conveyance system construction in Gadsden, Arizona; water distribution system improvements in Huachuca City, Arizona; water system improvements and wastewater infrastructure improvements in Ambos Nogales; a water project environmental assessment in Naco, Sonora; wastewater treatment and collection improvements in Patagonia, Arizona; expansion of wastewater collection and treatment systems in San Luis Rio Colorado, Sonora; wastewater treatment plant reconstruction in Somerton, Arizona; and a wastewater collection system in the colonias in Yuma, Arizona.

Lastly, priorities set by the EPA's Border 2012 water task force focus on funding projects that will reduce monsoonal flood peaks that affect the Nogales, Sonora, watershed. Strategies for attenuation of flood peaks may include installation of detention basins, revegetation, and domestic rainwater collection. By reducing flood peaks, the task force seeks to offset sedimentation of wastewater infrastructure, reduce sanitary sewer overflows that impact the Nogales Wash, improve water quality resources in Ambos Nogales, and protect BEIF investments on both sides of the border (Huth and Tinney 2008; Norman, Feller, and Guertin 2008).

Urban Planning

Rapid population growth has led to a renewed focus on the human–environment interface and strategies that promote sustainable resource management. In this regard, urban and regional planning can, and should, play a pivotal role. But urban and regional planners are at times ill equipped to monitor and evaluate the environmental consequences of rapid population growth and urbanization.

Such is the case in Ambos Nogales, where, over the years, urban development has led to decreased water quality. Population growth rates in this twin city are more than double the national average, and existing facilities will soon be overburdened if growth trends continue. The longer-term prospects are even more troublesome in view of global climate change, where predictions point to increased aridity and decreased water availability in the region.

Scientists from the USGS and the University of Arizona responded to water-quality issues in Ambos Nogales by developing analytical tools that support local urban and regional planning efforts. The project involved the use of a coupled model to forecast the effects of urban development on downstream water quality (Norman 2007; Norman, Feller, and Guertin 2008). The model projected changes in the size of the twin city's urban area using the SLEUTH urban growth model and applied these projections to erosion-sedimentation models (Universal Soil Loss Equation and Spatially Explicit Delivery Model). The coupled model was used to identify areas potentially vulnerable to high erosion. Simulations were then conducted to evaluate the effects of excluding these areas from future urban growth under various land management schemes.

These analytic methods enhanced land use planning decisions in two ways. First, the coupled model enabled the investigation of alternative land management scenarios that respond to erosion and diminished water quality. These alternatives include, for example, land set-asides that protect critical areas in the watershed and replanting high-risk areas with native grasses. Second, the project broadened the scope of decision making by bringing planners, local leaders, and nonprofit organizations together. Planners, city officials in Nogales, Sonora, and leaders of the Ambos Nogales Revegetation Project were provided with maps that show areas of the watershed prone to erosion, as well as sustainable development zones. These maps can be used to slow or mitigate settlement in high-risk areas, thereby decreasing both air and water pollution in the years to come.

Summary

Public and environmental health are tied closely together by processes and factors that promote or lessen human health and well-being. Cities across the globe recognize these interdependencies and implement a range of programs that advance public health by ensuring the vitality and sustainability of human-built and natural environments. But health disparities color much of the world, because countries and cities often lack the resources needed to foster safe environments. Such is the case in the U.S.–Mexico borderlands, where rapid population growth, urbanization, and economic transition have exacerbated public health problems as the natural environment suffers the consequences of growth.

This chapter focused on the environmental consequences of urbanization in the borderland region of Arizona and Sonora. I demonstrated how public health is affected by environmental degradation that stems from urbanization and modes of development. I then pointed to several projects that aim to mitigate these environmental disturbances by monitoring urban growth, upgrading infrastructure, and providing tools that enable sound urban planning and land use decisions.

The future prospects for environmental health in the border region depend largely on cross-border cooperation, because natural environments do not recognize political boundaries. As scientists from both sides of the border continue to study the impacts of urban growth, sustainable development solutions will surface so that public health is improved. Urbanization and environmental degradation in Arizona colonias do not have to go hand in hand. The United States and Mexico have agreed to act jointly to address environmental and public health problems prevalent in border communities that are consistent with principles of environmental protection, resource conservation, and sustainable development.

Acknowledgments

I wish to thank Wes Ward and Hans Huth for their contributions to and careful review of this chapter.

15

Environmental Pollution and Quality of Life in Imperial Valley's Colonias

Kimberly Collins

WATER AND AIR POLLUTION are linked to numerous public health concerns in the Imperial Valley.[1] By many accounts, the New River is one of the most polluted rivers in North America. It runs north from the Mexicali watershed through the city of Mexicali, Baja California, Mexico, crosses the border at Calexico, and drains into the Salton Sea about 60 miles to the north. Mexicali's maquiladoras dump industrial pollutants into the river; then the city adds 10 to 20 million gallons of raw sewage per day, and agricultural runoff on the U.S. side of the border deposits a range of chemicals and pesticides by the time the river reaches the Salton Sea (Colorado River Basin Regional Water Quality Control Board 2008; Kopinack 2003). There are also serious air pollution problems in the Mexicali–Calexico corridor. In recent years, Mexicali and Imperial County have been designated nonattainment areas for three air pollutants (Ruiz 2005). Vehicular traffic, uncontrolled burnings, and unpaved roads all contribute to poor air quality and a range of public health issues.

The region's agricultural economy contributes significantly to environmental health problems. The Imperial Valley ranks as one of California's most productive agricultural regions, and agriculture has been a leading economic activity in the county for nearly a hundred years. But the agricultural economy relies on a vast reserve of cheap and exploitable farm labor, much of which comes from Mexico. It comes as no surprise that poverty and deprivation are widespread among the farmworker population. According to the U.S. Census Bureau (2008), 19 percent of the Imperial County population lived in poverty as of 2004, compared to 13 percent for the state. The California Employment Development Department (2007) indicates that in 2007, farmworkers and farm laborers in

El Centro, the Imperial County seat, earned an average annual income of $17,309, compared to $45,309 for the state as a whole.

Much of the farmworker population resides in the county's 15 formally designated colonias, where affordable farmworker housing has long been scarce and infrastructure problems are common. But in real terms, much of the county qualifies as a "colonia." Public health issues, therefore, revolve around farmworker health, long compromised by farm-related accidents and injuries, pesticide poisoning, and exposure to air- and waterborne pollutants (Mills and Yang 2007).

While there is ample evidence that environmental health is a critical issue in Imperial Valley, local colonia residents hold far different attitudes and perceptions. My research finds that residents reveal a high level of satisfaction with housing and local environmental conditions. This brings forward fundamental questions about what constitutes quality of life. What are the social and economic bases for establishing quality-of-life indicators? Who is ultimately positioned to set such standards for others, especially poor farmworkers?

This chapter looks at environmental health issues in Imperial Valley's colonias and examines residents' attitudes towards quality of life. The narrative draws on my experience as director of the California Center for Border and Regional Economic Studies, which is based at San Diego State University's Imperial Valley campus. As director, I am involved with many issues of border environmental health, farmworkers, and the local economy. In this chapter, I share some of what I have learned over the years.

The chapter begins with a profile of Imperial Valley's economy. I discuss the emergence of agriculture in the valley and then report major recent employment trends. Discussion then turns to colonias in the area, where I discuss formal definitions as they apply to Imperial Valley. This is followed by a review of environmental problems. The chapter concludes by summarizing the perspectives of Calexico residents' perceptions of quality of life and environmental health.

The Imperial Valley: A Short History of Work in the Region

Imperial County was founded in 1907: the fifty-eighth and most recent county in California. San Diego County borders to the west, Riverside

County abuts to the north, and the state of Arizona forms the eastern boundary. The Mexican state of Baja California lies to the south, and Mexicali–Calexico forms the major cross-border urbanized area in the region. As of 2006, Mexicali housed nearly 900,000 persons, while Calexico's 2007 population was approximately 170,000 (Instituto Nacional de Estadística Geografica Informática 2006; California Department of Finance 2007). The names of these two border cities reveal close historic ties, but the agricultural economy spreads well beyond their boundaries.

Agriculture in the Imperial Valley owes much to irrigation projects funded by the federal government years ago. As early as the 1850s, large-scale farming outfits expressed interest in bringing water from the Colorado River to the arid desert of southern California, but the first major project was launched in 1934 with construction of the All American Canal. The canal spanned a distance of 80 miles to bring water from the Colorado to the Imperial Valley and the Coachella Valley (in Riverside County). Over the years, the water delivery system was upgraded and expanded so that, currently, the Imperial Irrigation District receives enough water to irrigate 500,000 acres. Water is channeled to fields through a network of over 3,100 miles of delivery and drainage canals (Cohen 2004; U.S. Bureau of Reclamation n.d). This meets the needs of Imperial Valley farmers, who currently have over 487,000 acres in cultivation. But the longer-term prospects for irrigation in Imperial Valley are less certain. The Colorado River is already taxed to capacity, and the drought of recent years has led to conflicts about who (Arizona, California, Nevada) will receive scarce water resources in the years to come. Mexicali is affected, because it also receives water from the Colorado via dams and canals built by the Mexican government (Cohen 2004; Martin 2003; Nagler et al. 2005). Water resources may well determine the fate of Mexicali and the Imperial Valley as populations continue to grow.

While the agribusiness community has benefited from federal investments in irrigation, farmworkers across the county have been denied the fruits of taxpayer dollars. This inequality has historically been part of the economic structure in Imperial Valley. Agricultural interests insist that they need a large supply of cheap labor in order to grow and harvest food, but the low pay keeps farmworkers in poverty as they struggle to survive.

A few summary statistics reveal the extent of deprivation among the county's workers. Imperial County is one of the poorest counties in

California. As of 2006, there were over 12,000 persons employed in agriculture (21 percent of the county's total labor force), but even so, the unemployment rate stands at around 16–18 percent (California Employment Development Department 2007). The abundance of labor keeps wages low so that farmers and ranchers maximize profits. Per capita income is approximately $16,000, and the median household income hovers near $37,000 (U.S. Census Bureau 2006). There are approximately 3.4 persons per owner-occupied dwelling, and the two largest cities in the valley have a first-time homebuyer program to assist with down payments. Home ownership is out of reach for many living in the area, with a median housing value of $245,000. This means that many households must spend over 50 percent of their net income to buy a home (Collins 2007). Many families live in substandard housing but consider these dilapidated structures their homes. In 2007, for example, the Imperial County government tried to evict residents living in dilapidated mobile homes in the City of Holtville. Residents resisted, because, unfit or not, those were their homes. This highlights the overall problem of housing in the region (Lusk 2007).

These data demonstrate differences between the haves and have-nots and define the power and dominance of agriculture interests in the valley. Farmworkers fight to survive and turn to the government for support when wages cannot secure basic needs such as health care and decent housing. Thus, agribusiness relies on the government to supplement the low incomes of workers. In sum, workers live on the margins economically and are disenfranchised from the decision-making process because they have no power.

Even as Imperial County grows and diversifies its economic base, its history continues to affect the current economy and environment. This is partly due to the county's political power structure and the perceptions of stakeholders who seek economic growth by luring business to the Valley. Those working in economic development often complain that people are not proud to be from Imperial County, which hampers business recruitment efforts. This problem is so severe that the Imperial Valley Economic Development Corporation (2007) initiated a campaign that asks local residents to speak in one positive voice about the county's assets. In effect, they seek to mask the deeper inequities that color social and economic relations in Imperial County.

The government sector is also part of the economic power structure. As of 2006, the government sector employed 17,577 persons, or 31 percent of the county's total labor force (California Employment Development Department 2007). Government jobs include county-level social service positions that assist those living on the margins, workforce development programs that respond to the county's high unemployment, and city employees. There are also a large number of state employees working at two state prisons, and the U.S. Border Patrol continues to add personnel in response to the "border crisis."

The services sector is the third-largest employer in the county, trailing agriculture and the government sector. For present purposes, this sector includes professional and personal services, retailing, and the leisure and hospitality industry. The service industry employs 8,618 persons, or 15 percent of the county's 2006 labor force (California Employment Development Department 2007). The service industry meets local needs and also caters to cross-border shoppers from Mexicali. Local market studies estimate that as many as 400,000 border crossers are potential Imperial Valley consumers.

Agriculture in the Imperial Valley was made possible by costly federal investments in irrigation. These projects benefited the agribusiness community and set in motion a pattern of dominance that remains today. Farmworkers provide the backbreaking work that enables agriculture to prosper, but wages are kept low because of the vast reserve of labor. The government supplements worker incomes by providing basic needs so that they can continue working the fields that reap huge profits for farmers and ranchers.

Colonias in the Imperial Valley

Colonias have been defined in many ways. One approach is to define them by race or communities that are dominated by Latinos (Galarza 1964; González and Fernandez 2002; Vaught 1997). These settlements are not located particularly on, or near, the border but are formed based on an economic system in need of cheap, primarily Latino labor. While the poor inhabit the county's colonias, many residents across Imperial Valley are impoverished, have few economic possibilities, and live in substandard housing. This suggests that a more appropriate definition lies closer to colonias as defined in the Chicano(a) literature, where they are considered largely Latino areas developed because of the availability of cheap labor (Vaught 1997). With this broader definition in hand, the entire Imperial Valley could be defined as a colonia. Latinos or Hispanics account for 76 percent of the population (U.S. Census Bureau 2006), and immigrants move to the area every year.

Nevertheless, the most-often-used definition of colonias follows from federal policies. These guidelines were set forth in the Cranston-Gonzalez National Affordable Housing Act, passed in 1990, and require that colonias are located within 150 miles of the border in order to receive official designation from federal agencies (U.S. Department of Housing and Urban Development 2006). Colonias must also demonstrate the lack of physical infrastructure and/or dilapidated housing to qualify for federal assistance. Federal agencies have used these guidelines to designate fifteen colonias in Imperial County, nine in San Diego County, and eight in Riverside County. However, the federal government omits colonias if county populations exceed one million. This means that colonias in San Diego County are excluded from some federal funding opportunities. Similarly, colonias in Riverside County are not located near the border, so they are also excluded from some federal programs. The Environmental Protection Agency (EPA), for example, funds large-scale infrastructure projects in the border region through the North American Development Bank (NADBank). To be considered for funding, colonias must be located within 62 miles of the border (Esparza and Donelson 2008).

The 15 federally designated colonias in the Imperial Valley fall within the jurisdiction of county or city governments (Mukhija and Monkkonen 2006). Nine are located outside of city boundaries and are therefore within the administrative domain of the county government. These include Bombay Beach, Heber, Niland, Ocotillo, Palo Verde, Poe, Salton Sea Beach, Seeley, and Winterhaven. The remaining six colonias lie within the jurisdiction of municipal governments: two colonias in the city of Imperial (East and South Colonias); two in Calexico (C. N. Perry and Kloke); one in Brawley (Brawley County Water District); and one in El Centro (El Dorado). All of these jurisdictions have received funding through HUD's CDBG set-aside program.

The first colonias to receive official designation in 1991—Kloke, C. N. Perry, and Poe—are older communities located in unincorporated areas of the county. Kloke and C. N. Perry were eventually annexed by the city of Calexico. The Poe colonia, located outside the city of Brawley, has yet to be annexed. Poe's future has been long debated, with the county lobbying for annexation and the city resisting the move. In 1993, unincorporated areas near the Salton Sea (Bombay Beach and Salton Sea) were designated as colonias, as were poorer communities also located in the unincorporated territory of the county (Heber, Ocotillo, Palo Verde). In the same year, colonias in Imperial and El Centro also received official designation. The communities near the Salton Sea were settled in the 1940s and 1950s but were abandoned in more recent years as environmental degradation engulfed the sea. The two remaining colonias, Niland and Seeley, received official designation in 2002. They are located in unincorporated areas of the county. As with the other colonias, Niland and Seeley house poverty-stricken residents. In these remote areas, poverty led to substandard housing that the county cannot service with adequate water and sewage facilities in the absence of special use districts. Thus, residents continue to live in unhealthful environments.

In 2002, the Imperial County Planning and Development Services Department developed a master plan to address the issues of colonias within its jurisdiction. The master plan defines colonias as areas with high rates of poverty, a high percentage of low-income households, and a lack of physical and social services (County of Imperial 2002). Colonias in unincorporated areas still have problems with potable water and sewer infrastructure. Other challenges identified in the plan include poor-quality housing, high levels of environmental contamination, the lack of transportation infrastructure, and the absence of street lighting and other public services enjoyed by most people in Imperial Valley. It should be emphasized, however, that these problems do not affect all colonias equally. As part of the planning process, surveys were conducted with colonia residents. It is noteworthy that many respondents indicated satisfaction with the standard of living in their communities. As I will discuss later in this chapter, these sentiments are similar to those held by Imperial Valley residents.

In concluding this section, it is important to stress that the issues related to formally designated colonias apply to much of Imperial Valley. It is also important to acknowledge the positive steps taken by county planners and economic development specialists as they attempt to confront these problems. But the greatest obstacle is the struggle between the old rural guard—those who made their wealth from agriculture and the current system of government assistance for workers—and the new urban elites who seek to diversify the economy and modify the system. This struggle has been played out in a number of environmental issues in the region, and most have not been resolved to date.

Environmental and Quality-of-Life Challenges in Imperial Valley

The environments of Calexico and Mexicali are linked through common watersheds and airsheds. Geographically, the Imperial Valley is lower in elevation than Mexicali, so water flows north to the Salton Sea. Such is the case with the New River, often depicted as the most contaminated river in North America, which has been discussed at federal, state, and local levels of government for nearly 50 years. The underlying problem is that the New River served as the principal drainage for raw sewage back when communities in the valley were founded. It still carries residential, industrial, and agricultural waste from Mexicali through Calexico, causing much concern in Imperial Valley. A local Calexico city commission was formed in 2000 to lobby for federal or California state funds to enclose segments of the New River that pass through the city. The commission championed an underground, covered channel that resembles work completed in Mexicali (Calexico New River Committee n.d.). However, the state of California refused to fund the project, arguing that it is a cross-border problem that should be resolved at the federal level. The channel has not been built, and the New River remains a critical risk to public health.

Air quality is another serious public health problem in the border region. Calexico and Mexicali share an airshed that is contaminated with emissions from industry; a large and poorly maintained vehicle fleet; diesel truck emissions; agricultural, trash, and other uncontrolled burning; unpaved roads; and dust and sand blown in from the desert.

The level of air contaminants varies according to source (Ruiz 2005). Imperial County and Mexicali both exceeded the U.S. one-hour ozone standard every year from 1997 through 2003.[2] In Imperial County and Mexicali, ozone problems peaked in 1999, with over 20 and 15 noncompliance days respectively. Since then the number of noncompliant days has declined considerably for both Imperial County and Mexicali.

Carbon monoxide (CO) has also been a major source of air pollution, far more so in Mexicali than in Imperial Valley. This is to be expected, because the Mexican government imposes fewer restrictions on industries and vehicles, both of which contribute significantly to CO pollution. For example, in 1998 Mexicali recorded 80 days of the year in which the CO eight-hour standard was exceeded (Ruiz 2005). The number of noncompliant days fell considerably since then, to fewer than 40 days by 2003. Finally, particulate matter smaller than 10 microns (PM10) has been a serious problem in Mexicali, but less so in Imperial County. For nearly 50 days in 2000, PM10 levels in Mexicali surpassed EPA standards. Levels have fallen since then but remain unacceptably high.

The Imperial Valley population is exposed to serious health impacts that result from water- and airborne pollution (Carranza et al. 2004). There are high rates of childhood asthma, and respiratory infections are common in the region. The New River has been linked to several public health issues due to high levels of contamination and waterborne pathogens (Lares-Villa et al. 1993; U.S. Department of Health and Human Services 1996). There is considerable concern about high incidences of cancer, especially among those living near the New River. This has not been proven scientifically, although many in the community hold this perception. Even so, only a few environmental organizations or nonprofits have addressed issues of environmental health.

The EPA's Border 2012 initiative is the primary effort to combat air pollution in the region. Through the Border 2012 program, the EPA joined forces with the Mexican Secretariat for the Environment and Natural Resources (SEMARNAT) task force. There are also a few community-based groups that provide outreach and disseminate information on asthma. These groups discuss the problem of air quality as it relates to public health. Yet the response from the community has been limited. Residents are generally disenfranchised from the system, and poverty is the central concern. Local governments have also been slow in responding to community concerns about public health. These issues are pursued in the next section.

Quality-of-Life Perspectives

In 2005, I conducted a survey during the months of April and May that included 97 Imperial Valley residents. The survey sought to assess their perceptions of local quality of life, including environmental health (Collins 2005). Among other things, the survey found that most people believe their quality of life is good, are satisfied with housing, and view their communities positively. Even though communities have high levels of environmental contamination and/or lack public services and infrastructure, local residents are happy with their homes. More than 72 percent of respondents rated their quality of life as excellent, and nearly 26 percent indicated it was good. When asked how satisfied they are with living in their respective cities, 77 percent indicated that they were very satisfied, and 21 percent were satisfied. Only a small percentage of residents were not satisfied (2 percent) or rated their quality of life as poor (1 percent) (Collins 2005). These results support Imperial County's Colonia Master Plan, mentioned previously, where residents interviewed saw their communities favorably even though they lack adequate public services and housing is substandard. Even so, over 50 percent of respondents I surveyed believed the government was doing little, or nothing, to improve the environment. It may be that survey participants hid true beliefs for numerous reasons, but these results are the best indication of how residents perceive their local environmental conditions.

Two concerns surface from the sentiments held by local residents. First, the slow response by local government and the seeming lack of concern on the part of residents are mutually reinforcing. Where the cycle begins and ends is unclear, but the result is that environmental issues are not adequately addressed. The second concern deals with residents' perception of quality of life. It seems as though residents on average live where they want based on their priorities of what is important. What one person finds uninhabitable, another person may find acceptable. It is important that we understand the nuances of quality of life, because they may well explain why solutions to environmental health problems are so slow in coming.

Definitions and Theories about Quality of Life

Perhaps the most important question is, How is quality of life determined? A practical understanding of quality of life includes the process of selecting and defining social indicators that represent aspects of an individual's life. Quality-of-life indicators as described by Liu consist of many variables that represent a person's life. These include economics, politics, environment, health, education, and a series of social indicators (Liu 1976). Theoretically, Liu views quality of life as "the status of human happiness and satisfaction at a particular point in time for the given physical and psychological conditions with which the individual in question is confronted" (Liu 1976, 79). But Liu's definition looks more at the individual living within a specific space and time, and others may hold different views.

Dissart and Deller's (2000) review of the urban and regional planning literature examines perceptions of quality of life. In defining the term, Dissart and Deller build on the following basic assumptions: "(1) it refers to human life only, (2) it is rarely if ever used in the plural, (3) it is used as a single indivisible generic term whose meaning can be clarified, and (4) it is difficult to classify into any discrete category of related social sciences" (Dissart and Deller 2000, 136). These assumptions lay the framework for understanding quality of life through an interdisciplinary analysis of the system in which people live. Dissart and Deller measure quality of life through "three major philosophical approaches . . . : (1) characteristics of quality of life dictated by normative ideals based on religious, philosophical, or other systems; (2) the satisfaction of preferences (choice utility); and (3) the experience of individuals" (Dissart and Deller 2000, 137). Their measurement positions individuals at the center of quality of life and seeks to understand their perceptions of the ingredients that produce quality of life.

In contrast, Szalai and Andrews define quality of life as a "collective attribute that adheres to groups or categories of people, not to individuals" (Szalai and Andrews 1980, 16). This definition, therefore, looks to collective perceptions that apply broadly to populations. In this case, social variables are approached as community-wide indicators, not individuals. Szalai and Andrews (1980) argue that quality-of-life variables are more than social indicators: they describe the observable conditions of life and individual perspectives and assessments.

Quality of Life Revisited

It is fitting to conclude the discussion of quality of life by comparing Calexico to other small cities and micropolitan areas of the United States.

Heubusch's (1997) research uses quality-of-life indicators that cover climate and environment, diversions (amusement, shopping, and the like), economics, education, community assets, health care, housing, and public safety. While some may argue with his selection of variables, most would agree that they include a broad base of factors involved with quality of life. According to his study, the Calexico–El Centro–Brawley region fell to the bottom. Out of 193 localities, these Imperial Valley communities took the 181st position.

These results bring into question the fundamental understanding of quality of life as described by Liu (1976) and Dissart and Deller (2000) versus Szalai and Andrews (1980). In the first case, the individual in her or his broader system (circumstances) determines quality of life, while in the second case, quality of life applies to entire communities. My survey research suggests that Liu's and Dissart and Deller's depiction is applicable to Imperial Valley residents, while Heubusch (1997) built on Szalai and Andrews's approach. This may well explain the divergent perceptions of quality of life in the Imperial Valley.

But in real terms, the perceptions of quality of life held by Imperial Valley residents are problematic. Foremost, change will be slow in coming as long as residents are satisfied and do not demand it. Residents who are content are highly unlikely to request assistance from local, state, and federal agencies. Second, if government acts on its own, policies and initiatives move ahead without citizen input. Such was the case with evictions in Holtville (described above), which were met with stern opposition by local residents. In many ways, this is also what the Cranston-Gonzalez National Affordable Housing Act has done. It has created a revenue stream for areas that do not have the services expected in other communities across the country, even though residents are not actively seeking help.

Given the complex nature of social relations in the Imperial Valley, it is easy to see why change is difficult. The landed elite have little interest in promoting change among farmworkers, because their subsistence lifestyles keep profits high. On the other hand, farmworkers are content with their situation, because, in many respects, their lives have improved. Such perceptions of quality of life are difficult to change, because they are reproduced from generation to generation, and the constant influx of immigrants reinforces attitudes and perceptions. In the end, it may well be that community education projects are the most viable means of bringing change to the valley. Workers must first be informed of the severity of problems, then equipped with advocacy skills before they engage in community organizing. Such efforts have proven successful in colonias of other border states (Esparza and Donelson 2008), and they may well pay off in the Imperial Valley.

Summary

Impoverishment is real in the Imperial Valley. By most standards, people survive in conditions that resemble the poorest regions of the world. In this chapter, I showed how these conditions stem from the long history of economic development in the region. The agricultural economy prospered from federal investments in irrigation projects and the large supply of Mexican farmworkers. These workers were not paid enough to support themselves or their families, so a system of government assistance arose. I also demonstrated how, and why, the population on both sides of the border is exposed to extreme environmental health hazards. Confronting public health problems is difficult, because residents are generally satisfied and see little need for improvement. Without residents' demanding change, substandard living conditions will continue, and improvements will come only when the government decides to step in. Local government has been reluctant to take action, but the federal government is dealing with air and water quality. Even so, the funds allocated to the region are insufficient to make a real and lasting impact. As the California border region continues to grow, more industry and automobiles will impact the environment. Without community action, living conditions in the Imperial Valley will not change, and the cycle of poverty and impaired environmental and human health will continue.

Notes

1. In keeping with the local vernacular, throughout the chapter I use the terms Imperial Valley and Imperial County interchangeably.

2. The National Ambient Air Quality Standards were set by the U.S. Clean Air Act of 1990. The one-hour ozone standard is 0.12 ppm and set once an area exceeds the standard for three consecutive years. The eight-hour carbon monoxide standard is

9 ppm not to be exceeded more than once a year. The PM10 standard for a 24-hour period is 150 micrograms per cubic meter of air. This standard is set by a three-year average, in which "the 98th percentile of 24-hour concentrations at each population-oriented monitor within an area must not exceed 65 micrograms per cubic meter of air (U.S. Environmental Protection Agency 2005).

PART IV

Conclusion: Reflections and Directions

16

A Sustainability Praxis for the Future of Colonias Development and Colonias Studies

William D. Smith

THIS CHAPTER HAS two objectives. The first is to synthesize what appears to emerge from this volume's meeting among scholars and practitioners. My account draws on the concept of praxis in a broadly critical-theoretical understanding of that term—the mobilization of theory and analysis to enrich the imagination as it goes about the concrete process of building a more just and equitable world. The second objective concerns methodological avenues that, in my estimation, will enhance the future of what I call (perhaps prematurely) Colonia Studies. This section of the chapter argues for finer-grained, longer-term, policy-committed ethnographic research as a way to bring methodological breadth and depth to our engagement with colonia communities. These two dimensions, praxis and research methodology, are mutually reinforcing.

Praxis

One argument that brings various of the authors in this volume together—scholars as well as practitioners—is to take the "regulatory approach" to task. This approach tends to construe development levels almost exclusively in terms of basic service infrastructure. Through it, governments explain away their own apathy toward "pirate" settlements by faulting unscrupulous developers for inadequate services. It sometimes adds insult to injury by holding resource-strapped residents themselves responsible for bringing their neighborhoods up to code. As Ward (1999) argues, the regulatory approach seems designed to regulate colonias out of existence (see also Hill 2003).

Those of us intent on calling the regulatory approach on the carpet argue that it should give way to a more organic, resident-centered, "from below" orientation vis-à-vis development. Institutional support should open itself to local imagination, local social capital, and local process. All authors in this volume would likely agree on this point, but Giusti (chapter 2), Arizmendi, Arizmendi, and Donelson (chapter 6), Henneberger, Carlisle, and Paup (chapter 7), Mealey (chapter 10), and Peña and Rosenthal (chapter 12) treat it directly. Here I want to flesh out the implications of that criticism in terms of praxis, or project. My principal argument is twofold. First, questioning development as usual should lead us to a more manifestly critical and structural angle on colonia problems. Several authors of these chapters suggest that race and racism should receive due emphasis in our analyses of colonias as some of the most protractedly disadvantaged neighborhoods in "a country that too often ignores the poor," as Esparza and Donelson indicate in the book's introduction. Many of us speak of the regulatory approach, poverty, and discrimination, even racism, all in the same breath (Hill 2003). To appropriate one of Paul Farmer's productive concepts, this is a "structural violence" point of view that I think should bring to Colonias Studies some degree of theoretical unity. As Sabo, Ingram, and Wennerstrom (chapter 13) seem to imply, we might also consider the power of human rights as a framing discourse for advancing colonia claims to a brighter future. Second, when we move from theory to practice—praxis—more robust theorizing should lead us toward a more creative and colonia-empowering conception, planning, and carrying out of colonia projects. What is required of us, I believe, is to think and do colonia development in ways more adequate to colonia community autonomy and self-determination.

Preliminarily, however, we in Colonia Studies should recognize that "development" itself, both in the social sciences and in community organizing across the planet, has become a quite fraught concept. Since "development discourse" hit the social science of modernization in the late 1980s through an interdisciplinary critical development studies (CDS), scholars have been coming to grips with the relative power of empires, states, and powerful institutions to implement modernization in out-of-the-way places.[1] Much recent work has begun to question the notion that development on the ground is a one-way process in which hegemonic social forces work their priorities into local institutions and identities.[2]

Anthropologists of modernity have pretty much consolidated the argument that "development" does not designate a simple process of a local people's incorporation into the reach of modernity as the metropole configures it. People neither swallow whole some imposed modernity nor reactively defend "the local" against it. The targets of development, rather, mount "counterdevelopment" responses, both personally and collectively, that shape the outcome of the development process (Galjart 1981, quoted in Arce and Long 2000). In so doing, they often bring "tradition" to bear on the process, repositioning tradition, breathing new life into it, sometimes discovering it in the course of coming up with new ways to pursue development.[3] In Arce and Long's view, development ethnography should investigate real worlds "made up of living ensembles of imagined and felt experiences" (Arce and Long 2000, 2) that encompass both the modern and traditional.

This literature has dealt largely with the "developing world," and so its applicability to colonia contexts may require translation. As Esparza and Donelson point out in this book's introduction, colonias often enough look like the Third World, and many colonia residents have social and cultural roots there. And recent processes in the global economy have upset the older center-periphery models of world systems theories. One finds the First World in a network of economic elites across the globe; one finds pockets of the developing world everywhere—Los Angeles, after all, is being called "the capital of the Third World" (Rieff 1997; Sawhney 2002). Still, the whole category of "tradition" may be less immediate in the colonia milieu than in the culture-clash dynamics between metropole and periphery that so many scholars in CDS have documented. For the moment, I want simply to counterpose to received ideas of modernization some alternative ideas about ways forward in Colonias Studies, inspired in no small measure by this volume.

I think we need holistic trains of thought to counter the path-of-progress conceit that still exists in the heart of a still-stubborn modernization theory, even in Colonias Studies. This is an argument implicit, perhaps, in all chapters that insist on seeing colonia realities in larger political economic perspective, whether it be Pavlakovich-Kochi and Esparza's (chapter 4) attention to transborder economy and border policy or May's (chapter 11) systems approach to understanding colonia public health, which helps set up the more critical structural line taken by Sabo, Ingram, and Wennerstrom (chapter 13). There are many ways to think holistically; we can, for example, consider how a host of problems revolve around one fundamental issue, for example, housing. I think Henneberger, Carlisle, and Paup (chapter 7) invite us to think about housing as *homebuilding;* that is, as a foundation for belonging, for physical and mental health. That perspective brings Colonias Studies in line with important currents in activist scholarship on homelessness in the United States (e.g., Hopper 2003).

Building on that chapter, Donelson and Holguin (chapter 8) suggest a salutary point of departure in colonias development work. Up to this volume, most of the colonias literature has dealt in some way with conventional infrastructure delivery and economic development. Given the significance of sustainability for all of us, including colonia residents, it is high time we push for green building as a viable alternative for colonia *affordable* housing. Donelson and Holguin are guardedly optimistic that adobe, rammed earth, and straw bale construction would take root, especially in the historically deeper colonias of Arizona and New Mexico with more traditional architecture. Innovative new housing projects have been developed in Indian communities in Arizona and New Mexico, and the chapter concludes with two case studies in Doña Ana County, New Mexico, that suggest that energy-efficient building can surmount the host of cultural and regulatory challenges it has to confront. These challenges are formidable, to be sure. Would-be green homebuilders anywhere face regulatory resistance, and, thus far, government-sponsored housing programs have been reticent to embrace green building. Furthermore, the sentiment is strong and widespread among colonia residents that low-cost alternative materials mean substandard materials. This resonates with failures to get adobe construction widely accepted in colonias on the Mexican side of the border, including in the colonia in which I have been working, Agua Prieta, Sonora. Despite its advantages, and despite plenty of local expertise, adobe has made little headway in self-help or philanthropic house building in Agua Prieta. Conventional fired bricks and cinder block (and even plywood) are preferred because they are more modern, and somehow express upward mobility; whereas adobe, despite its practical advantages, represents rurality, the past, the retrograde. This state of affairs points up that sustainability initiatives in colonia development are in part an educational process that questions the elements of modernity inculcated by the culture of modernization. The entire set of givens under the category "standard of living" is ripe for rethinking. In Mexico at any rate, to bring all this down to the vicissitudes of everyday life, we need to see that energy-efficient materials such as adobe or straw bale would reduce families' need to burn trash in homemade woodburning stoves to keep warm in winter (health-compromising, needless to say; and note that fire is the most common and devastating environmental problem in urban slums worldwide—see Davis 2006 on "slum ecology"). That sort of consistent and deliberate connection building through reflection-in-education would help all of us—colonia residents and the outsiders who work with them—nest a holistic approach to housing in a yet more holistic comprehension of public health.

Sabo, Ingram, and Wennerstrom (chapter 13) help us grasp ways in which colonia organizations are already forging connections and nesting. After systematically describing the structural conditions that prejudice health in border communities, including access to health insurance and punitive legislation targeting undocumented immigrants, the authors stump for the community health worker (CHW) approach, whose primary protagonist is the promotor(a). Their chapter makes clear that in some CHW cases, health workers/leaders, as organic intellectuals and deeply connected advocates, are using health as a kind of fulcrum for community organizing around social justice in general. The implication here is that grassroots projects oriented mainly to one problem, be it health, housing, or economic development, can be mobilized for bigger or other things. The potential of "from-below" projects like the CHW approach to attack a host of issues and to attack root issues like poverty and discrimination is extremely suggestive. For those of us interested in using our work to promote colonia empowerment and sustainability, we might posit public health as a kind of master rubric. That is, the rubric "public health" could exceed its capacity as a heuristic for understanding what is ultimately at stake in colonia development: the health of bodies and minds, and all the social implications that follow. We could actually *work*—in health-care delivery systems themselves, in housing, in local natural resource management, in economic sustainability, in nutrition, in community education—from the standpoint that these are all aspects of health. Further, the authors suggest that we may find an important synergy with human rights as a promising avenue for pressing claims. If, as

Paul Farmer has so convincingly argued (1999, 2005), we must shift the paradigm of public health toward human rights, then, in colonias work, two powerful terrains of redressing discrimination come together.

These chapters demonstrate that, without dismissing the pressing need for better standards of living in the economy as presently constituted, we can still break out of the received wisdom of colonias development. Does economic development always have to be about business and employment conventionally understood? Could sustainability—green building, self-help food production—for its own sake and for community well-being be worked into conceptions of economic development, as well as of rights?

Organizations on the Mexican side of the border that I am collaborating with are asking these kinds of questions. How do we consider such questions if we wish to move from criticism to construction? Prior to shifting to border studies, my own work looked closely at the concept and practice of autonomy, mainly in the context of indigenous rights organizations in Mexico building on the energy of the Zapatista Rebellion (Smith 2004). But autonomy, or self-determination, is a transferrable concept, able to frame the aspirations as well as the nuts and bolts of the development initiatives of stressed communities everywhere, especially during a historical conjuncture like our own. To borrow Marx's famous phrase, much that is solid seems to be melting into air. As energy economies fall deeper into crisis, as we wring our hands about dwindling and decaying farmland, as we prognosticate that future wars will be fought over the most basic of resources, water, and as we face the prospect of debt and financial instability and diminishing soft money and reduced public budgets, "sustainability" is ineluctably the order of the day, even if that concept falls victim to distortion by greenwashing or gets hollowed out as a buzzword. That, in fact, should worry us, as should the inertia of the institutions and global power elites and cultures of consumption too invested in the status quo to get serious, and immediately, about alternative paths. In other words, do we have time to counter that inertia before planetary systems collapse? This is not doomsaying; it is simply another earnest call to put our money where our mouth is. Although one should always be respectful before the priorities and immediate needs of real people in real time and place *as they themselves understand and express them,* it makes sense to think about colonias in just this sort of urgent big picture. One thing my friend Jose Luis Ramirez, Mexican Director of the binational organization DouglaPrieta Works (DPW), has taught me is that we can make a virtue of necessity by plugging a specific colonia's bid for development into the larger projects of our time. In addition to advancing market-led entrepreneurial programs like carpentry and sewing cooperatives, he and I are initiating a permaculture program that will include household kitchen gardens, water conservation, nopal cactus production for consumption and sale, small livestock, and natural building. Step-by-step, we are converting a city lot of construction fill dirt into an outdoor classroom for community instruction in integrated permaculture principles and practices. We are also working toward partnering with a nearby rural community of farmers, ranchers, artisan millers, and cheese makers, likewise interested in permaculture. Ultimately, the objective is to build a regional network of projects, each of which would form a building block toward sustainable regional subsistence systems. In so doing, we are seeking to tap both local knowledge and cutting-edge sustainability theory and practice to consolidate more self-determined futures. We want to diminish colonia residents' dependency, both on government assistance programs and on (usually) U.S.-led charity missions.

DPW represents one attempt at counterdevelopment, integrating elements of tradition and (post)modernity. Through our efforts in DPW, we are hoping to realize the potential of praxis. Praxis is critical in disposition, premised on the understanding that culture can be a force for disorder as well as for order (Bauman 1999). Indeed, the world culture underpinning modernization schemes has left a lot of disorder in its wake. And praxis is about directing, again, critically, our labor to transform the world and be transformed thereby (Bhaskar 1989; Hoffman 1975; Korsch 1971; Mepham and Ruben 1979)—transformed, in this context, into bearers of a more constructive culture of development. And here is where colonia development takes on focus and gets very interesting, even exciting. Many of the authors in this book agree that present bureaucracies, because of their ideological commitments and material limitations, are failing colonias. And yet those institutions have produced seeds that one might nurture. Sweat equity self-help housing, the CHW approach, and promotor(a)s pursuing a host of grassroots agendas are all beginnings that could be massaged toward a fuller-blown armature for autonomy as the central goal of praxis. Thus, I do not believe we should cease being witnesses to history and leave off decrying the intractable poverty and discrimination colonia residents continue to endure. But again, we might follow the "postdevelopment" scholars and activists (see Rahnema and Bawtree 1997) coming out of a long period of *critical* development studies whose program at the end of the day was to tear down the development concept altogether. Now it is time to be positive both attitudinally and in terms of actually producing something that works—something that is not only livable but constructive for the planet—and making that matter as an example for other localities. Thus, a particular colonia's process links up with the larger, piecemeal process toward global sustainability that will be the cumulative outcome of a constellation of local and regional initiatives, buoyed up (hopefully) by the hard-won support of necessary new directions in national and international policy (Keare 2001). One can think about such a road as an activist mission in the already applied scientific field of Colonia Studies.

Praxis Ethnogaphy

The world has been talking about sustainability for about four decades. If we want to move Colonias Studies beyond becoming merely another voice in this crowded discourse, we need to base both our ideas and our pragmatics on richer methodologies. Of course, not all praxis-inspired programs would look like DPW permaculture. If we take counterdevelopment seriously at all, each of us will take it to the streets consonant with the specific profile of a specific colonia setting and pool of assets.

How do we make praxis something more substantive than a set of notions in progressive professionals' heads by really bringing colonia residents into it? At the same time, how do we deepen the functional relationship between scholar-researchers and practitioners that this volume introduces? As this volume shows and as I have argued, Colonia Studies scholars and practitioners working in colonias are defining themes and arguments that bring a certain unity of the field into focus. One methodological move that I think will be critical in defining, deepening, and enlivening this unity concerns ethnography. Not the "objective," cultural relativist, observe-and-document-the-daily-life-of-people sort of ethnography, but the "barefoot" ethnography that Nancy Scheper-Hughes has described (1995), whose ethos demands that we call the world like we see it and not be afraid to change it (see also Hackenberg and Hackenberg 1999). Further, as an applied anthropologist I remain committed to a participatory action research (PAR) approach that enfranchises research "subjects" from beginning to end of the research process (van Willigan 2002). PAR, inspired by Paolo Freire's "pedagogy of the oppressed" (see Arizmendi, Arizmendi, and Donelson, chapter 6), recognizes that the research process itself as well as its outcomes may be greatly enhanced when community members play an active role in designing research methodologies, carrying them out, and processing data. It is a critical pedagogy, an exploratory investigative process that begins with everyday social experience and builds conceptual complexity from that level up. PAR is, of course, not new to many applied social scientists working in colonias, but we have not come close to realizing its potential, especially as we revitalize it through the sustainability praxis that I am arguing is incumbent on all of us. For one thing, PAR, and indeed applied social science work in general, has often been single-problem-oriented and short-lived in the actual field ("rapid ethnographic assessment," in the parlance of applied anthropology). We need sustained, holistic research and action over a longer haul.

To make my case for this type of collaborative ethnography, and to consolidate my arguments regarding theory and researcher-practitioner cooperation, let me consider those issues through the provocative questions suggested in the volume's final chapter, Collins's (chapter 15) account of local perceptions of environmental threat in a Calexico colonia. Collins sounds an important cautionary note. Even if we bring to our work, both as researchers and workers in the trenches, a theoretically informed idea of what is to be done, we cannot presume that colonia residents will agree with us. Collins indicates that in Imperial Valley colonias, residents are highly satisfied with housing and environmental conditions, even though both are deplorable by most accounts. She continues by noting that colonia residents are far more concerned with issues of income and overall well-being for their children than with environmental and public health. Of course, colonia residents may not be positioned to perceive certain environmental threats. They might also be concerned that calling attention to their discontent will prejudice them somehow, especially if they are undocumented workers. Further, we must always be sensitive to how communities perceive us as researchers.

But praxis ethnography is a two-way street. Collins's chapter raises the questions of whether we should allow people to be satisfied with present conditions and whether it is okay for researchers and practitioners to rest on what colonia residents tell them. I think she would agree that we do not want to fall into the binary-oppositional frame of mind that judges our models of the world as colonialist the minute we wish to apply them to the people we study and work with. I have already suggested that countering the negative dimensions of development cultures in colonias means that someone has to step up and judge them wanting, and sustainability will be an educative process perhaps more for colonia residents than for "us." In the Imperial Valley and many other places, environmental dangers, economic disadvantage, and racial discrimination are inextricable. These are cases of environmental injustice whether affected communities tell us so or not. Collins spends a good bit of the chapter detailing how deprived—from "our" perspective—Imperial Valley farmworkers are, and she is clear that the agribusiness establishment there is responsible for a landscape of haves and have-nots. She calls the uncritical views of her survey respondents "problematic." I agree. Based on these research findings, residents do not see the relationship between environmental security and their children's safety and security. Moreover, partly because of this elision, the state feels little obligation to pressure agro-industry to clean up its act. From my standpoint as an aspiring holistic praxis researcher, I wonder whether it is feasible to design an integrated PAR project around the theme of security, a master rubric potentially as fertile as public health or social justice, and certainly embracing these two. Here and elsewhere, not only would a policy-interventionist PAR ethnography explore the wells of creative thinking and action such a holism might uncover, it would also help bridge whatever gaps exist between colonia residents, researchers, NGOs, and maybe even policymakers as we confront the urgencies of the era.

Summary

In sum, the book takes a critical and valuable step in establishing colonias as a field of study worthy of its own identity. The book provides an excellent portrayal of economy, housing, and public/environmental health in borderland colonias and brings forward many of the issues that underpin problems. This concluding chapter suggested pathways for bridging theory and practice and thus advancing Colonia Studies in the years ahead. In view of the mounting social, economic, and environmental/public health problems that confront the borderlands, the need to address colonia issues head-on will only deepen.

Notes

1. Major works in this line of investigation include Apffel-Marglin and Marglin 1990; Sachs 1992; Tsing 1993; Ferguson 1994; Escobar 1995; Gupta 1998. More regionally, we might look forward to bringing Colonia Studies into conversation with critical scholarship on land use and land-related social policies that have prejudiced or threaten both people and natural resources in the Southwest and southern California (de Buys 1999; Hackenberg and Benequista 2001; Sheridan 2001, 2006).

2. See Comaroff 1985; Comaroff and Comaroff 1993; Hobart 1993; Brow 1996; Cooper and Packard 1997; Scott 1998; Arce and Long 2000.

3. "Discovering" is not the same as "inventing"—see Hobsbawm and Ranger 1983—even if discovering involves an interpretation of tradition firmly situated in present concerns.

Works Cited

Agency for Healthcare Research and Quality. 2005. *2005 National Health Disparities Report*. Rockville, MD: U.S. Department of Health and Human Services.

Aguirre International. 2005. *The California Farm Labor Force Overview and Trends from the National Agricultural Workers Survey*. Burlingame, CA: Aguirre International.

Allensworth, Elaine, and Refugio Rochin. 1996. *White Exodus, Latino Repopulation, and Community Well-Being: Trends in California's Rural Communities*. Research Report no. 13, Julian Samora Research Institute. East Lansing: Michigan State University.

Allmendinger, Philip. 2002. *Planning Theory*. New York: Palgrave.

Alvarez, Robert. 1995. The Mexican–U.S. Border: The Making of an Anthropology of Borderlands. *Annual Review of Anthropology* 24: 447–470.

Amnesty International. 2007. Femicide in Ciudad Juárez and Chihuahua, Mexico Photo Exhibition. Available via http://www.amnestyusa.org/women/juarez/photoexhibit.html?tr=y&auid=2173748; accessed 18 December 2008.

Anderson, Joan, and Martín de la Rosa. 1991. Economic Survival Strategies of Poor Families in the U.S.–Mexico Border Region. *Journal of Borderlands Studies* 6: 51–68.

Anderson, Joan, and James Gerber. 2007. *Fifty Years of Change on the U.S.–Mexico Border: Growth, Development, and Quality of Life*. Austin: University of Texas Press.

Appfel-Marglin, Frederique, and Stephen Marglin. 1990. *Dominating Knowledge: Development, Culture, and Resistance*. Oxford: Clarendon Press.

Applebome, Peter. 1989. At Texas Border, Hope for Sewers and Water. *New York Times*, January 3, p. 1.

Arce, Alberto, and Norman Long. 2000. Reconfiguring Modernity and Development from an Anthropological Perspective. In *Anthropology, Development and Modernities*, ed. Alberto Arce and Norman Long, pp. 1–31. London: Routledge.

Arcury, Thomas, and Sara Quandt. 2007. Delivery of Health Services to Migrant and Seasonal Farmworkers. *Annual Review of Public Health* 28: 345–363.

Arizona American Friends Service Committee. 2008. *What Is Arizona AFSC?* Available via http://www.afsc.org/ht/d/ContentDetails/i/4898; accessed 18 December 2008.

Arizona Department of Commerce. 2008a. *Arizona Workforce Report.* Available via http://www.workforce.az.gov/admin/uploadedPublications/.

Arizona Department of Commerce. 2008b. *Arizona Community Economic Base Studies.* Available via http://www.azcommerce.com/Research/BaseStudies/.

Arizona Department of Environmental Quality. 2006. *Air Quality Monitoring Research Programs.* Available via http://www.azdeq.gov/environ/air/monitoring/border.html; accessed 31 December 2008.

Arizona Department of Health Services. 2003. *Arizona Community Health Profiles.* Phoenix: Arizona Primary Care Area Program. Available via http://www.azdhs.gov/hsd/chpweb/2003/profiles.htm; accessed 30 December 2008.

Arizona Department of Health Services. 2007. *Santa Cruz County Report for the 2007 Youth Risk Behavior Survey.* Phoenix: Steps to a Healthier Arizona Initiative, Arizona Department of Health Services, Public Health Prevention Services.

Arizona Secretary of State. 2002. *State of Arizona Official Canvass.* Available via http://www.azsos.gov/election/2002/General/Canvass2002GE.pdf; accessed 30 December 2008.

Arizona Workforce Informer. 2008. 2001–2008 Nonfarm Jobs Data. Available via http://www.workforce.az.gov/?PAGEID=67&SUBID=142; accessed 18 December 2008.

Arnold, Chester, and C. James Gibbons. 1996. Impervious Surface Coverage: Emergence of a Key Environmental Factor. *Journal of the American Planning Association* 62: 243–258.

Arreola, Daniel, and James Curtis. 1993. *The Mexican Border Cities: Landscape Anatomy and Place Personality.* Tucson: University of Arizona Press.

ASU Stardust Center for Affordable Homes and the Family. 2006a. Nageezi House: 2005. Affordable + Sustainable Design/Build fact sheet. Available via http://stardust.asu.edu/; accessed 18 December 2008.

ASU Stardust Center for Affordable Homes and the Family. 2006b. *Guadalupe House:* 2006. Affordable + Sustainable Demonstration Home project fact sheets. Available via http://stardust.asu.edu/; accessed 18 December 2008.

Auchincloss, Amy, Ana Roux, Daniel Brown, Christine Erdmann, and Alain Bertoni. 2008. Neighborhood Resources for Physical Activity and Healthy Foods and Their Association with Insulin Resistance. *Epidemiology* 19: 146–157.

Bandy, Dewey. 2004. *Farm Worker Cooperative Housing: Training Needs Assessment.* California Coalition for Rural Housing. Available via http://www.calruralhousing.org/publications; accessed 18 December 2008.

Bastidea, Elena, Israel Cuéllar, and Paul Villas. 2001. Prevalence of Diabetes Mellitus and Related Conditions in a South Texas Mexican American Sample. *Journal of Community Health Nursing* 18: 75–84.

Bastidea, Elena, Shelton Brown, and José Pagán. 2008. Persistent Disparities in the Use of Health Care on the U.S./Mexico Border: An Ecological Perspective. *American Journal of Public Health* 98: 1987–1994.

Bauman, Zygmunt. 1999. *Culture as Praxis.* London: Sage.

Beach, Dana. 2002. Coastal Sprawl: *The Effects of Urban Design on Aquatic Ecosystems in the United States*. Arlington, VA: Pew Oceans Commission.

Bee, Ed. 2004. Small Business Vitality and Economic Development. *Economic Development Journal* 3(3): 7–15.

Belden, Joseph, and Robert Wiener. 1999. *Housing and Rural America: Building Affordable and Inclusive Communities*. Thousand Oaks, CA: Sage.

Belshe, Kimberly, and Sandra Shewy. 2003. *Border Health Status Report 2002–2003. California Department of Health Services*. Available via http://www.cdph.ca .gov/programs/cobbh/Documents/BorderHealthStatusBorder-2002–2003 .pdf; accessed 22 December 2008.

Bhaskar, Roy. 1989. *Reclaiming Reality: Philosophical Underlabouring*. London: Verso.

Blaesser, Brian, and Alan Weinstein. 1989. *Land Use and the Constitution: Principles for Planning Practice*. Chicago: Planners Press.

Blakely, Edward. 1994. *Planning Local Economic Development: Theory and Practice*. London: Sage.

Border Low Income Housing Coalition. 1993. Border Housing and Community Development Partnership Plan. Paper presented to Gov. Ann Richards, June 1993, Austin. Available via http://www.texashousing.org/documents/files/bhcdp.pdf; accessed 18 December 2008.

Boser, Richard, Tory Ragsdale, and Charles Duvel. 2002. Recycled Foam and Cement Composites in Insulating Concrete Forms. *Journal of Industrial Technology* 18: 2–5. Available via http://www.nait.org.

Bowden, Virginia, Frederick Wood, Debra Warner, Cynthia Olney, Evelyn Olivier, and Elliot Siegel. 2006. Health Information Hispanic Outreach in the Texas Lower Rio Grande Valley. *Journal of the Medical Library Association* 94: 180–189.

Boyer, Elizabeth, Christine Goodale, Norbert Jaworski, and Robert Howarth. 2002. Anthropogenic Nitrogen Sources and Relationships to Riverine Nitrogen Export in the Northeastern USA. *Biogeochemistry* 57: 137–69.

Bradshaw, William, Edward Connelly, Madeline Cook, James Goldstein, and Justin Pauly. 2005. *The Costs and Benefits of Green Affordable Housing*. Cambridge, MA: New Ecology.

Brooks, Kenneth, Peter Ffolliott, Hans Gregersen, and John Thames. 1997. *Hydrology and the Management of Watersheds*, 2nd ed. Ames: Iowa State University Press.

Brow, James. 1996. *Demons and Development*. Tucson: University of Arizona Press.

Brulle, Robert, and David Pellow. 2006. Environmental Justice: Human Health and Environmental Inequalities. *Annual Review of Public Health* 27: 103–24.

Buckwalter, Paul. 2003. Building Power: Finding and Developing Leaders in Arizona Congregations. *Social Policy* 33: 2–8.

Buelna, Genoveva, and Rumana Riffat. 2007. Preliminary Environmental Monitoring of Water Quality in the Rio Grande in the Laredo–Nuevo Laredo Region. *Journal of Environmental Science and Health, Part A* 42: 1379–90.

Bureau of Economic Affairs. 2007. Gross Domestic Products by State, 2006. Bureau of Economic Affairs, Regional Economic Accounts. Available via http://www .bea.gov/newsreleases/regional/gdp_state/2007/gsp0607.htm; accessed 25 June 2009.

Caetano, Raul, Suhasini Ramisetty-Mikler, Lynn Wallisch, Christine McGrath, and Richard Spence. 2008. Acculturation, Drinking, and Alcohol Abuse and Dependence among Hispanics in the Texas-Mexico Border. *Alcoholism: Clinical and Experimental Research* 32: 314–321.

Calexico New River Committee. n.d. City of Calexico New River Committee. Available via http://www.calexiconewriver.org/; accessed 6 January 2009.

California Coalition for Rural Housing. 2007. Programs. Available via http://www .calruralhousing.org/programs; accessed 18 December 2008.

California Department of Finance. 2007. Population Estimates and Components of Change—July 1, 2000–2007. Available via: http://www.dof.ca.gov/HTML/ DEMOGRAP/ReportsPapers/Estimates/E6/E6-00-05/E-6_Report_00-07 .php; accessed 6 January 2009.

California Department of Food and Agriculture. 2007. *California Agriculture Resource Directory 2007.* Sacramento: California Department of Food and Agriculture.

California Employment Development Department. 2007. Labor Market Information. Available via http://www.labormarketinfo.edd.ca.gov/; accessed 6 January 2009.

California Housing Law Project. 2001. AB 3526: Farmlabor Housing Protection Act of 1992. Available via http://www.housingadvocates.org/default.asp?ID=115; accessed 18 December 2008.

California Institute for Rural Studies. 2000. *Suffering in Silence: A Report on the Health of California's Agricultural Workers.* Woodland Hills, CA: California Endowment.

Carranza, Reyna, Marco Antonio, Kimberly Collins, Margarito Quintero Núñez, and Luis Vildósola Reyes. 2004. *Examinando la Asociación de PM10 con las enfermedades respiratorias de la población urbana de Mexicali.* Un Estudio de Series de Tiempo. Baja California: Mexicana de Ingeniería Biomédica.

Carroll, Susan. 2006. "Colonia" Problem Growing in Arizona. *Arizona Republic,* January 23, p. 1A.

Carter, Nicole, and Leonard Ortolano. 2004. Implementing Government Assistance Programmes for Water and Sewer Systems in Texas Colonias. *Water Resources Development* 20: 553–564.

Castells, Manuel. 2000. Materials for an Exploratory Theory of the Network Society. *British Journal of Sociology* 51: 5–24.

Centers for Disease Control and Prevention. n.d. United States–Mexico Border Environmental Health Issues. Available via http://www.cdc.gov/nceh/hsb/ borderhealth/; accessed 22 December 2008.

Centers for Disease Control and Prevention. 2004. Health Disparities Experienced by Hispanics–United States. *Morbidity and Mortality Weekly Report* 53: 935–937.

Chapa, Jorge, and David J. Eaton. 1997. *Colonia Housing and Infrastructure*. Austin: University of Texas, LBJ School of Public Affairs.

Chaves, Mark. 2004. *Congregations in America*. Cambridge: Harvard University Press.

Chavez, Leo. 1991. *Shadowed Lives: Undocumented Immigrants in American Society*. Orlando: Harcourt College Publishers.

Cisneros, Ariel. 2001. Texas Colonias: Housing and Infrastructure Issues. *Border Economy*, June, pp. 19–21.

City of El Cenizo. n.d. Available via http://www.cityofelcenizo.com/index.htm; accessed 18 December 2008.

City of Pharr Water Billing. 2007. City of Pharr. Available via http://tx-pharr2 .civicplus.com/index.asp?NID=66; accessed 18 December 2008.

Clark, Margaret, and Tracy Huston. 1992. *Directory of Microenterprise Programs*. Washington, D.C.: Aspen Institute.

Clement, Norris. 2003. *The U.S.–Mexican Border Environment: U.S.–Mexican Border Communities in the NAFTA Era*. San Diego: San Diego State University Press and Southwest Center for Environmental Research and Policy.

Coachella Valley Housing Coalition. 2001. Programs. Available via http://www .ruralisc.org/cvhc.htm; accessed 18 December 2008.

Cohen, Jeffrey. 2004. Colorado River Delta. *BioScience* 54: 386–391.

Cohen, Stuart, and Maia Ingram. 2005. Border Health Strategic Initiative: Overview and Introduction to a Community-Based Model for Diabetes Prevention and Control. *Preventing Chronic Disease* 2(1) [serial online]. Available via http://www.cdc.gov/pcd/issues/2005/jan/04_0081.htm; accessed 30 December 2008.

Cohen, Stuart, Joel Meister, and Jill Guernsey de Zapien. 2004. Special Action Groups for Policy Change and Infrastructure Support to Foster Healthier Communities on the Arizona–Mexico border. *Public Health Reports* 119: 40–47.

Collins, Kimberly. 2005. *Local Government Capacity and Quality of Life in the U.S.–Mexican Border: The Case of Calexico and Mexicali*. Ph.D. diss., Applied Social Sciences, El Colegio de la Frontera Norte, Tijuana, Baja California, Mexico.

Collins, Kimberly. 2007. *CCBRES Bulletin* 8, nos. 9–10.

Collins-Dogrul, Julie. 2006. Managing U.S.–Mexico Border Health: An Organizational Field Approach. *Social Science & Medicine* 63: 3199–3211.

Colorado River Basin Regional Water Quality Control Board. 2008. Introduction to the New River/Mexicali Sanitation Program. Available via http://www.swrcb .ca.gov/rwqcb7/water_issues/programs/new_river/nr_intro.shtml; accessed 6 January 2009.

Comaroff, Jean. 1985. *Body of Power, Spirit of Resistance*. Chicago: University of Chicago Press.

Comaroff, John, and Jean Comaroff. 1993. *Modernity and Its Malcontents: Ritual and Power in Post-Colonial Africa*. Chicago: University of Chicago Press.

Comité de Bienestar. 2008. Strategies and Accomplishments Fact Sheet. Available via http://www.ruralisc.org/comite.htm; accessed 18 December 2008.

Community Housing Improvement Program. 2008. Mutual Self-Help Housing. Available via http://www.chiphousing.org/nodes/self_help_housing; accessed 18 December 2008.

Consumer Action. 2005. Micro Business Basics. Building a Sound Financial Foundation. Money Wise—A Consumer Action Publication. Available via http://www.consumer-action.org/modules/articles/micro_business_basics_english; accessed 18 December 2008.

Cooper, Frederick, and Randall Packard. 1997. *International Development and the Social Sciences.* Berkeley: University of California Press.

Corbett, Jim. 1991. *Goatwalking: A Guide to Wildland Living.* Bergenfield, NJ: Viking Press.

Corkery, Eileen, Carmen Palmer, Mary E. Foley, Clyde B. Schechter, Leah Frisher, and Sheila H. Roman. 1997. Effect of a Bicultural Community Health Worker on Completion of Diabetes Education in a Hispanic Population. *Diabetes Care* 20: 254–257.

County of Imperial. 2002. *Colonia Master Plan.* El Centro, CA: Imperial County Community and Economic Development.

Crowe, Jessica. 2006. Community Economic Development Strategies in Rural Washington: Towards a Synthesis of Natural and Social Capital. *Rural Sociology* 74: 573–596.

Cunningham, Peter, Michelle Banker, Samantha Artiga, and Jennifer Tolbert. 2006. *Health Coverage and Access to Care for Hispanics in New Growth Communities and Major Hispanic Centers.* Washington, D.C.: Kaiser Family Foundation.

Curtis, Sarah. 2004. *Health and Inequality.* Thousand Oaks, CA: Sage.

Czerniak, Robert J., and Adrian Esparza. 2004. Colonias in Texas, New Mexico and Arizona: Economic and Business Development Strategies. Unpublished report prepared for the U.S. Department of Housing and Urban Development, December 2004.

Dannenberg, Andrew, Richard Jackson, Howard Frumkin, Richard Schieber, Michael Pratt, Chris Kochtitzky, and Hugh Tilson. 2003. The Impact of Community Design and Land-Use Choices on Public Health: A Scientific Research Agenda. *American Journal of Public Health* 93: 1500–1508.

Davidhizar, Ruth, and Gregory Bechtel. 1999. Health and Quality of Life within Colonias Settlements along the United States and Mexico Border. *Public Health Nursing* 16: 301–306.

Davies, Christopher, and Robert Holz. 1992. Settlement Evolution of Colonias along the U.S.–Mexico Border. *Habitat International* 16: 119–142.

Davis, Mike. 2006. *Planet of Slums.* New York: Verso.

Davis, Tony. 2000. Wildcat Subdivisions Fuel Fight over Sprawl. *Arizona Daily Star,* April 24, p. 1A.

de Buys, William. 1999. *Salt Dreams: Land and Water in Low-Down California.* Albuquerque: University of New Mexico Press.

Desert Alliance for Community Empowerment. 2008. Housing Services. Available via http://www.dace-rancho.org/DACE_Housing.htm; accessed 18 December 2008.

Diaz, David. 2005. *Barrio Urbanism: Chicanos, Planning and American Cities*. New York: Routledge.

Dissart, J.-C., and Steven C. Deller. 2000. Quality of Life in the Planning Literature. *Journal of Planning Literature* 15: 135–161.

Dolhinow, Rebecca. 2005. Caught in the Middle: The State, NGOs and the Limits to Grassroots Organizing along the U.S.–Mexico Border. *Antipode* 37: 558–580.

Donelson, Angela. 2004. The Role of NGOs and NGO Networks in Meeting the Needs of U.S. Colonias. *Community Development Journal* 39: 332–344.

Donelson, Angela, and Adrian Esparza. 2007. Undocumented Immigrants and Quality of Life in New Mexico and Arizona Colonias. *Journal of Borderlands Studies* 22: 39–52.

Donelson, Angela, and Esperanza Holguin. 2001. Homestead Subdivision/Colonias and Land Market Dynamics in Arizona and New Mexico. Paper presented at the conference on Irregular Settlement and Self-Help Housing in the United States: Memoria of a Research Project, at the Lincoln Institute of Land Policy, September 2001, Cambridge, Massachusetts.

Doyle, Timothy, and Ralph Bryan. 2000. Infectious Disease Morbidity in the U.S. Region Bordering Mexico, 1990–1998. *Journal of Infectious Diseases* 182: 1503–1510.

Dunn, Timothy J. 1996. *The Militarization of the U.S.–Mexico Border, 1978–1992*. Austin: The Center for Mexican American Studies, University of Texas at Austin.

Earle, Duncan. 1999. The Border Colonias and the Problem of Communication: Applying Anthropology for Outreach. In *Life, Death and In-Between on the U.S.–Mexico Border*, ed. Martha Loustaunau and Mary Sanchez-Bane, 23–38. Westport, CT: Bergin and Garvey.

Edgcomb, Elaine, and Joyce Klein. 2005. *Opening Opportunities, Building Ownership. Fulfilling the Promise of Microenterprise in the United States*. Washington, D.C.: Aspen Institute.

Ehrenberg, Ronald, and Robert Smith. 2000. *Modern Labor Economics: Theory and Public Policy*. New York: Addison Wesley Longman.

Elac, John. 1972. *The Employment of Mexican Workers in U.S. Agriculture, 1900–1960: A Bi-national Economic Analysis*. Ph.D. diss., UCLA.

Elder, John, Guadalupe Ayala, Nadia R. Campbell, Donald Slymen, Eva T. Lopez-Madurga, and Moshe Engelberg. 2005. Interpersonal and Print Nutrition Communication for a Spanish-Dominant Latino Population: Secretos de la Buena Vida. *Health Psychology* 24: 49–57.

Eldridge, Jennifer. 2002. Health Care Access for Immigrants in Texas. Working paper from the Policy Research Project Expanding Health Care Coverage for the Uninsured. Austin: The LBJ School of Public Affairs, University of Texas–Austin.

Eng, Eugenia, and Rebecca Young. 1992. Lay Health Advisors as Community Change Agents. *Family and Community Health* 15: 24–40.

Escobar, Arturo. 1995. *Encountering Development*. Princeton, NJ: Princeton University Press.

Esparza, Adrian, and Angela Donelson. 2008. *Colonias in Arizona and New Mexico: U.S.–Mexico Border Poverty and Community Development Solutions.* Tucson: University of Arizona Press.

Esparza, Adrian, and Andrew J. Krmenec. 1999a. City Systems and Industrial Market Structure. *Annals of the Association of American Geographers* 89: 267–89.

Esparza, Adrian, and Andrew J. Krmenec. 1999b. Entrepreneurship and Producer Services Markets. *Growth and Change* 30: 216–236.

Esparza, Adrian, Javier Chavez, and Brigitte Waldorf. 2001. Industrialization and Land Use Change in Mexican Border Cities: The Case of Ciudad Juárez, México. *Journal of Borderlands Studies* 16: 15–30.

Esparza, Adrian, Brigitte Waldorf, and Javier Chavez. 2004. Localized Effects of Globalization: The Case of Ciudad Juárez, Chihuahua, Mexico. *Urban Geography* 25: 120–138.

Evans, Gary, and Elyse Kantrowitz. 2002. Socioeconomic Status and Health: The Potential Role of Environmental Risk Exposure. *Annual Review of Public Health* 23: 303–331.

Fairlie, Robert W. 2001. *Earnings Growth among Disadvantaged Business Owners.* Final Report to the Office of Advocacy, U.S. Small Business Administration. Available via http://www.sba.gov/ADVO/research/rs209tot.pdf; accessed 18 December 2008.

Farmer, Paul. 1999. *Infections and Inequalities.* Berkeley: University of California Press.

Farmer, Paul. 2005. *Pathologies of Power.* Berkeley: University of California Press.

Farris, Anne, Richard Nathan, and David Wright. 2004. *The Expanding Administrative Presidency: George W. Bush and the Faith-Based Initiative.* Albany: Rockefeller Institute of Government Roundtable on Religion and Social Welfare Policy.

Federal Reserve Bank of Dallas. 2007. Texas Colonias: A Thumbnail Sketch of the Conditions, Issues, Challenges and Opportunities. Available via http://dallasfed.org/ca/pubs/colonias.html; accessed 22 December 2008.

Ferguson, James. 1994. *The Anti-Politics Machine.* Minneapolis: University of Minnesota Press.

Fernández-Kelly, Patricia. 1983. *For We Are Sold, I and My People: Women and Industry in Mexico's Frontier.* Albany: State University of New York Press.

Forbes, Kathryn. 2007. Bureaucratic Strategies of Exclusion: Land Use Ideology and Images of Mexican Farm Workers in Housing Policy. *Human Organization* 66: 196–209.

Freire, Paolo. 1970. *Pedagogy of the Oppressed.* New York: Continuum.

Frey, John Carlos, dir. 2006. *Invisible Mexicans of Deer Canyon.* Los Angeles: Gatekeeper Productions. Available via http://www.invisiblemexicans.com/; accessed 20 December 2008.

Fronstin, Paul. 2005. Sources of Health Insurance and Characteristics of the Uninsured: Analysis of the March 2005 Current Population Survey. EBRI Issue brief, no. 287. Washington, D.C.: Employee Benefit Research Institute.

Frumkin, Howard. 2003. Healthy Places: Exploring the Evidence. *American Journal of Public Health* 93: 1451–1456.

Galarza, Ernesto. 1964. *Merchants of Labor: The Mexican Bracero Story*. Charlotte, NC: McNally & Loftin.

Galarza, Ernesto. 1977. *Farm Workers and Agribusiness in California: 1947–1960*. South Bend, IN: University of Notre Dame Press.

Galjart, Benno. 1981. Counterdevelopment: A Position Paper. *Community Development Journal* 16: 88–96.

Ganster, Paul, and David E. Lorey. 2008. *The U.S.–Mexican Border into the Twenty-First Century*. Lanham, MD: Rowman and Littlefield.

Garcia, Alexandra, Evangelina Villagomez, Sharon Brown, Kamiar Kouzekanani, and Craig Hanis. 2001. The Starr County Diabetes Education Study: Development of the Spanish-Language Diabetes Questionnaire. *Diabetes Care* 24: 16–21.

Garcia, Guillermo. 1999. Border Battle Centers on "Spanish-Only" Town. *USA Today*, December 17, 1999, section A, p. 21.

Gerber, James. 1999. The Effects of a Depreciation of the Peso on Cross Border Retail Sales in San Diego and Imperial Counties. *San Diego Dialogue*. Available via http://www.sandiegodialogue.org/pdfs/tax_summary.pdf; accessed 19 December 2008.

Gibson, Lay J., Raphael Gruener, Bruce Wright, and Vera Pavlakovich-Kochi. 2008. Closing the Industry–Community Gap through Community Engagement: High Tech/Biotech's New frontier. Project report prepared for the U.S. Department of Commerce, Economic Development Administration, Western Regional Office, Seattle, Washington.

Gilmer, Todd, and Richard Kronick. 2001. Calm before the Storm: Expected Increase in the Number of Uninsured Americans. *Health Affairs* 20: 207–210.

Giusti, Cecilia, Jane Larson, Peter Ward, Flavio de Souza, and Marlynn May. 2006. Land Titling in Starr County Colonias along the Texas–Mexico Border. *Projections—Mismatched Boundaries* 6: 36–55.

Global Green USA. 2007. *Blueprint for Greening Affordable Housing*. Washington, D.C.: Island Press.

González, Gilbert, and Raúl Fernandez. 2002. Empire and the Origins of Twentieth-Century Migration from Mexico to the United States. *Pacific Historical Review* 71: 19–57.

Gruben, William, and Sherry Kiser. 2001. NAFTA and Maquiladoras: Is the Growth Connected? *Border Economy*, June, pp. 22–24. Available via http://www.dallasfed.org/research/border/tbe_gruben.pdf; accessed 25 January 2009.

Gupta, Akhil. 1998. *Postcolonial Developments*. Durham, NC: Duke University Press.

Haass, Jeffrey, Gayle Miller, Anne Haddix, Laurence Nickey, and Thomas Sinks. 1996. An Economic Analysis of Water and Sanitation Infrastructure Improvements in the Colonias of El Paso County, Texas. *International Journal of Occupation and Environmental Health* 2: 211–221.

Hackenberg, Robert A., and Nick Benequista. 2001. The Future of an Imagined Community: Trailer Parks, Tree Huggers, and Trinational Forces Collide in the Southern Arizona Borderlands. *Human Organization* 60: 153–158.

Hackenberg, Robert A., and Beverly Hackenberg. 1999. You Can Do Something! Forming Policy from Applied Projects, Then and Now. *Human Organization* 58: 15–28.

Hadley, Jack, and Peter Cunningham. 2004. Availability of Safety Net Providers and Access to Care of Uninsured Persons. *Health Services Research* 39: 1527–1546.

Haffner, Steven M., Andrew Diehl, Braxton Mitchell, Michael Stern, and Helen Hazuda. 1990. Increased Prevalence of Clinical Gallbladder Disease in Subjects with Non-Insulin-Dependent Diabetes Mellitus. *American Journal of Epidemiology* 132: 327–335.

Haffner, Steven M., Donald Fong, Michael P. Stern, Jacqueline A. Pugh, Helen P. Hazuda, Judith K. Patterson, W. A. Van Heuven, and R. Klein. 1988. Diabetic Retinopathy in Mexican Americans and Non-Hispanic Whites. *Diabetes Care* 37: 878–884.

Hall, Peter. 1996. Microenterprise. *World Watch* 9: 10–19.

Hanis, Craig, Robert Ferrell, Sara Barton, Lydia Aguilar, Ana Garzaibarra, Brian Tulloch, Charles Garcia, and William Schull. 1983. Diabetes among Mexican Americans in Starr County, Texas. *American Journal of Epidemiology* 118: 659–668.

Hansen, Lisa, Polly Feigl, Manuel Modiano, Jose Lopez, Sylvia Escobedo Sluder, Carol Moinpour, and Paula Donner. 2005. An Educational Program to Increase Cervical and Breast Cancer Screening in Hispanic Women: A Southwest Oncology Group Study. *Cancer Nursing* 28: 47–53.

Hardin, Mary. 2006. Research as Ethical Practice: Academic Goals Aligned with Community Needs. In *From the Studio to the Streets: Service Learning in Planning and Architecture,* ed. Mary Hardin, 59–76. Sterling, VA: Stylus.

Harrison, Rebecca. 1995. *Houston Hispanic Entrepreneurs: Profile and Needs Assessment*. New York: Garland.

Harvey, David. 1985. *The Urbanization of Capital*. Baltimore: Johns Hopkins University Press.

Harvey, David. 2002. The Urban Process under Capitalism: A Framework for Analysis. In *The Blackwell City Reader,* ed. Gary Bridge and Sophie Watson, 116–124. Malden, MA: Blackwell.

Headd, Brian. 2000. The Characteristics of Small-Business Employees. *Monthly Labor Review* 123: 13–18.

Health Resources and Services Administration. 2000. *Assuring a Healthy Future along the U.S.–Mexico Border*. Rockville, MD: U.S. Government Printing Office.

Health Resources and Services Administration. 2007a. *Border County Health Workforce Profiles: Arizona*. Rockville, MD: U.S. Department of Health and Human Services. Available at http://bhpr.hrsa.gov/healthworkforce/border/arizona/; accessed 20 May 2009.

Health Resources and Services Administration. 2007b. *Border County Health Workforce Profiles: California.* Rockville, MD: United States Department of Health and Human Services. Available via http://bhpr.hrsa.gov/healthworkforce/border/california/; accessed 20 May 2009.

Health Resources and Services Administration. 2007c. *Border County Health Workforce Profiles: New Mexico.* Rockville, MD: U.S. Department of Health and Human Services. Available via http://bhpr.hrsa.gov/healthworkforce/border/newmexico/; accessed 20 May 2009.

Health Resources and Services Administration. 2007d. *Border County Health Workforce Profiles: Texas.* Rockville, MD: U.S. Department of Health and Human Services. Available via http://bhpr.hrsa.gov/healthworkforce/border/texas/; accessed 20 May 2009.

Heisler, S., H. Balentine, L. Bradley, and M. Garcia. 1999. *Ambos Nogales Hazardous Air Pollution and Particulate Matter Air Quality Study Final Report.* Phoenix, AZ: Arizona Department of Environmental Quality Document 0493–016–300.

Henkel, David S. 1979. *A Socio-economic Profile of the Border Region,* vol. 1. Santa Fe: New Mexico State Planning Office.

Henneberger, John. 2000. Despite Economic Growth, Little Credit and Few Options for Working Families: Affordable Housing on the Border. *Borderlines* 65: 1.

Henry, Mark. 1999. Home Tour: Dirt, Bushes and Flies for Farm Workers. *Press–Enterprise,* Riverside County, June 5, section B (Local), p. 6.

Hernandez, Reggie Romo, Charles Curtis, Alfredo Huete, and Stephen Nelson. 2005. Regeneration of Native Trees in the Presence of Invasive Saltcedar in the Colorado River Delta, Mexico. *Conservation Biology* 19: 1842–1852.

Herrera-Pérez, Octavio. 2004. *La Zona Libre: Excepción fiscal y conformación histórica de la frontera norte de México.* Mexico, D.F.: Secretaría de Relaciones Exteriores.

Herzog, Lawrence. 1990. *Where North Meets South: Cities, Space, and Politics on the U.S.–Mexico Border.* Austin: University of Texas, Center for Mexican American Studies.

Heubusch, Kevin. 1997. *The New Rating Guide to Life in America's Small Cities.* New York: Prometheus Books.

Heyman, Josiah. 1993. The Oral History of the Mexican American Community of Douglas, Arizona, 1901–1942. *Journal of the Southwest* 35: 186–206.

Hill, Sarah. 2003. Metaphoric Enrichment and Material Poverty: The Making of "Colonias." In *Ethnography at the Border,* ed. P. Vila, 141–165. Minneapolis: University of Minnesota Press.

Hispanic and Native American Center of Excellence. n.d. Available at http://hsc.unm.edu/SOM/excellence/US_Mex_CoE.shtml; accessed 1 July 2009.

Hobart, Mark. 1993. *An Anthropological Critique of Development: The Growth of Ignorance.* London: Routledge.

Hobsbawm, Eric, and Terrence Ranger. 1983. *The Invention of Tradition.* London: Cambridge University Press.

Hoffman, John. 1975. *Marxism and the Theory of Praxis.* New York: International Publishers.

Hoffrichter, Richard. 2003. The Politics of Health Inequities. In *Health and Social Justice: Politics, Ideology and Inequity in the Distribution of Disease,* ed. Richard Hoffrichter, 1–56. San Francisco: John Wiley and Sons.

Hopkins, Randall. 1988. Diversification Plays a Key Role in Rural Job Growth. *Arizona's Economy* (December): 1–4.

Hopper, Kim. 2003. *Reckoning with Homelessness.* Ithaca, NY: Cornell University Press.

Housing Assistance Council. 2003. Migrant and Seasonal Farm Worker Housing. Available via http://www.ruralhome.org/infoSheets.php?id=169; accessed 18 December 2008.

Housing Assistance Council. 2005. Housing in the Colonias. Available via http://www.ruralhome.org/infoSheets.php?id=162; accessed 1 July 2009.

Housing Assistance Council. 2007. *Affordable Green Building in Rural Communities.* Washington, D.C.: Housing Assistance Council. Available at http://www.ruralhome.org; accessed 18 December 2008.

Housing Authority of the County of Riverside. 2008. *Consolidated Plan for Riverside County.* Available via http://www.harivco.org/Resources/ConsolidatedPlanfor RiversideCounty/tabid/114/Default.aspx; accessed 18 December 2008.

Hufbauer, Gary C., and Jeffrey J. Schott. 2005. *NAFTA Revisited: Achievements and Challenges.* Washington, D.C.: Institute for International Economics.

Hunter, Jennifer, Jill Guernsey de Zapien, Catalina Denman, Eva Moncada, Mary Papenfuss, Danelle Wallace, and Anna Giuliano. 2003. Health Care Access and Utilization among Women 40 and Older at the U.S.–Mexico Border: Predictors of a Routine Check-up. *Journal of Community Health* 28: 317–33.

Hunter, Jennifer, Jill Guernsey de Zapien, Mary Papenfuss, Lourdes Fernandez, Joel Meister, and Anna Giuliano. 2004. The Impact of a *Promotora* on Increasing Routine Chronic Disease Prevention among Women Aged 40 and Older at the U.S.–Mexico Border. *Health Education & Behavior* 31(4 suppl): 18S–28S.

Huth, Hans, and Craig Tinney. 2008. Causes and Consequences of Monsoonal Flooding in Nogales, Sonora. In *Proceedings of a USGS Workshop on Facing Tomorrow's Challenges along the U.S.–Mexico Border—Monitoring, Modeling, and Forecasting Change within the Arizona-Sonora Transboundary Watersheds.* Ed. Laura M. Norman, Derrick D. Hirsch, and A. Wesley Ward. U.S. Geological Survey circular, no. 1322. Washington, D.C.: Department of the Interior. Available at http:pubs .usgs.gov/circ/1322/c1322.pdf.

Imperial County Community and Economic Development. 2003. *Colonias Master Plan.* El Centro, CA: Imperial County Community and Economic Development.

Imperial Valley Economic Development Corporation. 2007. *Imperial Valley Strategic Plan.* Available at http://www.ivedc.com/?pid=8; accessed 6 January 2009.

Ingram, Maia, Samantha Sabo, Janet Rothers, Ashley Wennerstrom, and Jill Guernsey de Zapien. 2008. Community Health Workers and Community Advocacy: Addressing Health Disparities. *Journal of Community Health* 33: 417–424.

Ingram, Maia, Emma Torres, Floribel Redondo, Gail Bradford, Chin Wang, and Mary O'Toole. 2007. The Impact of *Promotoras* on Social Support and Glycemic Control. *Diabetes Educator* 33 (supp. 6): 172S–178S.

Institute for Policy and Economic Development. 2006. *At the Crossroads: U.S./ Mexico Border Counties in Transition*. El Paso, TX: U.S./Mexico Border Counties Coalition.

Instituto Nacional de Estadística Geográfica Informática. 2006. *Demographic Data*. Available via http://www.inegi.org.mx/inegi/default.aspx; accessed 6 January 2009.

International Boundary and Water Commission. 2001. *Binational Nogales Wash United States/Mexico Groundwater Monitoring Program Final Report, August 2001*. Available at http://www.ibwc.state.gov/Files/Nogales_Report/Tableof Contents.pdf; accessed 31 December 2008.

Irwin, Alec, and Elena Scali. 2007. Action on the Social Determinants of Health: a Historical Perspective. *Global Public Health* 2: 235–256.

Joshu, Corinne, T. K. Boehmer, Ross Brownson, and Reid Ewing. 2008. Personal, Neighbourhood and Urban Factors Associated with Obesity in the United States. *Journal of Epidemiology and Community Health* 62: 202–208.

Jurik, Nancy, Gray Cavender, and Julie Cowgill. 2006. Searching for Social Capital in U.S. Microenterprise Development Programs. *Journal of Sociology & Social Welfare* 33: 151–170.

Keare, Douglas H. 2001. Learning to Clap: Reflections on Top-Down versus Bottom-Up Development. *Human Organization* 60: 159–165.

Keim, Sarah. 2005. The National Children's Study of Children's Health and the Environment: An Overview. *Children, Youth and Environments* 15: 240–256.

Kelly, David. 1999. Crackdown Panic Leads to Progress. *Press–Enterprise* (Riverside County), October 7, section B (Local), p. 6.

Kelly, David. 2007. Things Happened So Fast. *Los Angeles Times*, November 12. Available at http://articles.latimes.com/2007/nov/12/local/me-harvey12; accessed 20 December 2008.

Kelly, David. 2008. Judge Names Overseers for Duroville. *Los Angeles Times*, February 12, section B (Metro Desk), p. 2.

Koerner, Mona. 2002. Colonias in New Mexico: Rethinking Policy Approaches to Substandard Housing Problems. Paper presented at the urban issues colloquium Constructing Urban Space, LBJ School of Public Affairs, University of Texas, Austin, Texas.

Kopinack, Kathryn. 2003. Maquiladora Industrialization of the Baja California Peninsula: The Coexistence of Thick and Thin Globalization with Economic Regionalism. *International Journal of Urban and Regional Research* 22: 319–336.

Korsch, Karl. 1971. *Marxism and Philosophy*. New York: Monthly Review Press.

Krahnstoever-Davison, Kirsten, and Catherine Lawson. 2006. Do Attributes in the Physical Environment Influence Children's Physical Activity? A Review of the Literature. *International Journal of Behavioral Nutrition and Physical Activity* 3:19 [serial online].

Available at http://www.pubmedcentral.nih.gov.ezproxy1.library.arizona.edu/picpicren.fcgi?artid=1463001&blobtype=pdf; accessed 30 December 2008.

Kreiger, Nancy, and Nancy Zierler. 1996. What Explains the Public's Health? A Call for Epidemiological Theory. *Epidemiology* 7: 107–109.

Krmenec, Andrew J., and Adrian Esparza. 1993. Modeling Interaction in a System of Markets. *Geographical Analysis* 25: 354–68.

Landeck, Michael, and Cecilia Garza. 2002. Utilization of Physician Health Care Services in Mexico by U.S. Hispanic Border Residents. *Health Marketing Quarterly* 20: 3–16.

Lara, Marielena, Christina Gamboa, M. Iya Kahramanian, Leo Morales, and David Baustista. 2005. Acculturation and Latino Health in the United States: A Review of the Literature and Its Sociopolitical Context. *Annual Review of Public Health* 26: 367–397.

Lares-Villa, Fernando, Johan de Jonckheere, Hercules de Moura, Antonio Rechi-Iruretagoyena, Elizabeth Ferreira-Guerrero, Gabriela Fernandez-Quintanilla, Cuauhtémoc Ruiz Matus, and Govinda Visvesvara. 1993. Five Cases of Primary Amebic Meningoencephalitis in Mexicali, Mexico: Study of the Isolates. *Journal of Clinical Microbiology* 31: 685–688.

LaWare, Paul, and Hanadi Rifai. 2006. Modeling Coliform Contamination in the Rio Grande. *Journal of the American Water Resources Association* 42: 337–356.

Leach, Charles, Felix Koo, Thomas Kuhls, Susan Hilsenbeck, and Hal Jenson. 2000. Prevalence of Cryptosporidium Parvum Infection in Children along the Texas–Mexico Border and Associated Risk Factors. *American Journal of Tropical Medicine Hygiene* 62: 656–661.

Lemos, Maria, Diane Austin, Robert Merideth, and Robert Varady. 2002. Public-Private Partnerships as Catalysts for Community-Based Water Infrastructure Development: The Border WaterWorks Program in Texas and New Mexico Colonias. *Environment and Planning C: Government and Policy* 20: 281–295.

Lenzi, R. 1996. The Entrepreneurial Community Approach to Community Economic Development. *Economic Development Review* 14: 16–20.

Levy, John. 1995. *Essential Microeconomics for Public Policy Analysis.* Westport, CT: Praeger.

Levy, John. 2006. *Contemporary Urban Planning.* Upper Saddle River: Pearson Prentice Hall.

Libertad Latina. 2006. A Genocide Is Taking Hundreds of Lives in the Juarez City, Chihuahua State, Mexico, Mexico and El Paso, Texas (U.S.) Border Region. Available at http://www.libertadlatina.org/Crisis_Lat_Mexico_Juarez_Femicide.htm; accessed 18 December 2008.

Light, Ivan, and Carolyn Rosenstein. 1995. *Race, Ethnicity, and Entrepreneurship in Urban America.* New York: Aldine de Gruyter.

Liu, Ben-Chieh. 1976. *Quality of Life Indicators in U.S. Metropolitan Areas: A Statistical Analysis.* New York: Praeger.

Lopez, Robert. 2004. Residents Complain about Dirty Water. *Laredo Morning Times,* July 30, 2004, section A, p. 1.

Lorey, David. 1999. *The U.S.–Mexican Border in the Twentieth Century: A History of Economic and Social Transformation.* Wilmington, DE: Scholarly Resources.

Lusk, Brianna. 2007. Families Fight for Holtville Homes. *Imperial Valley Press,* October 16, 2007. Available at http://www.ivpressonline.com/articles/2007/10/17/news/news03.prt; accessed 6 January 2009.

Macias, Eduardo, and Leo Morales. 2001. Crossing the Border for Health Care. *Journal of Health Care for the Poor and Underserved* 12: 77–87.

Madanipour, Ali. 2003. *Public and Private Spaces of the City.* New York: Routledge.

Mandelbaum, Seymour. 2000. *Open Moral Communities.* Cambridge: MIT Press.

Markley, Debora, and Kevin McNamara. 1995. Sustaining Rural Economic Opportunity. *American Journal of Agricultural Economics* 77: 1259–1265.

Marmot, Michael, and Richard Wilkinson. 1999. *Social Determinants of Health.* New York: Oxford University Press.

Martin, Philip. 2002. Mexican Workers and U.S. Agriculture: The Revolving Door. *International Migration Review* 36: 1124–1142.

Martin, Philip. 2003. Impact on Farmworkers of Proposed Water Transfer from Imperial County. Available via http://www.ucop.edu/cprc/documents/farmwkrwatertransfer.pdf; accessed 6 January 2009.

Martin, Philip, and J. Edward Taylor. 1995. *Immigration and the Changing Face of Rural California.* Summary of the report of the conference held at Asilomar, CA, June 12–14, 1995.

Martin, Philip, and J. Edward Taylor. 1998. Poverty amidst Prosperity: Farm Employment, Immigration and Poverty in California. *American Journal of Agricultural Economics* 80: 1008–1014.

Martínez, Oscar J. 1977. Chicanos and the Border Cities: An Interpretive Essay. *Pacific Historical Review* 46: 85–106.

Martínez, Oscar J. 1978. *Border Boom Town: Ciudad Juárez Since 1848.* Austin: University of Texas Press.

Martínez, Oscar J. 1994. *Border People.* Tucson: University of Arizona Press.

Martínez, Oscar J. 2006. *Troublesome Border.* Tucson: University of Arizona Press.

Marus, Robert. 2006. Jim Towey to Leave White House Faith-Based Post for Academia. *Associated Baptist Press,* April 19, 2006. Available via http://www.abpnews.com/; accessed 18 December 2008.

May, Marlynn, Gloria Bowman, Kenneth Ramos, Larry Rincones, Maria Rebollar, Mary Rosa, Josephine Saldana, Adelina Sanchez, Teresa Serna, Norma Viega, Gregoria Villegas, Maria Zamorano, and Irma Ramos. 2003. Embracing the Local: Enriching Scientific Research, Education, and Outreach on the Texas–Mexico Border through a Participatory Action Research Partnership. *Environmental Health Perspectives* 111: 1571–1576.

May, Marlynn, and Richard Contreras. 2007. *Promotor(a)s,* the Organizations in Which They Work, and an Emerging Paradox: How Organizational Structure and Scope Impact *Promotor(a)s'* Work. *Health Policy* 82: 153–166.

McKnight, John. 1995. *The Careless Society: Community and Its Counterfeits.* New York: Basic Books.

McWilliams, Carey. 1939. *Factories in the Field: The Story of Migratory Farm Labor in California.* Boston: Little, Brown.

McWilliams, Carey. 1999. *Factories in the Field.* Berkeley: University of California Press.

Medius, Inc. 2005. *Vado/Del Cerro, New Mexico Colonias Recipe for Transformation: Comprehensive Plan 2005–2010.* Commissioned by U.S. Department of Housing and Urban Development, Policy, Development and Research Division.

Meister, Joel, and Jill Guernsey de Zapien. 1989. Un Comienzo Sano: A Model Prenatal Education Project. *Maternal and Child Health Education Resources* 4: 1–2.

Meister, Joel, and Jill Guernsey de Zapien. 2005. Bringing Policy Issues Front and Center in the Community: Expanding the Roles of Community Health Coalitions. *Preventing Chronic Disease* 2 (1) [serial online]. Available via http://www.cdc.gov/pcd/issues/2005/jan/04_0080.htm; accessed 30 December 2008.

Meister, Joel, Louise Warrick, Jill Guernsey de Zapien, and Anita Wood. 1992. Using Lay Health Workers: Case Study of a Community-Based Prenatal Intervention. *Journal of Community Health* 17: 37–51.

Mepham, John, and David-Hillel Ruben. 1979. *Issues in Marxist Philosophy.* Atlantic Highlands, NJ: Humanities Press.

Metzger, Raphael, Jane Delgado, and Robert Herrell. 1995. Environmental Health and Hispanic Children. *Environmental Health Perspectives* 103 (suppl 6): 25–32.

Mier, Nelda, Ann Millard, Isodore Flores, Esmeralda Sanchez, Bonny Medina, and Ester Carbajal. 2007. Community-Based Participatory Research: Lessons Learned from Practice in South Texas Colonias. *Texas Public Health Association Journal* 59: 16–18.

Mills, Paul, and Richard Yang. 2007. Agricultural Exposures and Gastric Cancer Risk in Hispanic Farm Workers in California. *Environmental Research* (104): 282–289.

Milofsky, Carl. 2003. Transorganizations and the Limits of Conventional Organizational Theory and Where Nonprofits Come From: Community and Organizational Emergence. Chapter from unpublished manuscript.

Mines, Richard. 2006. *Data on Crops, Employment and Farmworker Demographics: A Resource for CRLA Assistance.* Available via http://migration.ucdavis.edu/cf/files/MinesCAData.pdf; accessed 20 December 2008.

Moore, Steve. 2007. "Duroville" Owner Sues U.S. Official. *Press–Enterprise* (Riverside County), September 7, section B (Local), p. 1.

Mora, Maria. 2006. Self-Employed Mexican Immigrants Residing along the U.S.–Mexico Border: The Earnings Effect of Working in the U.S. versus Mexico. *International Migration Review* 40: 885–98.

Mora, Maria, and Alberto Dávila. 1998. Gender, Earnings, and the English-Skill Acquisition of Hispanic Workers. *Economic Inquiry* 36: 631–44.

Moyer, Laura, Kimberley Brouwer, Stephanie Brodine, Rebeca Ramos, Remedios Lozada, Michelle Firestone Cruz, Carlos Magis-Rodrigues, and Steffanie Strathdee. 2008. Barriers and Missed Opportunities to HIV Testing among Injection Drug Users in Two Mexico–U.S. Border Cities. *Drug and Alcohol Review* 27: 39–45.

Mukerjee, Shaibal. 2001. Selected Air Quality Trends and Recent Air Pollution Investigations in the U.S.–Mexico Border Region. *Science of the Total Environment* 276: 1–18.

Mukhija, Vinit, and Paavo Monkkonen. 2006. Federal Colonias Policy in California: Too Broad and Too Narrow. *Housing Policy Debate* 17: 755–80.

Mukhija, Vinit, and Paavo Monkkonen. 2007. What's in a Name? A Critique of "Colonias" in the United States. *International Journal of Urban and Regional Research* 31: 475–488.

Myerson, Allen. 1995. This Is the House That Greed Built: Texas Developers Profit from Squalor. *New York Times,* April 2, 1995. Available via http://www.nytimes.com/1995/04/02/business/this-is-the-house-that-greed-built.html?pagewanted=1; accessed 18 December 2008.

Nagler, Pamela, Osvel Hinojosa-Huerta, Edward Glenn, Jacqueline Garcia-Hernandez, Reggie Romo, Charles Curtis, Alfredo Huete, and Stephen Nelson. 2005. Regeneration of Native Trees in the Presence of Invasive Saltcedar in the Colorado River Delta, Mexico. *Conservation Biology* 19: 1842–1852.

Nash, Gerald E. 1977. *The American West in the Twentieth Century.* Albuquerque: University of New Mexico Press.

Nash, Gerald E. 1990. *World War II and the West: Reshaping the Economy.* Lincoln: University of Nebraska Press.

Nathan, Richard P., and David J. Wright. 2003. Is "Charitable Choice" Compatible with the First Amendment? Is It a Good Idea? Does It Work? Albany: Rockefeller Institute of Government Roundtable on Religion and Social Welfare Policy.

National Association of Community Health Centers. 2007. *Access Denied: A Look at America's Medically Disenfranchised.* Washington, D.C.: Robert Graham Center.

National Latino Research Center. 2004. *The Border That Divides and Unites: Addressing Border Health in California.* San Marcos, CA: National Latino Research Center.

National Rural Housing Coalition. 2005. *Serving America's Rural Housing and Community Development Needs.* Washington, D.C.: National Rural Housing Coalition.

Navarro, Anna, Karen Senn, Lori McNicholas, Robert Kaplan, Beatriz Roppe, and Mary Campo. 1998. Por La Vida Model Intervention Enhances Use of Cancer Screening Tests among Latinas. *American Journal of Preventive Medicine* 15: 32–41.

Nevins, Joseph. 2002. *Operation Gatekeeper.* New York: Routledge.

New Mexico Department of Finance and Administration, Local Government. 2007. New Mexico Colonias Initiative Overview. Fact Sheet.

New Mexico Department of Finance and Administration. 2008. Colonias at the New Mexico/Mexico Border: A Strategy for Transformation. Available via http://cpi .nmdfa.state.nm.us/content.asp?CustComKey=208015&CategoryKey=226962&pn =Page&DomName=cpi.nmdfa.state.nm.us; accessed 18 December 2008.

New Mexico Department of Workforce Solutions. 2008. Labor Market Information. Available via http://www.dws.state.nm.us/dws-lmi.html#data2; accessed 18 December 2008.

Nitze, William. 2003. Meeting the Water Needs of the Border Region: A Growing Challenge for the United States and Mexico. In *The U.S.–Mexican Border Environment: Binational Water Management Planning,* ed. Suzanne Michel, 145–184. SCERP Monograph Series, no. 8, Southwest Center for Environmental Research and Policy.

Norman, Laura. 2007. United States–Mexico Border Watershed Assessment: Environmental Modeling in Ambos Nogales. *Journal of Borderland Studies* 22: 79–97.

Norman, Laura, Angela Donelson, Edwin Pfeifer, and Alven Lam. 2006. *Colonia Development and Land Use Change in Ambos Nogales, United States–Mexican Border.* U.S. Geological Survey Open-File Report 2006-1112. Available via http:// pubs.usgs.gov/of/2006/1112; accessed 31 December 2008.

Norman, Laura, Mark Feller, and D. Phillip Guertin. 2008. Forecasting Urban Growth across the United States–Mexico Border. *Computers, Environment and Urban Systems* 33:150–159.

Norman, Laura, Jean Parcher, and Alven Lam. 2004. Monitoring Colonias along the U.S.-Mexico Border. U.S. Geological Survey Fact Sheet, USGS FS 2004–3070–Colonias. Available at http://egsc.usgs.gov/isb/pubs/factsheets/fs307004.html; accessed 31 December 2008.

NPR. 2003. *Farm Worker Housing in California.* Available at http://www.npr.org/ news/specials/housingfirst/nprstories/030607.migrant/index.html; accessed 18 December 2008.

Ogden, Cynthia, Margaret Carroll, Lester Curtin, Margaret McDowell, Carolyn Tabak, and Katherine Flegal. 2006. Prevalence of Overweight and Obesity in the United States, 1999–2004. *Journal of the American Medical Association* 295: 1549–55.

Olmstead, Sheila. 2004. Thirsty Colonias: Rate Regulation and the Provision of Water Service. *Land Economics* 80: 136–50.

Olney, Cynthia, Debra Warner, Greyssi Reyna, Fred Wood, and Eliot Siegel. 2007. MedlinePlus and the Challenge of Low Health Literacy: Findings from the Colonias Project. *Journal of the Medical Library Association* 95: 31–39.

Olsson, Karen. 2006. The Old College Try. *Texas Monthly* 34: 76–80.

Ortiz, Larry, Lydia Arizmendi, and Cornelius Llewellyn. 2004. Access to Health Care among Latinos of Mexican Descent in Colonias in Two Texas Counties. *Journal of Rural Health* 20: 246–52.

Pacheco, Vivian. 2007. *Si Se Puede*: Developing Farm Worker Housing in the 12th District. *Community Investments* 19: 9–12.

Pagán, José. 2004. *Work Displacement in the U.S.–Mexico Border Region*. Northampton, MA: Edward Elgar.

Pagán, José, and Mark Pauly. 2006. Community-Level Uninsurance and the Unmet Medical Needs of Insured and the Uninsured Adults. *Health Services Research* 41: 788–803.

Palerm, Juan Vicente. 1991. *Farm Labor Needs and Farm Workers in California: 1970 to 1989*. California Agricultural Studies Report no. 91-2. Sacramento: Employment Development Department.

Pappas, Gregory. 2006. Geographic Data on Health Inequities: Understanding Policy Implications. *PLOS Medicine* 3: 1461–1462.

Parchman, Michael, and Theresa Byrd. 2001. Access to and Use of Ambulatory Health Care by a Vulnerable Mexican American Population on the U.S.–Mexico Border. *Journal of Health for the Poor and Underserved* 12: 404–414.

Patrick, Michael, and William Renforth. 1996. The Effects of the Peso Devaluation on Cross-Border Retailing. *Journal of Borderlands Studies* 11: 25–41.

Pavlakovich-Kochi, Vera. 2006. The Arizona-Sonora Region: A Decade of Transborder Region-Building. *Estudios sociales. Revista de Investigación Científica* 14: 25–55.

Peach, James. 1997. Income Distribution along the United States Border with Mexico: 1970–1990. *Journal of Borderlands Studies* 12: 1–16.

Peach, James. 2007. NAFTA, Globalization and Poverty in El Paso. Lecture presented to the El Paso Community Foundation, 23 February 2007.

Peach, James, and James Williams. 2003. *Population Dynamics of the U.S.–Mexican Border Region*. San Diego: SCERP/San Diego State University.

Peoples' Self-Help. 2008. *Peoples' Self-Help Housing*. Available via http://www.pshhc .org; accessed 18 December 2008.

Perez, Leda, and Jacqueline Martinez. 2008. Community Health Workers: Social Justice and Policy Advocates for Community Health and Well-Being. *American Journal of Public Health* 98: 11–14.

Plocek, Keith. 2006. Lost in Translation. *Houston Press*, September 7, 2006. Available at http://www.houstonpress.com/2006-09-07/news/lost-in-translation; accessed 18 December 2008.

Pollinger, Jordan, and Héctor Cordero-Guzmán. 2007. The Question of Sustainability for Microfinance Institutions. *Journal of Small Business Management* 45: 23–41.

Power, Gerald, and Theresa Byrd. 1998. *U.S.–Mexico Border Health: Issues for Regional and Migrant Populations*. Thousand Oaks, CA: Sage.

Price, Joyce. 1999. Officially, They Speak No Ingles: It's Spanish Only for Town in Texas. *Washington Times*, August 14, 1999, section A, p. 1.

Ragan, Mark, and David J. Wright. 2005. The Policy Environment for Faith-Based Social Services in the United States: What Has Changed since 2002? Results of a 50-State Study. Albany: Rockefeller Institute of Government Roundtable on Religion and Social Welfare Policy.

Raheim, Salome. 1996. Micro-Enterprise as an Approach for Promoting Economic Development in Social Work: Lessons from the Self-Employment Investment Demonstration. *International Social Work* 39: 69–82.

Rahnema, Majid, and Victoria Bawtree, eds. 1997. *The Post-Development Reader.* London: Fernwood Books.

Ramos, Irma, Marlynn May, and Kenneth Ramos. 2001. Environmental Health Training of Promotoras in Colonias along the Texas–Mexico Border. *American Journal of Public Health* 91: 568–570.

Redlinger, Thomas, Kathleen O'Rourke, and James VanDerslice. 1997. Hepatitis among Schoolchildren in a U.S.–Mexico Border Community. *American Journal of Public Health* 87: 1715–1717.

Reed, Deborah. 2006. Poverty in California: Moving beyond the Federal Measure. *California Counts: Population Trends and Profiles* 7: 1–25. Public Policy Institute of California.

Resnik, David, and Gerard Roman. 2007. Health, Justice, and the Environment. *Bioethics* 21: 230–241.

Rieff, David. 1997. *Los Angeles: Capital of the Third World.* New York: Touchstone.

Riverside County Economic Development Agency. 2008. *Mobile Home and Agricultural Housing.* Available at http://www.rivcoeda.org/Default.aspx?tabid=568; accessed 18 December 2008.

Robles, Bárbara, and Héctor Cordero-Guzmán. 2007. Latino Self-Employment and Entrepreneurship in the United States: An Overview of the Literature and Data Sources. *Annals of the American Academy of Political and Social Science* 613: 18–31.

Rochin, Refugio. 1989. *The Changing Nature of American Agriculture and Its Impact on Hispanic Farm Labor: Topics for Research and Analysis.* Working Paper, no. 3. Davis: University of California–Davis.

Rochin, Refugio, and Monica Castillo. 1993. *Immigration, Colonia Formation and Latino Poor in Rural California: Evolving "Immiseration."* Occasional Paper series, no. 93-1. Claremont, CA: Tomas Rivera Center.

Rochin, Refugio, and Monica D. Castillo. 1995. Immigration and Colonia Formation in Rural California. Working Paper, Institute for the Study of Social Change. Center for Latino Policy Research. Berkeley: University of California–Berkeley. Available at http://works.bepress.com/refugio_rochin/2; accessed 22 December 2008.

Rochin, Refugio, Rogelio Saenz, Steve Hampton, and Bea Calo. 1998. *Colonias and Chicano/a Entrepreneurs in Rural California.* Research Report no. 16. East Lansing: Julian Samora Research Institute, Michigan State University.

Rodriguez, Michael, Jennifer Toller, and Patrick Downing. 2004. *Health of Migrant Farm Workers in California.* Policy Brief no. 4. Sacramento: California Research Bureau.

Rodríguez-Saldaña, Joel. 2005. Challenges and Opportunities in Border Health. *Preventing Chronic Disease* 2 (1) [serial online]. Available at http://www.cdc.gov/pcd/issues/2005/jan/04_0099.htm; accessed 22 December 2008.

Romero, Mary, and Serag Marwah. 2005. Violation of Latino Civil Rights Resulting from INS and Local Police's Use of Race, Culture and Class Profiling: The Case of the Chandler Roundup in Arizona. *Cleveland State Law Review* 52: 75–96.

Romney, Lee. 2005. Poor Neighborhoods Left Behind. *Los Angeles Times,* September 18, section B, p. 1.

Rosenthal, Lee, Noelle Wiggins, Nell Brownstein, S. Johnson, Angelina Borbon, Roberta Rael, Jill Guernsey de Zapien, Maia Ingram, Joel Meister, Jean Mcleod, Lakisha Williams, Yvonne Lacey, and Lisette Blondet. 1998. *The Final Report of the National Community Health Advisor Study: Weaving the Future.* A Policy Research Project of the University of Arizona funded by the Annie E. Casey Foundation. Tucson, AZ: University of Arizona.

Rothfeld, Michael. 2007. Schwarzenegger Calls for New Tack on Infrastructure. *Los Angeles Times,* November 28.

Ruiz, Gabriel. 2005. Preliminary Assessment of Air Quality in the California–Mexico Border. California Air Resource Board. Presentation at the Border 2012 Imperial-Mexicali Air Taskforce, January 13.

Runsten, David, Ed Kissam, and JoAnn Intili. 1995. Parlier: The Farmworker Service Economy. Paper presented at the Conference on the Changing Face of Rural California, June, Asilomar, California.

Rural Community Assistance Corporation. 2007. Agricultural Workers. Available via http://www.rcac.org/doc.aspx?51; accessed 18 December 2008.

Sachs, Wolfgang. 1992. *The Development Dictionary: A Guide to Knowledge as Power.* New York: St. Martin's.

Salant, Tanis, and John Weeks. 2007. Undocumented Immigrants in U.S.–Mexico Border Counties. Washington, D.C.: U.S./Mexico Border Counties Coalition. Available at http://www.bordercounties.org/; accessed 22 December 2008.

Sanders, Cynthia. 2004. Employment Options for Low-Income Women: Microenterprise versus Labor Market. *Social Work Research* 28: 83–92.

Sassen, Saskia. 2001. *The Global City: New York, London and Tokyo.* Princeton, NJ: Princeton University Press.

Sawhney, Deepak Narang. 2002. *Unmasking L.A.: Third Worlds and the City.* New York: Palgrave.

Schatan, Claudia, and Liliana Castilleja. 2005. *The Maquiladoras Electronics Industry and the Environment along Mexico's Northern Border.* Montreal: Commission for Environmental Cooperation.

Scheper-Hughes, Nancy. 1995. The Primacy of the Ethical. *Current Anthropology* 36: 409–440.

Schur, Claudia, and Jacob Feldman. 2001. *Running in Place: How Job Characteristics, Immigrant Status, and Family Structure Keep Hispanics Uninsured.* Washington, D.C.: Commonwealth Fund.

Scott, James. 1998. *Seeing Like a State*. New Haven: Yale University Press.

Seid, Michael, Gregory Stevens, and James Varni. 2003. Parents' Perceptions of Pediatric Primary Care Quality: Effects of Race/Ethnicity, Language, and Access. *Health Services Research* 38: 1009–1032.

Self-Help Enterprises. 2004. Programs. Available via http://www.selfhelpenterprises .org; accessed 18 December 2008.

Servon, Lisa. 2006. Microenterprise Development in the United States: Current Challenges and New Directions. *Economic Development Quarterly* 20: 351–367.

Servon, Lisa, and Timothy Bates. 1998. *Microenterprise as an Exit Route from Poverty: Recommendations for Programs and Policy Makers*. CES 98-17. Washington, D.C.: U.S. Census Bureau, Center for Economic Studies,. Available via http://econpapers .repec.org/paper/cenwpaper/98-17.htm; accessed 18 December 2008.

Shaffer, Ron. 1989. *Community Economics: Economic Structure and Change in Smaller Communities*. Ames: Iowa State University Press.

Shaffer, Ron, Steve Deller, and David Marcouiller. 2006. Rethinking Community Economic Development. *Economic Development Quarterly* 20: 59–74.

Sheridan, Thomas E. 2001. Cows, Condos, and the Contested Commons: The Political Ecology of Ranching on the Arizona-Sonora Borderlands. *Human Organization* 60: 141–152.

Sheridan, Thomas. 2006. *Landscapes of Fraud: Mission Tumacácori, the Baca Float, and the Betrayal of the O'odham*. Tucson: University of Arizona Press.

Sherman, Jennifer, Don Villarejo, Anna Garcia, Stephen McCurdy, Ketty Mobed, David Runsten, Kathy Saiki, Steven Samuels, and Marc Schenker. 1997. *Finding Invisible Farm Workers: The Parlier Survey*. Davis: California Institute of Rural Studies.

Sklair, Leslie. 1993. *Assembling for Development: The Maquila Industry in Mexico and the United States*. San Diego: Center for U.S.–Mexican Studies, University of California.

Sleavin, William J., Daniel L. Civco, Sandy Prisloe, and Laurie Giannotti. 2000. Measuring Impervious Surfaces for Non-Point Source Pollution Modeling. University of Connecticut Laboratory for Earth Resources Information Systems. Available at http://nemo.uconn.edu/tools/impervious_surfaces/pdfs/Sleavin_etal_2000.pdf.

Small Business Administration. 1998. *Characteristics of Small Business Employees and Owners*. Washington, D.C.: SBA Office of Advocacy. Available via http://www .sba.gov/advo/stats/ch_em97.pdf; accessed 18 December 2008.

Small Business Administration. 2007. Programs and Services to Help You Start, Grow and Succeed. Available at http://www.sba.gov/services/contractingopportunities/ sizestandardsizesta/size/index.html; accessed 18 December 2008.

Small Business Administration. Office of Advocacy. 2008. Frequently Asked Questions. Available at http://www.sba.gov/advo/stats/sbfaq.pdf; accessed 18 December 2008.

Smith, William D. 2004. The Topology of Autonomy: Markets, States, Soil, and Self-Determination in Totonacapan. *Critique of Anthropology* 24: 403–429.

Soja, Edward. 1980. The Socio-Spatial Dialectic. *Annals of the Association of American Geographers* 70: 207–225.

South County Housing. 2005. Resident Services. Available via http://www.scounty .com/nh.htm; accessed 18 December 2008.

State of California. 2002. Notice of Funding Availability. Community Development Block Grant Program, Department of Housing and Community Development, Sacramento, California.

State of California. 2005. California 2005–10 Consolidated Plan. Department of Housing and Community Development. Available via http://www.hcd.ca.gov/ hpd/hrc/rep/fed/conplano5-1ofinal.pdf; accessed 18 December 2008.

Staudt, Kathleen. 1998. *Free Trade? Informal Economies at the U.S.–Mexico Border.* Philadelphia: Temple University Press.

Steinbeck, John. 1939. *The Grapes of Wrath.* New York: Viking Press.

Stoddard, Ellwyn R. 1987. *Maquila: Assembly Plants in Northern Mexico.* El Paso: Texas Western Press.

Strauss, David. 2005. Farm Labor Housing: An Overview. *Rural Voices* 10: 2–6.

Street, Richard. 2004. *Beasts of the Field: A Narrative History of California Farmworkers, 1769–1913.* Stanford, CA: Stanford University Press.

Stringer, Jeffrey W., and Cary Perkins. 1997. *Kentucky Forest Practice Guidelines for Water Quality Management 1997.* Lexington: Cooperative Extension Service at the University of Kentucky. College of Agriculture.

Stuesse, Angela. 2001. *Lessons Learned from Community-Based Organizing in El Cenizo: Strategies for Claiming Rights and Resources in a Texas Colonia.* Paper presented at research workshop Irregular Settlement and Self-Help Housing in the United States, September 21–22, 2001. Lincoln Institute of Land Use Policy, Cambridge, Massachusetts.

Swider, Sue. 2002. Outcome Effectiveness of Community Health Workers: An Integrative Literature Review. *Public Health Nursing* 19: 11–20.

Szalai, Alexander, and Frank M. Andrews. 1980. *The Quality of Life: Comparative Studies.* Beverly Hills: Sage.

Taylor, Edward, Philip Martin, and Michael Fix. 1997. *Poverty amid Prosperity: Immigration and the Changing Face of Rural America.* Washington, D.C.: Urban Institute.

Taylor, Jessamy. 2004. *The Fundamentals of Community Health Centers.* Washington, D.C.: National Health Policy Forum.

Taylor, Lori. 2001. The Border: Is It Really a Low-Wage Area? *Border Economy* June, pp. 6–8.

Texas Association of Community Health Centers. n.d. Map of Member Locations. Available at http://www.tachc.org/About/Membership/Member_Locations.asp; accessed 24 December 2008.

Texas Attorney General. 2007a. Colonias Prevention. Available at http://www.oag .state.tx.us/consumer/border/colonias.shtml; accessed 18 December 2008.

Texas Attorney General. 2007b. Historical Sketch of Texas Laws Related to Colonias Remediation and Prevention. Austin, TX: Office of Texas Attorney General.

Available at http://www.oag.state.tx.us/consumer/border/history.shtml; accessed 18 December 2008.

Texas Department of Housing and Community Affairs. 1997. Colonias Self Help Center (SHC) Program. Austin: TDHCA. Available at http://www.tdhca.state .tx.us/oci/centers/index.jsp; accessed 18 December 2008.

Texas Department of Human Services, Office of Strategic Research and Development. 1998. *The Colonias Factbook: A Survey of Living Conditions in Rural Areas of South Texas and West Texas Border Counties.* Austin: The Department.

Texas Department of State Health Services. Texas Primary Care Office. 2007. Promotor(a) Community Health Worker Training and Certification Program. Available at http://www.dshs.state.tx.us/chpr/chw/default.shtm; accessed 24 December 2008.

Texas House. 1995a. Bill 1001. Local Government Code, chapter 232.

Texas House. 1995b. Bill 2726. Texas Government Code, chapter 1372.

Texas House 2005. Bill 1823. Texas Local Government Code, chapter 212.

Texas Secretary of State. 2008. *What Is a Colonia?* Available at http://www.sos.state .tx.us/border/colonias/what_colonia.shtml; accessed 18 December 2008.

Texas Secretary of State. Colonia Initiatives Program. 2006. *Tracking the Progress of State-funded Projects That Benefit Colonias.* SB 827 final report. Available at http://www.sos.state.tx.us/border/forms/sb827_111706.pdf; accessed 18 December 2008.

Texas Senate. 1989. Bill 2. Texas Water Code, chapters 15 and 16.

Texas Senate. 1995a. Bill 336. Texas Property Code, chapter 5.

Texas Senate. 1995b. Bill 459. Texas Housing Trust Fund.

Texas Senate. 1995c. Bill 1509. Texas Government Code, chapter 2306.

Texas Senate. 1999. Bill 1421. Texas Water Code, chapter 363.

Texas Senate. 2001. Bill 1. General Appropriations Act.

Texas Senate. 2001. Full Senate Passes Sen. Lucio's Landmark Bill Regulating Proliferation of Colonias with Amendment to Expand Law Statewide. Press release. March 6. Available via http://www.senate.state.tx.us/75r/senate/members/ dist27/pr01/p030601a.htm; accessed 18 December 2008.

Texas Senate. 2003. Limited Ordinance Making Authority Bill Passes to Curb Proliferation of Colonias. Press release. Available via http://www.senate.state.tx.us/ 75r/senate/members/dist27/pr03/p030603a.htm; accessed 18 December 2008.

Texas Water Development Board. 2000. Economically Distressed Areas Program press release. June 7. Available at http://www.twdb.state.tx.us/publications/ press_releases/Editorials/EDAP.htm; accessed 18 December 2008.

Texas Water Development Board. 2001. *A Report on the Activities in the Texas–Mexico Border Region.* Available via http://www.twdb.state.tx.us/publications/reports/ Colonias/State%20of%20the%20Border%20Report2.pdf; accessed 18 December 2008.

Texas Workforce Center. 2008. County Profiles. Available at http://www.txcip.org/ tac/census/CountyProfiles.php; accessed 18 December 2008.

Tinker-Salas, Miguel. 1997. *In the Shadow of the Eagles: Sonora and the Transformation of the Border during the Porfiriato.* Berkeley: University of California Press.

True, Philip. 1996. Shantytown, U.S.A.: The Boom on the Border. *Progressive* 60 (January). Available at http://www.thefreelibrary.com/Shantytown%2c+U.S.A .%3a+the+boom+on+the+border.-a017963638; accessed 25 January 2009.

Tsing, Anna. 1993. *In the Realm of the Diamond Queen.* Princeton, NJ: Princeton University Press.

Twin Plant News. 2000–2007. Available via http://www.twinplantnews.com/; accessed 7 January 2009.

United Nations. 2007. Human Development Reports. Available via http://hdr.undp .org/en/humandev; accessed 18 December 2008.

United Nations. 2008. *The Millennium Development Goals Report, 2008.* Available at http://www.un.org/millenniumgoals/pdf/The%20Millennium%20Development %20Goals%20Report%202008.pdf; accessed 30 June 2009.

U.S. Bureau of Reclamation. n.d. Boulder Canyon Project and All American Canal System. Available at http://www.usbr.gov/dataweb/html/allamcanal.html; accessed 6 January 2009.

U.S. Census Bureau. 1990. 1990 Summary Tape File 1, Table H41. Available via http://factfinder.census.gov; accessed 18 December 2008.

U.S. Census Bureau. 2000a. U.S. Census of Population Detailed Characteristics for New Mexico. Available via http://factfinder.census.gov/servlet/DatasetMain PageServlet?_progpro=DEC&_tabId=DEC1&_submenuId=datasets_1&_lang= en&_ts=225112578922; accessed 19 December 2008.

U.S. Census Bureau. 2000b. *The 2000 Dicennial Census.* Available via http:// factfinder.census.gov/servlet/DatasetMainPageServlet?_program=DEC& _submenuId=datasets_0&_lang=en; accessed 18 December 2008.

U.S. Census Bureau. 2002. *Census 2000.* Available via http://www.census.gov/ main/www/cen2000.html; accessed 18 December 2008.

U.S. Census Bureau. 2005. County Business Patterns, Arizona. Available via http:// www.census.gov/econ/cbp/index.html; accessed 19 May 2009.

U.S. Census Bureau. 2006. *American Community Survey.* Available via http://www .census.gov/acs/www/; accessed 6 January 2009.

U.S. Census Bureau. 2008. State and County Quick Facts. Available via http:// quickfacts.census.gov/qfd/; accessed 18 December 2008.

U.S. Commission on Civil Rights. 2002. Presentation before the commission on the Civil and Human Rights Implications of U.S. Southwest Border Policy. November 14. Available via http://www.usccr.gov/pubs/migrant/present/main.htm; accessed 30 December 2008.

U.S. Conference of Catholic Bishops. 2005. *Justice, Peace and Human Development: A Catholic Social Teaching.* Publication no. 5-315. Washington, D.C.: USCCB Publishing.

U.S. Department of Health and Human Services. 1996. *The New River Petitioned Public Health Consultation, Imperial County, California.* Atlanta: The Department.

Available via http://www.sci.sdsu.edu/salton/NewRiverPPHCons.html; accessed 6 January 2009.

U.S. Department of Health and Human Services. 2007. Community Health Worker National Workforce Study. U.S. Department of Health and Human Resources, Human Resources and Services Administration. Available at http://bhpr.hrsa .gov/healthworkforce/chw/; accessed 24 December 2008.

U.S. Department of Housing and Urban Development. 2003. Community Planning and Development Division Directors Notice: Use of HUD Resources to Assist Colonias. Available at http://www.hud.gov/offices/cpd/lawsregs/ notices/2003/03-10.doc; accessed 18 December 2008.

U.S. Department of Housing and Urban Development. 2004. *Delivering Results to Colonias and Farmworkers.* Washington, D.C.: U.S. Department of Housing and Urban Development. Available at http://www.hud.gov/groups/frmwrkcoln/ English_01.pdf; accessed 18 December 2008.

U.S. Department of Housing and Urban Development. 2006. Colonias Quick Facts. Available at http://www.hud.gov/offices/cpd/communitydevelopment/ programs/colonias/index.cfm; accessed 22 December 2008.

U.S. Department of Housing and Urban Development. 2008. Case Study: Farm Worker Housing. Torres Martinez Desert Cahuilla Indians. Available via http:// www.hud.gov/local/shared/working/groups/frmwrkcoln/casestudies/torres .cfm?state=nm; accessed 18 December 2008.

U.S. Environmental Protection Agency. 2002. *National Water Quality Inventory. 2000 Report.* EPA-841-R-02–001. Washington, D.C.: Office of Water.

U.S. Environmental Protection Agency. 2005. National Ambient Air Quality Standards (NAAQS). Available at http://www.epa.gov/air/criteria.html; accessed 6 January 2009.

U.S. Environmental Protection Agency. 2006. *Polluted Runoff (Nonpoint Source Pollution): Managing Urban Runoff.* Pointer No. 7. EPA841-F-96–004G. Available at http://www.epa.gov/owow/nps/facts/point7.htm; accessed 31 December 2008.

U.S. Environmental Protection Agency. 2007a. *U.S.–Mexico Environmental Program: Border 2012. Implementation and Mid-Term Report.* Available via http://www .epa.gov/border2012/docs/implementation_2007_eng.pdf; accessed 22 December 2008.

U.S. Environmental Protection Agency. 2007b. *Green Book: Criteria Pollutants.* Available at http://www.epa.gov/oar/oaqps/greenbk/o3co.html; accessed 31 December 2008.

U.S. Environmental Protection Agency. 2007c. *Status Report on the Water and Waste-Water Infrastructure Program for the U.S.–Mexico Borderlands.* Available via http://www.epa.gov/OWM/mab/mexican/mxsumrpt.htm; accessed 31 December 2008.

U.S. Environmental Protection Agency. 2008. U.S.–Mexico Border 2012 Program. Available via http://www.epa.gov/Border2012/; accessed 22 December 2008.

U.S. Geological Survey. 2006. Colonias Monitoring Project. Available at http://geography.wr.usgs.gov/science/colonias2.html; accessed 22 December 2008.

U.S. Geological Survey. 2008. U.S.–Mexico Border Environmental Health Initiative. Project Areas. Available at http://borderhealth.cr.usgs.gov/projareas.html; accessed 22 December 2008.

U.S. National Center for Health Statistics. 2006. *Health, United States, with Chartbook on Trends in the Health of Americans.* Hyattsville, MD: United States National Center for Health Statistics.

U.S./Mexico Border Counties Coalition. 2002. *Medical Emergency: Costs of Uncompensated Care in Southwest Border Counties.* Available via http://www.bordercounties.org/; accessed 22 December 2008.

U.S.–Mexico Border Health Association. n.d. Available at http://www.usmbha.org/; accessed 22 December 2008.

U.S.–Mexico Border Health Commission. 2003. *Healthy Border 2010: An Agenda for Improving Health on the United States–Mexico Border.* Available at http://www.borderhealth.org/files/res_63.pdf; accessed 30 December 2008.

USA–Mexico Border Health. 2008. *Assistance on Health Information and Funding Resources.* Available via http://borderhealth.raconline.org/; accessed 9 January 2009.

van Willigan, John. 2002. *Applied Anthropology: An Introduction.* 3rd ed. New York: Bergin and Garvey.

Vargas, Lucinda. 2001. Maquiladoras. Impact on Texas Border Cities. *Border Economy,* June, pp. 25–29.

Vaught, David. 1997. Factories in the Field Revisited. *Pacific Historical Review* 66: 149–184.

Ventura County Ag Futures Alliance. 2002. Farm Worker Housing: A Crisis Calling for Community Action. Issue Paper, no. 2, June. Available at http://agfuturesalliance.org/files/FWH_Report.pdf; accessed 8 January 2009.

Villarejo, Don, and Marc Schenker. 2007. *Environmental Policy and California's Farm Labor Housing.* Davis, CA: John Muir Institute of the Environment, University of California–Davis, Environmental Infrastructure Policy Papers Grants Program. Available at http://johnmuir.ucdavis.edu/research/whitepapers.html; accessed 18 December 2008.

Vint, Bob, and Christina Neumann. 2005. *Southwest Housing Traditions: Design Materials Performance.* Washington, D.C.: U.S. Department of Housing and Urban Development, Office of Policy Development and Research. Available via http://www.huduser.org; accessed 18 December 2008.

Wallack, Lawrence. 2003. The Role of Mass Media in Creating Social Capital: A New Direction for Public Health. In *Health and Social Justice: Politics, Ideology, and Inequity in the Distribution of Disease,* ed. Richard Hoffrichter, 594–625. San Francisco: John Wiley and Sons.

Wallisch, Lynn, and Richard Spence. 2006. Alcohol and Drug Use and Dependence in Urban Areas and Colonias of the Texas-Mexico Border. *Hispanic Journal of Behavioral Science* 28: 286–307.

Ward, Peter M. 1999. *Colonias and Public Policy in Texas and Mexico: Urbanization by Stealth*. Austin: University of Texas Press.

Ward, Peter, Flavio de Souza, Cecilia Giusti, Jane Larson, and Marlynn May. 2003. *The CRG Colonia Lot Titling Program in Rio Grande City, Starr County, Texas*. Final Report to the Ford Foundation and Community Resource Group. Austin: University of Texas at Austin, LBJ School of Public Affairs.

Warren, Mark. 2001. *Dry Bones Rattling: Community Building to Revitalize American Democracy*. Princeton, NJ: Princeton University Press.

Weaver, Thomas. 2001. Time, Space and Articulation in the Economic Development of the U.S.–Mexico Border Region from 1940 to 2000. *Human Organization* 60: 105–120.

Weinberg, Michelle, Stephen Waterman, Carlos Lucas, Veronica Falcon, Pablo Morales, Luis Lopez, Chris Peter, Alejandro Gutiérrez, Ernesto Gonzalez, Ana Flisser, Ralph Bryan, Enrique Valle, Alfonso Rodriguez, Gerardo Hernandez, Cecilia Rosales, Javier Ortiz, Michael Landen, Hugo Vilchis, Julie Rawlings, Francisco Leal, Luis Ortega, Elaine Flagg, Roberto Conyer, and Martin Cetron. 2003. The U.S.–Mexico Infectious Disease Surveillance Project: Establishing Binational Surveillance. *Infectious Emerging Diseases* 9: 97–102.

Weisbrod, Glen, and Brett Piercy. 2007. New Tools for Economic Development Targeting and Strategy. *Economic Development Journal* 6: 30–38.

Wilson, Patricia A. 1992. *Exports and Local Development: Mexico's New Maquiladoras*. Austin: University of Texas Press.

Wilson, Robert, and Peter Menzies. 1997. The Colonias Water Bill: Communities Demanding Change. In *Public Policy and Community: Activism and Governance in Texas,* ed. Richard Wilson, 229–274. Austin: University of Texas Press.

Winter, Stephen, Michael Crosbie, Peter Stratton, Bambi Tran, and Gordon Tully. 2004. *A Community Guide to Basic and Cost-Saving Construction in the American Southwest*. Washington, D.C.: U.S. Department of Housing and Urban Development, Office of Policy Development and Research, Affordable Housing Research and Technology Division. Available at http://www.huduser.org/publications/destech/cost_saving.html; accessed 19 May 2009.

Witmer, Anne, Sarena Seifer, Leonard Finocchio, Jodie Leslie, and Edward O'Neil. 1995. Community Health Workers: Integral Members of the Health Care Work Force. *American Journal of Public Health* 85 (Pt 1): 1055–58.

Wolch, Jennifer. 1990. *The Shadow State: Government and Voluntary Sector in Transition*. New York: Foundation Center.

World Health Organization. 1986. The Ottawa Charter for Health Promotion. First International Conference on Health Promotion, Ottawa, 21 November 1986. WHO/HPR/HEP/95.1. Available via http://www.who.int/hpr/NPH/docs/ottawa_charter_hp.pdf; accessed 30 December 2008.

World Health Organization. 2008. *The World Health Report 2008*. Available via http://www.who.int/whr/2008/whr08_en.pdf; accessed 7 January 2009.

Youth Risk Behavior Surveillance System. 2007. Data and Statistics. Available via http://www.cdc.gov/HealthyYouth/yrbs/index.htm; accessed 30 December 2008.

Yuma Private Industry Council. 2002. *Workforce & Economic Development Summit: Analysis of Workforce Interviews.* Yuma, AZ: YPIC.

Zúñiga, Victor, and Rubén Hernández-León. 2005. *New Destinations: Mexican Immigrants in the United States.* New York: Russell Sage Foundation.

About the Editors

Angela J. Donelson is President of Donelson Consulting, LLC, a firm that specializes in community development for local governments and nonprofits in the border region. Donelson has a Ph.D. in Geography and Regional Development from the University of Arizona, and a master's degree in Regional and Community Planning from Kansas State University. She worked previously as the U.S. Department of Housing and Urban Development's (HUD) representative to Arizona's colonias. Donelson has also worked in city government and in the private sector as an urban and regional planner. Her published research appears in journals such as the *Journal of Community Development* and the *Journal of Borderlands Studies*. Donelson recently co-authored *Colonias in Arizona and New Mexico: Border Poverty and Community Development Solutions* (with Adrian Esparza), published by the University of Arizona Press (2008).

Adrian X. Esparza is an Associate Professor in the School of Natural Resources at the University of Arizona. He received his Ph.D. in Regional Science from the University of Illinois–Urbana, and a master's degree in Urban and Regional Planning from the University of Arizona. His research focuses on exurban land development in the southwestern United States and urbanization in the U.S.–Mexico border region. Esparza has published numerous articles in regional science, planning, and borderlands journals and in 2008 coauthored (with Angela Donelson) *Colonias in Arizona and New Mexico: Border Poverty and Community Development Solutions* (University of Arizona Press). He was Director of the North American Regional Science Council from 2000 to 2005 and has received awards from the Association of Collegiate Schools of Planning (ACSP) and the North American Regional Science Council.

About the Contributors

David Arizmendi is a faculty instructor at South Texas College and is President and CEO of the Azteca Community Loan Fund, a community development financial institution (CDFI) that serves the financial needs of colonia residents. He has a B.S. in Economics and an M.S. in Sociology from the University of Texas Pan–American. From September 1999 through September of 2006, Arizmendi served as the Executive Director of Proyecto Azteca, a nationally known community housing development corporation that operates a self-help housing program in Hidalgo County, Texas, and founded Iniciativa Frontera, a community/economic development organization working on the Texas/Mexico border. In 1997 Arizmendi was recipient of the Leonard Lesser Award from the Center for Community Change. He was selected as a 2001 Fannie Mae James A. Johnson Fellow, and in the same year was named a Rockefeller 2001 Next Generation Leadership Fellow. In 2004, Arizmendi received the Housing Assistance Council's Skip Jason Community Service Award.

Lydia G. Arizmendi is Associate Professor in the Department of Social Work at the University of Texas at Pan American. She holds an M.S.W. from the University of Michigan and a law degree from the University of California at Davis. Arizmendi worked for 18 years as a legal services attorney in California and Texas, serving farmworkers and colonia residents, and developed extensive expertise in the areas of social welfare policy and community development. Between 1990 and 1997, while employed with Texas Rural Legal Aid, she directed the Texas RioGrande Legal Aid (TRLA) Colonias Project, partnering with numerous organizations to develop and assist colonia resident–driven organizations throughout the Texas border region.

Kristin Carlisle is Policy Director of the Texas Low Income Housing Information Service (TxLIHIS). Carlisle holds a B.A. degree in Journalism from the University of Texas at Austin. Since 2004, she has worked as a housing advocate at both the federal and state levels. She played a crucial role in securing legislative support for the state's first significant increase in funding for affordable housing. Prior to joining TxLIHIS, Kristin worked as a legislative aide to Congressman Charles Gonzalez. Kristin has published research on affordable housing and community development in *Shelterforce* magazine and the *Journal of Affordable Housing and Community Development Law*. She is the coordinator of Housing Texas and is a member of the Austin Tenants' Council board of directors.

Kimberly Collins is Assistant Professor of Public Administration and is Director of the California Center for Border and Regional Economic Studies (CCBRES) at the Imperial Valley campus of San Diego State University. Collins received her Ph.D. from El Colegio de la Frontera Norte in Tijuana, Baja California, and an M.A. in Political Science from San Diego State University. Her research deals with U.S.–Mexican border policy, especially quality-of-life issues, urban/rural planning and development, and local governance and federalism in the United States and Mexico. Collins is also involved with environmental policy at the federal, state, and local levels.

Robert J. Czerniak is Associate Vice President for Research at New Mexico State University. He also served as Associate Dean for Research in the College of Arts and Sciences. He received his Ph.D. from the University of Colorado–Boulder in 1979, and a master's degree from Wayne State University. For the past 24 years he has been a Professor of Urban Planning and Geography and was the director of the Urban Planning Program at NMSU from 1983 to 2004. His areas of specialization are land use and transportation planning, the use of GIS in planning applications, and community development. He has studied the formation, boundary delineation, legal status, and economic structure of colonias in New Mexico and Texas.

Cecilia Giusti is Assistant Professor in the Landscape Architecture and Urban Planning (LAUP) Department at Texas A&M University. She received her Ph.D. from the University of Texas at Austin, and a master's degree in Development Studies from the Institute of Social Studies at The Hague, the Netherlands. She was the recipient of a prestigious Housing and Urban Development (HUD) Urban Scholar Fellowship in 2002–3. Her research focuses on sustainable development with emphasis on regional economics, microbusiness, land tenure, gender, and housing markets. She also works in the area of Latin American development and Latino issues in the United States.

David Henkel Jr. is Associate Professor of Community and Regional Planning at the University of New Mexico. He received his Ph.D. in the Sociology of Development from Cornell University, and a master's degree in South Asia Regional Studies from the University of Pennsylvania. Henkel specializes in human ecology, land suitability analysis, and the relation between human communities and natural systems, including agriculture, forestry, rangelands, and riparian health. He has worked extensively in the New Mexico–Chihuahua border region since 1976 on transboundary resource management and environmental justice, and his recent analysis of rural development has drawn upon similarities among European, Mexican, and New Mexican approaches to cultural identity and sustainable planning.

John Henneberger is Co-director of the Texas Low Income Housing Information Service (TxLIHIS) and is an adjunct instructor at the University of Texas at Austin's School of Community and Regional Planning. He holds a B.A. in History from the University of Texas at Austin. Henneberger is one of Texas's leading authorities on low-income housing and is recognized as an innovator for combining housing with preservation strategies to effect comprehensive community revitalization. Over the past 27 years, he has worked for low-income communities, helping to establish eight nonprofit community development corporations that have built or rehabilitated over 500 homes. Henneberger is co-founder of the Border Low Income Housing Coalition, founder of the Texas Community Reinvestment Coalition, and a past board member of the National Low Income Housing Coalition. Henneberger's advocacy work won TxLIHIS the Texas Outstanding Public Service Award from his public-interest colleagues.

David Hohstadt is a GIS analyst with the Office of the New Mexico State Engineer, where he works on adjudication of water rights. He earned his master's degree in Applied Geography from New Mexico State University (NMSU), and a B.A. from California State University at Sacramento. Hohstadt specializes in colonias economic development and spent several years working on a U.S. Department of Housing and Urban Development (HUD) project that investigated economic development in New Mexico's colonias.

Esperanza "Espy" A. Holguin is the Colonias Program Specialist for the Department of Housing and Urban Development (HUD) and is the colonias representative in the southwest border region. She was born and educated in Mexico and is a 1987 graduate of the International Institute of Municipal Clerks. Holguin assists colonias in New Mexico, Arizona, and western Texas with a variety of community development needs. Prior to joining HUD, Holguin owned and operated a consulting firm that assisted U.S.–Mexico border communities. She has over 18 years of experience in municipal government, and over 14 years of working with colonias. She has served on numerous boards and commissions at the local, state, and national levels.

Maia Ingram is Program Director of Community Based Evaluation Projects at the University of Arizona's College of Public Health. Ingram received a master's degree in Public Health (MPH) from the University of Arizona, and a B.A. from Northwestern University. She has more than 10 years of experience in developing and participating in community–academic partnerships and conducting participatory evaluation of community-based programs that utilize the community health worker model. Her research interests focus on the use of participatory action research to engage all partners in the process of policy and environmental change, primarily with communities on the U.S.–Mexico Border. She currently teaches courses on participatory action research and advocacy.

Oscar J. Martínez is Regents' Professor of History at the University of Arizona. He has authored and edited eight books and many articles, book chapters, and reviews. His most recent works include *Troublesome Border* (2nd ed., University of Arizona Press, 2006) and *Mexican Origin People in the United States* (University of Arizona Press, 2001). His current book project seeks to explain why Mexico is poorer than the United States. Martínez has served on the boards of several journals and professional associations. He is a former president of the Association of Borderlands Scholars and a founder of the *Journal of Borderlands Studies*.

Marlynn May is Associate Professor in the Texas A&M Health Sciences Center, School of Rural Public Health, and Health Services Research Scholar in Residence at St. Luke's Episcopal Health Charities, St. Luke's Episcopal Health System, Houston, Texas. He received his Ph.D. in Sociology and Social Ethics from the University of California at Berkeley and the Graduate Theological Union, Berkeley (joint degree), and an M.Div. in Religion and Society from Princeton University. May has worked with community health workers (CHWs) and community-based organizations along the border for a decade. His published research focuses on the work of CHWs and on community-based participatory research (CBPR) in community health development. May has several publications that investigate the role of *promotores(as)* in colonia health, CHW certification and training programs, and participatory research.

John Mealey is founding Executive Director of the Coachella Valley Housing Coalition (CVHC), one of California's most successful nonprofit housing organizations. Mealey received a B.A. degree from Temple University and in 2006 completed the Advanced Practitioners Program at Harvard University. Under Mealey's leadership, CVHC has built more than 3,500 homes for low-income persons living in Riverside and Imperial counties, one of California's most impoverished regions. The CVHC is engaged in an innovative cross-border project that will bring low-income housing to Mexicali, Mexico. Mealey has received numerous awards, including the 2006 James A. Johnson Fellowship awarded by the Fannie Mae Foundation, and the Sol Azteca Award for Executive Director given by the International Hispanic Awards and *La Prensa Hispana*. He is a board member of the California Coalition for Rural Housing, National Rural Housing Coalition, and the National Equity Fund.

Vinit Mukhija is Associate Professor in the Department of Urban Planning at the University of California at Los Angeles (UCLA) School of Public Affairs. He received his Ph.D. from the Massachusetts Institute of Technology (MIT), and a master's degree in urban design from the University of Hong Kong. Mukhija's research focuses on affordable housing in developing countries and Third World–like housing conditions in the United States. He is interested in the globalization of ideas and institutions of housing and land development. In 2003 he published *Squatters as Developers? Slum Redevelopment in Mumbai* (Ashgate). His current research focuses on the rise of formal institutions in the changing real estate markets of Indian cities, and on the growing informality in California's colonias and trailer parks.

Laura M. Norman is a Research Physical Scientist at the U.S. Geological Survey, where she has worked since 1998. She received her Ph.D. in Watershed Management from the University of Arizona. Norman's research focuses on the U.S.–Mexico border, where she uses virtual models to predict pollution rates and to measure the consequences of pollution abatement under varying management scenarios. She specializes in geographic information systems (GIS) and the use of satellite imagery to overcome political boundaries and research environmental systems. Urban growth, sustainable development, nonpoint source pollution, and acid-mine drainage comprise the bulk of her analyses. Norman has published several articles on U.S.–Mexico environmental health, cross-border policy, and regional planning.

Karen Paup is Co-director of the Texas Low Income Housing Information Service (TxLIHIS). Paup holds a B.A. degree in Liberal Arts from the University of Texas at Austin and a master's degree in Urban Affairs from the University of Delaware. Her work with community-controlled housing development includes helping colonia residents in South Texas develop community development corporations (CDCs) and staffing the Texas Residents Network, which works in public and other subsidized housing. Paup is Vice Chair of the City of Austin's Community Development Commission. Her work was recognized by the Center for Community Change through their Leonard Lesser Award for outstanding work with impoverished communities.

Vera Pavlakovich–Kochi is Senior Regional Scientist in Eller College's Economic and Business Research Center, and adjunct Associate Professor in the Department of Geography and Regional Development at the University of Arizona. She received her Ph.D. from Kent State University and a master's degree from the University of Zagreb, Croatia. Pavlakovich–Kochi was previously Director of the University of Arizona's Regional Development Program in the Office of Economic Development. Her research deals with regional economic development on the U.S.–Mexico border, especially the maquiladora economy and transborder trade. Her publications appear in numerous regional development and borderlands journals, and she coedited *Challenged Borderlands* (Ashgate, 2004) in collaboration with scholars from Mexico and several European universities.

Sergio Peña has a doctorate in urban and regional planning and a master's degree in International Affairs from Florida State University. Dr. Peña is a research scholar at El Colegio de la Frontera Norte, a think tank institution whose mission is to study socioeconomic, environmental and cultural phenomena at the U.S.–Mexico border. He is the author of several articles dealing with urban and cross-border planning topics published in various peer-reviewed journals, among them the *Journal of Borderlands Studies, International Habitat Journal, International Journal of Sociology and Social Policy, Frontera Norte,* and *Water International.* He coedited a book entitled *Binational Planning and Crossborder Cooperation in the USA–Mexico Border.*

E. Lee Rosenthal is an Assistant Professor in Health Promotion at the University of Texas at El Paso. She received her Ph.D. in Public Policy from the University of Massachusetts at Boston and a master's degree in Public Health from the University of California at Berkeley. Her most-known contribution in the CHW field is her work as the director/initiator of the National Community Health Advisor Study (University of Arizona, 1998) and as consultant/initiator of the Community Health Worker Evaluation Tool Kit (University of Arizona, 2000); both projects were funded by the Annie E. Casey Foundation. More recently she was Co-Director of the U.S. Department of Education–funded Community Health Worker National Education Collaborative, and she is a Co-Investigator on a National Institutes of Health–funded study of Russian and other immigrants.

Samantha Sabo is the Program Director for Transborder Initiatives with the University of Arizona's Zuckerman College of Public Health. She received a master's degree in Public Health, concentrating in Family and Child Health, from the University of Arizona, and a B.A. degree in Health Sciences and Latin American Studies from California State University, Chico. Sabo developed binational public health experience through her work with the U.S.–Mexico Border Health Commission and the Arizona Department of Health Services–Office of Border Health. Her areas of specialization include maternal and child health, indigenous peoples, immigration and migration, agricultural workers, and participatory action research. She collaborates on several border and binational research and evaluation projects with a variety of community-based agencies and Mexican academic institutions.

William D. Smith is Associate Professor in the Anthropology Department of Western Oregon University. He received his M.A. and Ph.D. degrees in Anthropology from Stanford University. He researches grassroots community organizing in Mexico's northern border colonias and collaborates with DouglaPrieta Works, a community organization in the Douglas, Arizona–Agua Prieta, Sonora, borderlands.

Ashley Wennerstrom is a doctoral candidate in Public Health Policy and Management at the University of Arizona's Mel and Enid Zuckerman College of Public Health. She received a master's in Public Health (MPH) from the University of Arizona. Her research interests include fossil fuel depletion as a public health issue, food security, border health, corporate social responsibility in agriculture, and community health worker advocacy.

Index